Ohio Scenes and Citizens

Ohio Scenes and Citizens

BY GRACE GOULDER

THE WORLD PUBLISHING COMPANY
CLEVELAND AND NEW YORK

Published by The World Publishing Company
2231 West 110th Street, Cleveland 2, Ohio

Published simultaneously in Canada by
Nelson, Foster & Scott Ltd.

Library of Congress Catalog Card Number: 64-12464

FIRST EDITION

WP564

TO
MY HUSBAND
Robert James Izant

Contents

Acknowledgments

PRACTICALLY all the material in this book has appeared in altered form in the *Sunday Magazine* of the *Plain Dealer*, Cleveland, in my series of articles, "Ohio Scenes and Citizens" and "Ohioans in Europe." I appreciate the editors' permission to reproduce the stories. For their guidance and encouragement, I wish to thank Lawrence J. Hawkins, editor of the magazine, and Philip W. Porter, executive editor of the *Plain Dealer*, who has given me the benefit of his counsel since inception of the series. In years of adventuring through my native state so many persons have welcomed and aided me that my quest has been continually one of pleasure, rather than a task. For unfailing co-operation in many ways, I am grateful to members of the staff of the Ohio Historical Society and of the Martha Kinney Cooper Ohioana Library Association, particularly to its founder, Mrs. Cooper. Two Cleveland repositories of riches, the Cleveland Public Library and Western Reserve Historical Society, have been my main research centers. I am delighted to have this opportunity to express gratitude for generous assistance in the library by Miss Donna L. Root, head of the history and biography department, and her associate, Miss Janet Coe Sanborn, as well as others in the department. In the Historical Society, Alene Lowe White has tracked down many an elusive item for me and I offer her my thanks. Lastly, my deep gratitude is tendered my husband, Robert James Izant, whose participation in every phase of this undertaking has been so complete that he is rightly coauthor.

GRACE GOULDER

Great Elm
Hudson, Ohio
October 18, 1963

MICHIGAN
INDIANA
KENTUCKY
O
H
I
WILLIAMS
FULTON
LUCAS
Toledo
OTTAWA
Put-in-Bay
Sandusky
Vermilion
WOOD
SANDUSKY
Fremont
ERIE
Milan
DEFIANCE
HENRY
PAULDING
SENECA
Norwalk
PUTNAM
HANCOCK
HURON
VAN WERT
WYANDOT
CRAWFORD
RICHLAND
ALLEN
HARDIN
MERCER
AUGLAIZE
Iberia
Blooming Grove
MARION
Marion
MORROW
LOGAN
UNION
SHELBY
KNOX
DELAWARE
DARKE
Delaware
CHAMPAIGN
MIAMI
LICKING
FRANKLIN
Westerville
Greenville
CLARK
MADISON
Columbus
PREBLE
MONTGOMERY
FAIRFIELD
GREENE
PICKAWAY
Lancaster
Dayton
Wilberforce
FAYETTE
Washington Court House
WARREN
BUTLER
CLINTON
HOCKING
ROSS
Lebanon
VINTON
Chillicothe
HAMILTON
Cincinnatti
CLERMONT
HIGHLAND
PIKE
JACKSON
Pt. Pleasant
BROWN
ADAMS
Jackson
SCIOTO
Georgetown
Ripley
GALLIA
Mt. Vernon Furnace
LAWRENCE
Ironton

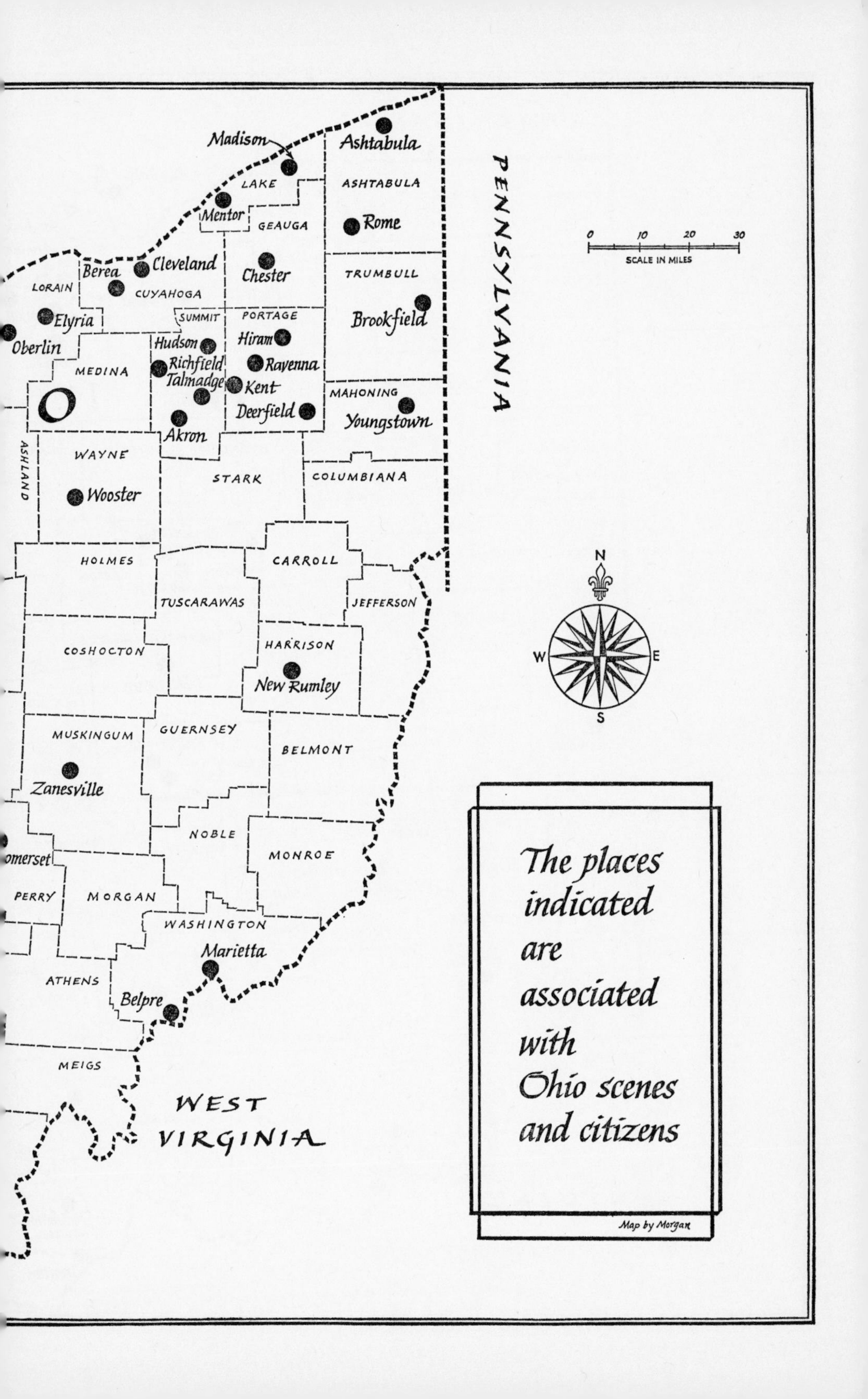

Madison
Ashtabula
LAKE
ASHTABULA
PENNSYLVANIA
Mentor
GEAUGA
Rome
0
10
20
30
SCALE IN MILES
Cleveland
Berea
Chester
TRUMBULL
LORAIN
CUYAHOGA
Elyria
SUMMIT
PORTAGE
Brookfield
Oberlin
Hudson
Hiram
Richfield
Rayenna
MEDINA
Talmadge
Kent
MAHONING
O
Deerfield
Youngstown
Akron
ASHLAND
WAYNE
STARK
COLUMBIANA
Wooster
N
HOLMES
CARROLL
TUSCARAWAS
JEFFERSON
HARRISON
COSHOCTON
W
E
New Rumley
S
MUSKINGUM
GUERNSEY
BELMONT
Zanesville
NOBLE
omerset
MONROE
PERRY
MORGAN
WASHINGTON
Marietta
ATHENS
Belpre
MEIGS
WEST
VIRGINIA
The places indicated are associated with Ohio scenes and citizens
Map by Morgan

CANADA
WASHINGTON
MONTANA
NORTH DAKOTA
MINNESOTA
OREGON
Soda Springs
SOUTH DAKOTA
IDAHO
WYOMING
Rohnerville
Red Bluff
NEBRASKA
Counci Bluffs
Omaha
NEVADA
San Francisco
Denver
Pottawatomie
Lawrence
UTAH
COLORADO
Kansas City
CALIFORNIA
Osawatomie
KANSAS
PACIFIC OCEAN
OKLAHOMA
ARIZONA
NEW MEXICO
N
W
E
TEXAS
Houston
Places associated with Ohio scenes and citizens
Map by Morgan

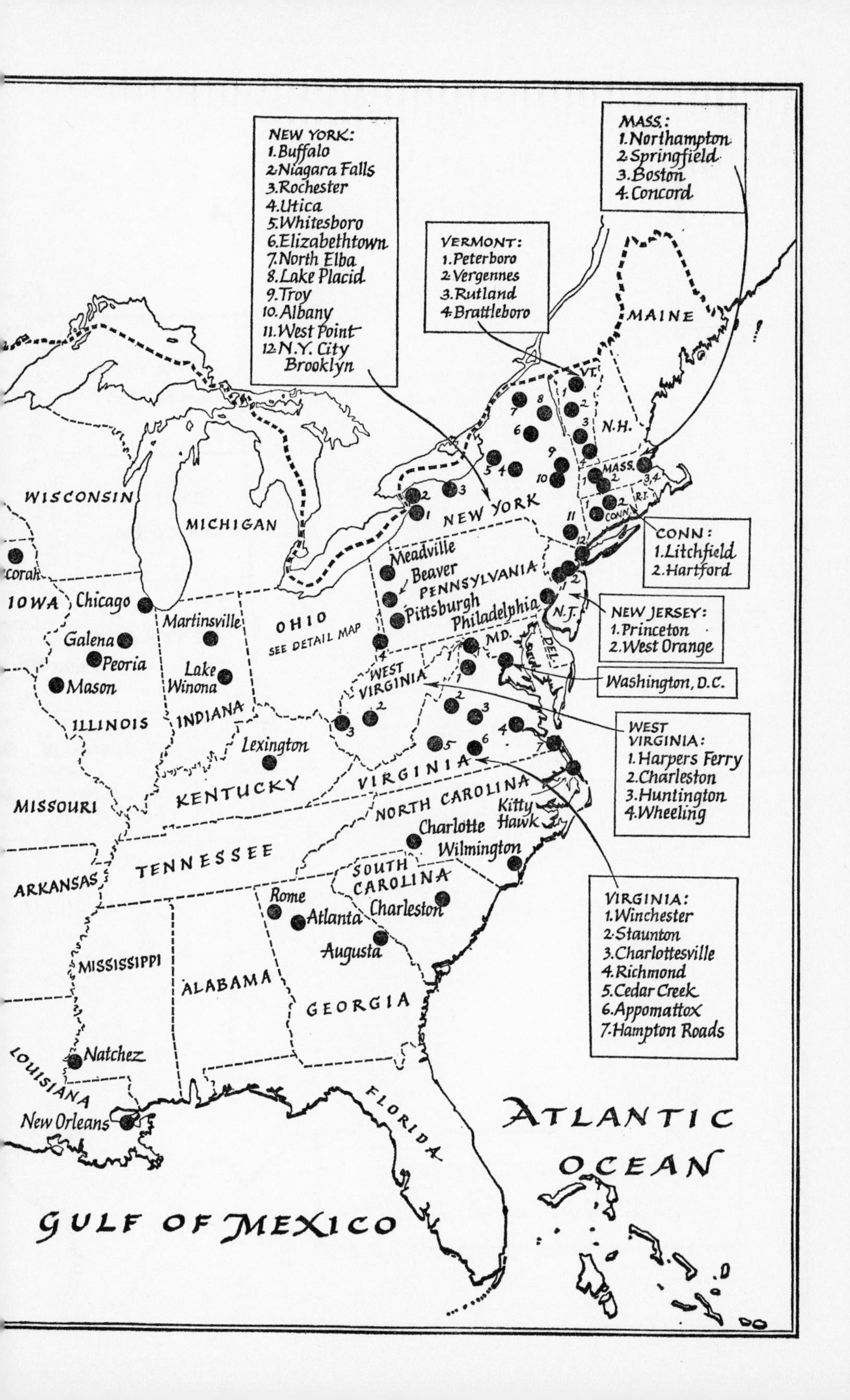

NEW YORK:
1.Buffalo
2.Niagara Falls
3.Rochester
4.Utica
5.Whitesboro
6.Elizabethtown
7.North Elba
8.Lake Placid
9.Troy
10.Albany
11.West Point
12.N.Y. City Brooklyn
VERMONT:
1.Peterboro
2.Vergennes
3.Rutland
4.Brattleboro
MASS.:
1.Northampton
2.Springfield
3.Boston
4.Concord
CONN:
1.Litchfield
2.Hartford
NEW JERSEY:
1.Princeton
2.West Orange
Washington, D.C.
WEST VIRGINIA:
1.Harpers Ferry
2.Charleston
3.Huntington
4.Wheeling
VIRGINIA:
1.Winchester
2.Staunton
3.Charlottesville
4.Richmond
5.Cedar Creek
6.Appomattox
7.Hampton Roads
MAINE
VT.
N.H.
MASS.
R.I.
CONN.
NEW YORK
WISCONSIN
MICHIGAN
Decorah
IOWA
Chicago
Galena
Peoria
Mason
ILLINOIS
Martinsville
Lake Winona
INDIANA
OHIO
SEE DETAIL MAP
Meadville
Beaver
PENNSYLVANIA
Pittsburgh
Philadelphia
N.J.
MD.
DEL.
WEST VIRGINIA
Lexington
KENTUCKY
VIRGINIA
MISSOURI
NORTH CAROLINA
Kitty Hawk
Charlotte
Wilmington
TENNESSEE
ARKANSAS
SOUTH CAROLINA
Charleston
Rome
Atlanta
Augusta
MISSISSIPPI
ALABAMA
GEORGIA
Natchez
LOUISIANA
New Orleans
FLORIDA
ATLANTIC OCEAN
GULF OF MEXICO

Ohio Scenes and Citizens

Paul Laurence Dunbar

THE YOUTH running the elevator had a dictionary and *The Century* magazine stowed under his stool. He kept a pad of paper handy, too. Between rides he scribbled away, hunched on his perch, or he pored over the magazine, the high-brow monthly of the 1890s.

He was writing poetry and dreaming of someday seeing it in *The Century*. He had been writing poems since age thirteen, which seemed a long while back to the nineteen-year-old elevator operator in Dayton's Callahan Building.

Already a few of his verses had appeared in local newspapers. He was not paid for them, but his name was printed in boldface type: Paul Laurence Dunbar.

Time to write, time to read and study—maybe the far possibility of college. All this he longed for. However, he had to make a living —if his four-dollar weekly wage could be so construed. The elevator job was the best he could get. There were not many opportunities for a Negro in Dayton in 1891.

Out of the twin obstacles of prejudice and poverty encompassing his people, this gifted one of them would sing of their trials and their yearnings, to become the first lyric voice of the African-American.

And he would become a poet for all Americans, white and black, and thus prove, as William Dean Howells said of him, "that . . . human unity and not race unity is the precious thing, the divine thing after all." It was Howells who launched Dunbar into fame, as he had many others of American literary greatness.

As Paul Dunbar stood at the threshold of attainment, the onrush of science and its accompanying inventions were overturning living patterns for all citizens. The Negro particularly felt the impact. He was free, but within Jim Crow social and economic confines, walled higher with each shift in the established order.

In the South he was shackled in a new kind of bondage—peonage. He was denied political redress. Lynchings were not uncommon. Bewildered and discouraged, the African looked back nostalgically on slave-day security while auction block and whipping post dimmed in memory.

White Americans, caught up in uncertainties of the new, likewise saw the past in a rosy aura. To both races, in different ways, the old that was going fast seemed good.

Dunbar reflected his Negro contemporaries' preoccupation with the carefree patterns of their ante-bellum status, as in his "At Candlelightin' Time":

> When I come in f'om de co'n-fiel' aftah wo'kin' ha'd all day . . .
> Den de happy hours dat foller are de sweetes' of de day . . .
> So I jes' teks up my banjo, an' I plays a little chune.

At the same time, Dunbar was alive to the current plight of his race and proclaimed it in "To the South":

> Now all is changed, within the rude stockade,
> A bondsman whom the greed of man has made
> Almost too brutish to deplore his plight,
> Toils hopeless on from joyless morn till night.

Though he associated all his life with whites, the poet, none the less, was proud of being a Negro, as he chorused in his "Ode to Ethiopia":

> O Mother Race! to thee I bring
> This pledge of faith unwavering
> This tribute to thy glory.

Dunbar became a vogue for Negroes and whites not because of or in spite of being black, but because his appeal was universal.

Perhaps his is too mellifluous, too gentle a tune to pipe the protest of insistent, present-day Negroes. After all, he believed a poet's major concerns were not sociological or reform, as he makes clear in "Choice":

> They please me not—these solemn songs
> That hint of sermons covered up.

'Tis true the world should heed its wrongs,
But in a poem let me sup,
Not simples brewed to cure or ease
Humanity's confessed disease,
But the spirit-wine of a singing line,
Or a dew-drop in a honey cup!

Dunbar's themes were human emotions of joy and grief, God's handiwork, nature's loveliness. These he presented melodiously in masterly rhythm whether his verse was dialect or literary English.

Dunbar probably would win few awards from today's poetry juries. This brings up the speculation as to how Tennyson and Wordsworth would fare at the hands of the *avant-garde*.

Dunbar sang to the accompaniment of his era and what he sang must be listened to in relation to that era. His own origins hardly could have been humbler. He was born in 1872 in the Negro quarter of Dayton. His parents, Joshua and Matilda Dunbar, were former slaves. The Dunbars were poor. His father had died when Paul was twelve. His mother took in washing to help support them. Paul knew hardship firsthand. Yet his boyhood had not been an unhappy one.

His personal travail began, paradoxically, with the achievement of an urgent goal—his graduation from high school a few days before his nineteenth birthday. To keep him in school those four years, Matilda doubled the laundry bundles and went out by the day to work in Dayton homes. After school hours Paul rustled errands and any odd job he could find.

Together, he and his mother laid aside for school clothes and schoolbooks whatever dimes and nickels and pennies they dared spare from rent and food needs. There never was quite enough to fill all the crevices, but somehow "Ma" managed.

When he enrolled in Central High, Paul was the solitary Negro in the school. His color made no difference. White schoolmates like Orville Wright were his friends. He spent any free time on Saturdays in the Wright barn watching Orv and his brother Wilbur tinker with a printing press they had evolved for publishing a magazine of their own editing. They called Paul The Deacon, and once they dropped in among the personals: "The Deacon is in good health." All their schoolfellows knew who was meant and laughed good-naturedly at the joke. Paul was popular and admired for the rhymes he was always turning out.

By unanimous vote he was taken into the coveted literary society of the school, and in his senior year was elected president. He was appointed editor-in-chief of the school paper. His great triumph came when his entry was chosen as class song. The stern and hard-to-please head of the music department wrote the music for it.

Commencement exercises in the Opera House closed that evening with the girls in their fluffy long-skirted white dresses and the boys in their Sunday best singing lustily the eight stanzas of "the beautiful farewell song composed by Paul L. Dunbar, colored member of the class," as next day's newspaper reported.

Matilda Dunbar, seated in the audience, saw her boy walk up on the platform and receive his diploma just like the white boys. Tears furrowed her alert, black face when she heard Paul's song. No white mother's son had written that. . . . She knew all the long years' struggle, all the backbreaking labor had been worth-while.

Paul and Ma read with elation the newspaper account next morning, and a few minutes later the young graduate started out, proud and confident, in search of work.

A high school education was less common and more of an accomplishment then than now. Only forty-three, nine boys and thirty-four girls, had been graduated in Paul's class. Any boy holding a diploma—and gained with such a record as his—would have felt as Paul did, that he had qualifications for maybe a start on one of the city's newspapers, or a chance at clerical work.

Editors who had printed his poems turned him down, giving no reason. Advertised vacancies in business firms suddenly were filled when he applied. Some department heads bluntly told him they could not hire a Negro. Finally, at the plant of the National Cash Register Company they hired him in the loading room. He was too slight to lift heavy freight and after a day or two he had to quit.

Handling an elevator was something a person could do who had had no training in Greek and Latin. Knowing chemistry and memorizing Shakespeare's sonnets had nothing to do with getting the cage up and down from floor to floor. All this Paul knew. The salary was far less than he had expected—less, in fact, than what was being paid white schoolmates not as able as he.

However, he took the post gladly. He would earn almost enough in a week to meet the monthly rent of the poor little house where he and Ma lived. He wanted desperately to begin paying her back, to begin easing her burden a little. He knew better than anyone that it was her steadfact vision of education for him that had opened his other world of books.

Mrs. Dunbar was a remarkable woman. She had learned to read and write not long before, at adult classes in a Dayton night school. At sixteen, a plantation owner had bought her as wife for his slave, Willis. After emancipation they took their owner's name—Murphy. Left a widow, with two boy babies, she came to Dayton, where she had relatives.

Here she met her second husband, Joshua Dunbar, twenty years her senior. He was a skilled plasterer and also a Union Army veteran. In slave days he had been "rented" out by a shrewd master who made nice profit from his labor and therefore worked him as hard as possible. Joshua escaped via the Underground Railroad and enlisted in a Massachusetts colored regiment. He died in the Soldiers' Home in Dayton.

The Murphy boys married and settled in Chicago. As youngsters they sometimes resented their mother's indulgence of Paul, who frequently was excused from filling the wood box and other chores. As they grew older, however, a loyalty developed among them. Always at ease with children, Paul became a doting uncle to his nieces and nephews.

Ma and Paul lived by themselves in Dayton. An unusual depth of companionship, affection, and understanding unfolded between them.

When Matilda had been a little slave girl in Kentucky she occasionally was allowed to sit at the back of the living room while her master read aloud to the family from such diverse favorites as Charles Dickens, Alexander Pope, Keats, and Shelley. The privileged moments were highlights in the child's drab existence. There were poignant incidents, too, with sobs and consequent punishments, when she was dragged off to bed before the conclusion of some particularly telling episode. Meager as was this exposure to letters, it awakened a basic awareness of words, especially the cadence of poetry. This endowed the illiterate child with a lifelong reverence for learning.

Intuitively she detected a keenness and sensitivity about her Paul that set him apart. She resolved that somehow he would have the schooling she missed. He was free and she was free. No one could sell or separate them . . .

Paul was never robust. He lacked energy for the rough-and-tumble games of other boys. When neighborhood children played on the sidewalks or at hearty games in back yards, Paul was more likely to be indoors tagging after his mother from room to room, begging her to tell about her days in the South.

Ma was a born storyteller, painter of vivid word pictures. She omitted the bitter parts—like the story of the day she turned seven. On this day her mother, sobbing uncontrollably, kissed her, explaining she, Matilda's mother, had been sold. Little Matilda, bereft and helpless, watched, as her mother, along with some farm animals, was carted off to live on another plantation. Mrs. Dunbar never told her son about that, nor about husbands and wives torn apart when "good" owners died or fell on bad times and their "chattels" had to be liquidated.

Instead, she related the merry hours in cabin dooryards, when the day's hoeing and harvesting were done, the chitt'lings and beaten biscuits were ready, "An' de co'n pone's hot." Ma wanted to keep Paul safe from sadness.

The boy, whose speech carried no more hint of "darky" dialect than his school associates', early caught the inflection of his mother's phrases. When she took him to call on friends, former houseboys and cotton pickers "from 'way down South," his sharp ear absorbed their speech and he never forgot it.

Faithfully, with his pen, he would echo the riches of this treasure-trove—the agrarian South's Negro vernacular, folk speech of an American ethnic group.

For the first few years after high school, Paul retained his elevator post. Everywhere his color blocked his efforts to find a position better suited to his capabilities. On the other hand, the elevator had its advantages.

Passengers noticed the unusual young man, stopped to chat, became his friends. They came from many sections of the country and he gained a good deal by listening to the varied speech. Best of all, there were lax intervals between the summoning of the bell. He put such breathing spells to good use, reading or capturing on paper lines that constantly danced in his thoughts.

Off duty, he wrote. He mailed out poems to publishers everywhere. Many were printed. They brought no cash returns or, at best, a check now and then for a few dollars. Nonetheless, he continued to write and to send forth his product.

He and some of his classmates had formed a dramatic and debating club. Their amateur programs helped develop his natural platform presence, a blend of pleasing modesty and convincing poise. He had a deep, rich voice and a fine delivery. He began giving free recitals before Negro church and social clubs. At first his numbers were selected from traditional, classic authors.

Soon he was substituting his own compositions, often acting out passages with a few graceful, telling steps to accent the rhythm. Now requests came from white as well as colored groups and he asked a small fee.

One of his former teachers who had attended a reading secured a place for him on the program of the Western Association of Writers, then holding a convention in Dayton. The date, as it happened, was his twentieth birthday. The coincidence proved an auspicious omen. He obtained leave from his elevator long enough to present an original poem by way of greeting to delegates, who were impressed with the dignity and culture of the Negro boy and his verses.

The following morning, on bringing his elevator to the main floor, he found three of the audience of the day before waiting to see him. Among them was a newspaper editor, Dr. James N. Matthews, from Mason, Illinois.

Dunbar was honored by the callers, but also embarrassed. Breaking into the conversation the elevator bell would sound and, excusing himself, he then hurried for his passengers. Matthews patiently waited out the interruptions, gathered a good deal of Paul's story, and obtained several poems from him. Back home he printed the poems with something about the poet.

Poems and article caught the eye of James Whitcomb Riley, Hoosier rhymester, beloved and renowned from coast to coast. The successful Riley sent the obscure Dunbar words of prophetic commendation, calling him "a singer who should command wide and serious attention." Such a boost from such a source offered a stimulus sorely needed at the moment by the "singer."

At the conclusion of his recitals, more and more people came to him to say they would like to be able to read his poems as well as listen to them. Why didn't he put them in book form? These queries gave substance to a secret ambition.

If in his innermost self he shared Ma's incredulous "Will anyone publish a Negro's book?" he downed the doubt. He thumbed through a pile of his verses Ma had been cherishing on the parlor table. Out of the mass he drew fifty-six. He took them to Orv Wright, who, with a partner, was operating a real print shop now.

Wright would like to have helped, he said, but he had no bookbinding facilities. He reminded Dunbar that his father, Milton

Wright, was a bishop of the United Brethren Church: "Why not go over to the United Brethren Publishing House," Orv said, "and see if they won't do it for you."

Bishop Wright was out of town. Had he been there to introduce Dunbar, the editor might not have dismissed him so curtly. As it was, the man made clear he was not interested in poetry. It didn't sell.

William Blocher, foreman of the job printing department, who had overheard some of the conversation, saw the utter dejection in the youth as he moved toward the door. He asked Paul to come into his office. Maybe something could be done about his book. He looked over the manuscripts, carefully estimated the cost at $125—and the firm's rule was money in advance.

Dunbar gathered up his papers and rose to leave. It would be a long time before he could amass that sum out of savings from his four dollars a week income.

Blocher stopped him. "I'll put up the money myself," he exclaimed impulsively. "You can pay me back from sales of the book."

Without this intervention of William Blocher, the world might never have heard of Paul Laurence Dunbar.

The collection of poems came out as *Oak and Ivy*, the book being issued in time for Christmas sales. When the delivery man from the printing house brought a bundle of the first books off the press to the Dunbar house, he asked Ma: "Who is this man Dunbar?" Ma answered: "He is just an elevator boy—and a poet."

She opened one of the books and stopped at the dedication, bewildered. Slowly she sounded out the words: "To Her who has ever been my guide, teacher and inspiration, my Mother, this little volume is affectionately inscribed."

Paul's elevator passengers bought the book; his friends of school days backed it. In two weeks he had sold enough at one dollar a copy to repay Mr. Blocher and have a nice sum left over. Ma and he celebrated Christmas with a dinner that was the best meal they ever had—and there were a few gifts, too.

The poems were the outpourings of youth, and several reached heights of his finest verse, as did "The Meadow Lark," with these lines:

> I can hear the song
> Of the meadow lark,
> As she flits and flutters.

And laughs at the thunder when it mutters.
O happy bird, of heart most gay
To sing when skies are gray!

Through *Oak and Ivy* Dunbar met two Toledoans, Dr. H. A. Tobey, head of the Toledo State Hospital, and Charles Thatcher, a lawyer. The meeting was a milestone for the poet, for they became his lifelong friends and benefactors. He had not relinquished his thought of college, and the men stood ready to arrange the finances. Paul's obligations unfortunately were too pressing.

"I am glad to say that for the past two or three years," he wrote Dr. Tobey, "I have been able to keep my mother from hard toil by which she raised and educated me."

Also, he had bought a house, an unpretentious dwelling, but an improvement on the place in which they had been living. For it he had assumed what to him was a heavy indebtedness. These responsibilities precluded college.

With his half brothers in Chicago, the World's Fair there in 1893 seemed a possible opportunity. The Negro civic leader Frederick Douglass, in charge of the Haitian exhibit, hired Paul as an assistant, but could pay him only five dollars a week. In a few weeks Dunbar was back in Dayton with Ma, resuming his role as elevator boy—and poet.

Finances were at such low ebb he was threatened with foreclosure on the house he was trying to buy. Yet the urge toward expression seemed never stilled. He had more poems ready for a new volume.

He was often in Toledo, giving programs arranged by Dr. Tobey, or visiting at the doctor's home. His circle of acquaintances widened. Among his good friends in the city were Mayor Samuel H. ("Golden Rule") Jones and Brand Whitlock, later mayor, and, in World War I, U.S. Ambassador to Belgium. These men saw Paul over his mortgage crisis, and more, they underwrote the publication of his next book, *Majors and Minors*. It came out in 1896.

Here was Dunbar grown mature and sure, compassionate yet firm. He ran the gamut deftly from pathos to humor, with much to say. The book included "When Malindy Sings," most quoted of all his poems, considered by many his best and a true evidence of genius.

Malindy is Matilda Dunbar singing at her washtub and ironing board:

Oh, hit's sweetah dan de music
  Of an edicated band;
An' hit's dearah dan de battle's
  Song o' triumph in de lan'.
It seems holier dan evenin'
  When de solemn chu'ch bell rings,
Ez I sit an' ca'mly listen
  While Malindy sings.

His own frustrations he etched with restraint, as in the sonnet "Fulfilment":

I grew a rose once more to please mine eyes.
All things to aid it—dew, sun, wind, fair skies—
Were kindly; and to shield it from despoil,
I fenced it safely in with grateful toil. . . .
At last, oh joy! the central petals burst apart.
It blossomed—but alas! a worm was at its heart!

Between the same covers was the jolly "When de Co'n Pone's Hot," with lines like these:

When de oven do' is opened,
  An' de smell comes po'in' out;
Why, de 'lectric light o' Heaven
  Seems to settle on de spot,
When yo' mammy says de blessin'
  An' de co'n pone's hot.

It included the eloquent eulogy to Douglass, who died in 1895:

Oh, Douglass, thou hast passed beyond the shore,
  But still thy voice is ringing o'er the gale!
Thou'st taught thy race how high her hopes may soar,
  And bade her seek the heights, nor faint, nor fail.

Dr. Tobey, who had sat up until midnight reading *Majors and Minors,* saw to it that a copy reached his friend James A. Herne, starring in his own play, *Shore Acres.* The actor-playwright in turn immediately posted off his enthusiastic reaction to Dunbar, adding that he would forward his copy to William Dean Howells.

Paul fingered Herne's letter in disbelief. He had spent fifty cents for a seat in the gallery to see Herne when the play was in Dayton the previous week. Now the great Herne was to intercede for him with the greater Howells—Howells who had attained Olympian heights as the arbiter of literary criticism in his "Life and Letters" department of *Harper's Weekly*, and in Dunbar's "Bible," *Century* magazine, where the renowned man's *Silas Lapham* had been serialized.

Paul shunted his thoughts to other matters. Herne was a busy man. He might forget about this promise regarding Mr. Howells and the book of a Negro he had never seen. Dunbar had tasted disappointment often enough to be cautious with his hopes.

One day Paul had a post card from Dr. Tobey—Get yourself a copy of *Harper's Weekly* and read what William Dean Howells thinks of you, was the message's import.

Paul rushed to the nearest newsstand. Leaning on the dealer's counter, he read every word. Howells had given his entire space to *Majors and Minors.*

After a startlingly brusque description of the poet as a Negro who "a generation ago . . . would have been worth, apart from his literary gift, twelve or fifteen hundred dollars under the hammer," Howells praises his style for "the jolly rush of its movement, its vivid picturesqueness, its broad characterization" . . . for "vistas into the simple, sensuous, joyous nature of his race [which] Mr. Dunbar opens."

Dunbar's "Negro [dialect] pieces" he rates "of like impulse with the works of Burns when he was most Scotch. . . . When Burns was least himself he wrote literary English, and Mr. Dunbar writes literary English when he is least himself."

He reproduced the first and last stanzas of "The Party," longest poem in the book: "Deh had a gread big pahty down to Tom's de othah night"; all of "When de Co'n Pone's Hot," which, he said, "delights me" and all of "When Malindy Sings," labeling it "purely and intensely black in its feeling . . ."

A race, Howells continued, which has reached Dunbar's heights "can no longer be held wholly uncivilized, and intellectually Dunbar makes a stronger claim for the Negro than any Negro has yet done." The critic admits he has been speaking of him as a black poet and "I should be speaking of him as a poet"; that "he is a real poet whether he speaks a dialect or writes a language." He concedes that the "non-Negro pieces . . . are good, very good . . . charming sketches . . . homely and tender poetry." He quotes the entire "Conscience and Remorse," which begins:

> "Good-bye," I said to my conscience—
> "Good-bye for aye and aye,"

And I put her hands off harshly,
And turned my face away;
And conscience smitten sorely
Returned not from that day.

In a crescendo of benignity, as if to offset his rough opening paragraphs, Howells presents Dunbar not alone as a poet but as one illustrating "human unity" and the fact that "God hath made of one blood all nations of men."

Concluding with the "hope that the reader likes as much as I like the strong full pulse of the music," he throws in practical information as to the publisher so that readers will have no difficulty acquiring a volume.

The review was carried in a special number of *Harper's,* covering William McKinley's nomination for the presidency. The edition circulated widely, particularly in Ohio, native state of the future President and the young poet. The rate of this issue was June 27, 1896. It was Paul's twenty-fourth birthday.

On that day Paul Laurence Dunbar was made. A new and shining literary star had been sighted and named by the all-seeing magic eye of Howells, who had discovered also such top-flight authors of the day as Hamlin Garland, Robert Herrick, and Stephen Crane, and was, if not the discoverer, at least the adviser and close friend of Mark Twain. Dunbar, too, was a celebrity.

Howells was authority infallible. If he designated Dunbar a poet of Negro vernacular, that was what he became. Ruefully the intellectual and literary-minded Dunbar might wish for equal recognition of his lyrics in standard English. It was as a singer in Negro dialect that the public was to take him to its heart.

Requests, snowballing with the weeks, rolled in on Dunbar for poems, articles, fiction, interviews, and public appearances. He wrote and kept on writing, hurried from one platform to another, trying, like a surprised well driller, to cap the gush while it lasted.

Dunbar made his first trip to New York City with his antenna ever alert to slights because of his skin. He hesitated to accept Howells' invitation to call at his Long Island summer home. His misgivings were accentuated when a haughty maid left him standing hat in hand on the steps. Howells, however, hurried to the door, took Dunbar's hand in both of his with the warmest cordiality, and invited him in for tea.

Dunbar's self-consciousness disappeared. The two talked about all manner of subjects, including Dayton. Howells as a boy had set type and delivered papers for his peripatetic editor father in Dayton. The important man reminded Dunbar that he, too, was born in Ohio. He had had a rugged boyhood and not nearly as good an education as Paul's . . .

Howells made arrangements for Dunbar to be booked by Major James B. Pond, who was Mark Twain's lecture manager, and later Howells'. He introduced him to Dodd, Mead and Company, who published his later books. As Dunbar prepared to go, Howells noted the evening had grown cold and insisted he borrow his overcoat.

Early the next year Dunbar sailed for England under the management of Major Pond's daughter, who proved a disappointment. The trip was a financial catastrophe for Dunbar, but it added to his prestige. The London press spoke of "the colored versifier . . . friend of William Dean Howells . . . as lionized . . . at receptions and parties." One of his recitals was before elite guests of a fellow Ohioan, John Hay, of Cleveland, then U.S. Ambassador to Great Britain.

Back in the United States, Paul married the love of his life, Alice Moore, native of New Orleans, then teaching school in the North. She was brilliant, beautiful, a light-skinned Negro, a contrast to dark Paul. He gave her as a wedding ring a plain circlet that had been Ma's. The marriage was a love match, but a stormy one.

Dunbar took a position at the Library of Congress obtained through Robert G. Ingersoll, who had met him on an Ohio lecture tour. Library hours were long, but did not curtail his writing. Howells obliged him by supplying the introduction to another volume, *Lyrics of Lowly Life,* his most popular book.

His name now established, he sold whatever he produced, whether poetry or prose. Plots of novels and short stories were woven largely around white characters, subject matter which reviewers considered unsure ground for him. It was not a valid criticism, Dunbar contended, pointing out that he had nearly as much contact with whites as with Negroes. Besides, didn't white authors invade the Negro domain in their books? His permanent place in American literature, however, was not won through his prose, but through his poetry.

Despite his success, money problems continued to plague him. With a wife and mother to support and his inner drive to create goading him on, the always frail Dunbar overtaxed his strength.

A cold quickly worsened into pneumonia. For weeks he lay desperately ill in their shabby New York apartment. Howells, hearing of his plight, climbed several flights of stairs to inquire about him.

He wrote again about Dunbar in an article, in *The North American Review,* on the New Poetry. Still complimentary, Howells noted a leveling off . . . Dunbar was carrying "his work *on* rather than *up;* but if he went no higher than the mark he struck at first he still would . . . be a part of our literary history."

This was 1899. On the platform he was a finished performer, unfailingly pleasing. Dunbar was at his zenith. Publishers and magazine and newspaper editors clamored for his manuscripts. Collections and separate poems appeared. When he mailed a copy of his *Lyrics of Sunshine and Shadow* to Dr. Tobey, he commented that it was his seventeenth book.

Dunbar collaborated in dramatic sketches and musical shows. His lyrics were set to music. Walter Damrosch wrote a score for "The Deserted Plantation." Carrie Jacobs Bond produced music for the much-sung "Lullaby," better known by its refrain, "Po' little lamb." Mary Turner Salter, Samuel Coleridge-Taylor, and others of similar standing, composed to his words.

The bout with pneumonia left its permanent scar—tuberculosis. He tried Colorado and the Catskills. Alice was with him. But he wanted Ma, too, and she went to him. Nothing checked his recurring hemorrhages and terrible coughing spells. To bolster his weakness when faced with speaking engagements or a publisher's deadline, some biographers state, he came to depend upon liquor. As a result, these writers claim, quarrels and recriminations developed between husband and wife.

It appears the cause of the rift lay less with his drinking than with a clash of temperaments between the two women he loved. Alice grew impatient and annoyed at the constant presence of Ma, her possessiveness and mothering of Paul. Ma was strong-willed. Alice, ambitious to be a writer in her own right, was high-strung.

Whatever the reason, Alice left Dunbar, refusing to see him in a reconciliation effort, or to answer his letters. The separation was a staggering blow to him, as revealed in numerous poems like "An Old Memory":

> O God! could all be altered,
> The pain, the grief, the strife,
> And wert thou—as thou shouldst be—
> My true and loyal wife! . . .

For I, alas like others,
  Have missed my dearest aim.
I asked for love. Oh, mockery!
  Fate comes to me with fame!

In midsummer 1903, with Alice out of his life forever, bearing in heart and body "a pain beyond my years," he returned to Dayton. Disposing of the first home, he bought another at 219 North Summit Street. It was a pleasant brick house on a shady street. A comfortable porch faced an extra lot for a garden.

He took a second-floor room as his study—"Loafing-Holt," he called it. Bookcases overflowed with autographed editions sent him by their authors. He put his typewriter beside a sunny window, laid out his smoking pipes, saw that Ma's old carpet-covered rocking chair was at hand. She had come to take care of him, to tempt his wayward appetite with his favorite dishes, to nurse and fuss over him.

Ma and he were

Home agin, an' home to stay. . . .

Say, it's nice a-gittin' back,
When yore pulse is growin' slack. . . .
Kind o' nice to set aroun'
On the old familiar groun',
Knowin' that when Death does come,
That he'll find you right at home.

Friends came in steady attendance, white as well as black. He was charming and gay as ever. No reference to the disease he could not shake off, or to the wife who was never out of his thoughts:

Thou art the blood of my heart o' hearts,
Thou art my soul's repose,
  But my heart grows numb
  And my soul is dumb;
Where art thou, love, who knows, who knows?

That very year of Dunbar's "homecoming," Orv and Wilbur Wright made their flight at Kitty Hawk. It was the week before Christmas, and in a few days Orv dropped around to tell Paul all about it. He stopped by now and then on his way to and from Huffman Field, where the brothers were intent on further experiments.

Mrs. Eugene Field, whose late husband was Dunbar's friend, made a special trip to Dayton to see him when she heard of his illness. Others arrived in their carriages to take the poet for drives. But he could go out less and less. And Ma had to cut short the calls. Dunbar was tiring more easily and growing steadily weaker. . . .

When he died on a snowy day in February, 1906, the passing of the thirty-four-year-old poet was page-one news in papers throughout the country. Alice Dunbar saw the headlines on her way to school. By Dunbar's will, she received one third of his royalty returns, the rest going to Ma. Alice mourned him as his widow, and when she married ten years later she signed herself Mrs. Robert Dunbar-Nelson.

At the simple funeral services in the Methodist Church he had attended, Dr. Tobey, deeply moved at the loss of his friend, was among the speakers. He read a letter from Brand Whitlock, then mayor of Toledo, who was absent due to his mother's illness. The dead man's "poetry had a quality of universality . . . he became not only a poet of his race . . . but of you and me and of all men everywhere." Whitlock added, he died of "tuberculosis, overwork—and heartbreak."

Dunbar in effect had written his own funeral sermon in what has been called his finest poem, "Compensation":

Because I had loved so deeply,
Because I had loved so long,
God in His great compassion
Gave me the gift of song.

Because I have loved so vainly,
And sung with such faltering breath,
The Master in infinite mercy
Offers the boon of Death.

He had asked to be buried under a willow tree. Ma saw to it that he had his wish and planted a willow beside his grave.

Three years after his death, on the anniversary of his birth, Dayton citizens erected a monument to him in the cemetery. It is a granite boulder bearing a plaque inscribed with his poem "A Death Song":

Lay me down beneaf de willers in de grass,
Whah de branch'll go a-singin' as it pass.

An' w'en I's a-layin' low,
I kin hyeah it as it go
Singin', "Sleep, my honey, tek yo' res' at las'."

More than a thousand witnessed the dedication—among the prominent, James Whitcomb Riley. Booker T. Washington, who entertained Dunbar at his Normal Institute at Tuskegee, Alabama, named him poet laureate of the Negro race.

The little willow tree his mother set out so hopefully did not grow, nor did successive plantings, including one by the Dayton Garden Club. But his words on the boulder were a comfort to Ma on her frequent trips to the cemetery—Paul was taking his "res' at las'."

Mrs. Dunbar continued to live in the North Summit Street house until her death in 1934. During these years she made a rite of seeing that every room in the house remained as in Paul's lifetime; his books and typewriter, his pipes in Loafing-Holt; the simple bedroom furnishings undisturbed; overstuffed Victorian pieces he had bought for the parlor left as he had placed them.

With the help of her granddaughter, Mrs. Helen Murphy Gillim, living near-by, Mrs. Dunbar maintained the house as a shrine to Paul. So many came to pay him homage that she was forced to institute visiting hours.

After Mrs. Dunbar's death the house, including the poet's personal possessions, became the property of the Ohio Historical Society, which administers it as a public museum. It also has been designated by the United States Department of the Interior as a National Historical Landmark, the only Ohio historic house to be so entitled to date.

Paul Laurence Dunbar's name is chiseled on public buildings in many parts of the country; on high schools, nursing homes, hospitals, banks, insurance company offices, theaters, apartment houses. Dayton's new public library has a tablet bearing his "Compensation," as does Dunbar House.

Fate, indeed, came to him with Fame.

Ulysses S. Grant

Rumbling along Georgetown's dusty main street one sultry July day in 1823 came a springless wagon overloaded with household goods and pulled by two fine, big horses. The driver was a young fellow named Jesse Grant.

He wore a suit of brown-speckled goods spun and sewed by his wife, Hannah, who sat on the hard seat beside him. Her dress was a light linsey-woolsey, also of her own making. Her keen eyes were shielded by a blue sunbonnet.

As best she could, she held their squirming, fat fifteen-month-old son, who was outfitted in a piece of the same cloth as Jesse's.

Hannah's father, John Simpson, had named the baby Hiram, perhaps because he was a Mason. His bookish wife, Hannah's stepmother, contributed Ulysses as a second name. This, shortened to 'Lyss, was what everyone called the baby—Lyss Grant.

Now that he had a son, Jesse meant to establish his own business—tanning—plus a home where the boy could grow up under his own roof. He was moving his little family and all their possessions from Point Pleasant in adjoining Clermont County. He had been successful enough there, but he believed prospects were better in Georgetown. It was by no means his first move.

Jesse, who was twenty-nine, had been a tanner since apprenticed as a lad to his older brother, Peter, in Maysville, Kentucky. He had left as soon as his indenture was fulfilled because he could not stomach slavery. Crossing into Ohio, he wandered about the northern part of the state, scene of his youthful years.

He had no trouble getting jobs in tanneries. One was in Hudson, at Owen Brown's, where Brown's son, John, six years younger than Jesse, was learning the business. The Browns held the same antislavery views as Jesse, which he was to recall years later when John Brown attacked Harpers Ferry and was hanged for it. . . .

Jesse's roaming nature had taken him finally to southern Ohio, to Point Pleasant on the Ohio River. He managed two tanneries and married Hannah. He installed his bride in a two-room house he rented. Here Lyss was born April 22, 1822.

The cabin was so close to the river that once at flood time a huge boulder had to be hoisted on its roof to keep it from floating downstream. But that was many years after the Grants had left it—when it had become famous as the birthplace of Ulysses Simpson Grant, commanding Union general in the Civil War and President of the United States from 1869 to 1877.

Jesse was earning good money. Nevertheless, he was dissatisfied. His house and the tanneries belonged to others, and he hankered to be his own boss and landlord.

In four years at Point Pleasant he had saved a neat bit—$1,100—after starting from nothing, only credit. Now he was ready for a new life. He picked Georgetown, seat of Brown County.

He was attracted to the place on many counts. There were good stands of oak, with bark to supply tannic acid necessary in his trade. Animal hides were plentiful, too, and the place was growing. Immigrants in steady influx were taking over virgin land, axing down giant trees to make way for farms. They would need leather for boots and harness for horses.

Georgetown, now a modern village of inviting mien, then looked mighty different as Grant headed his horses into Main Street. Construction was not yet begun on the well-designed county courthouse with its Greek columns and towering dome, which, happily, has survived unchanged. Its site, staked out amidst a crowding forest, adjoined the grazing commons.

Pigs wallowed in the mud and geese strutted, hissing at the Grants as they drove past. Their hound, tied under the wagon, barked back and strained at the rope that kept him from righting such insults.

Grant rented temporary quarters in a double house. The other occupants were Dr. George Bailey, physician; his wife, fated for a role in Lyss's life; and a son, Bartlett, a year older. They welcomed the strangers and invited them to supper.

After supper the Baileys helped unload the wagon, with its bed and feather tick, Hannah's spinning wheel and spindle, chairs, a good table, and well-made quilts. They were gifts from Hannah's family, prosperous farmers who lived in a fine brick house back in Clermont County. Some of these furnishings survive today as treasured Americana because they belonged to the parents of little Lyss.

Jesse conducted himself carefully. He bought lots on what has become Grant Avenue. The deed for this property was notarized by one of the coming political figures of the county, Justice of the Peace Thomas L. Hamer. Like Dr. Bailey, he, also, was destined to help shape the future of baby Grant.

In no time at all Jesse was laying out his tanyards, where skins would undergo foul-smelling treatment. Here was his one-horse mill for grinding bark.

Filling the hopper was an operation that Lyss, in a few years, would take over, detesting every step. Long after the Grants' day, the building where finished hides were stacked and sold was remodeled to become an attractive residence.

Opposite the mill, on a large lot that cost forty dollars, Jesse built his home, a two-story brick. It is as substantial now as in 1824, when he moved his family into it. Up the hill, on Water Street, a stone's throw away, Dr. Bailey erected a handsome Greek Revival-style house with soaring pillars and lofty pediments.

Thrifty Jesse prospered. He had no desire to have such a house as the Baileys'. He was greatly concerned, however, that his son have the best in education. He himself had been trying all his life to make up for his own lack of schooling. His library was the talk of Georgetown. There were thirty-five volumes on his shelves and he had read every one of them, some more than once.

Jesse was determined Lyss would have a better start than his. His mother had died when he was eleven. The family was then living in Deerfield, an early settled village in Ohio's Western Reserve. Jesse's father, Captain Noah Grant (he had fought at Bunker Hill and Yorktown) was not one to "lay up stores on earth," as his famous grandson, Ulysses, said of him in his memoirs. The Captain's five children were scattered, Jesse finding a home in Youngstown (Ohio) with Judge George Tod, a circuit-riding jurist of the Ohio Supreme Court.

Aristocratic Mrs. Tod was kind to the sad orphan who had come to help with the farming. Jesse adored her and spoke with veneration of her all his life. The Tods set their table with silver and china brought from their home in the East. Reared on crude pewter,

Jesse had never seen the like. He resolved that someday he would own silver and china and live like the Tods.

Too, the stay with the Tods fired him with a respect for education. There were books in the home and Mrs. Tod encouraged her ward to read them. She sent him to school for a "quarter term."

The Tods' baby, David, dogged Jesse everywhere. More than a century later, when David was Ohio's wartime governor (1862–64), Jesse's Lyss would be "Unconditional Surrender Grant," victor at Shiloh and Vicksburg and supreme commander of Union forces. . . .

Jesse saw to it that his children had the educational opportunities Georgetown offered. There were three schools operated on a subscription basis: one for the beginners; another for older children in a larger building, placarded now by the state because Lyss had been a pupil there; the third, a "higher school," where two men teachers, as Lyss remembered them, gave more attention to beatings than to books.

These places of learning didn't rate high with Jesse, so he sent his first-born (always the apple of his eye) to an Academy at Ripley, ten miles away on the Ohio River. This school was under the sponsorship of Presbyterians. Its director, the Reverend John Rankin, divided his time between pupils and fugitive blacks he aided to freedom on the Underground Railroad. Rankin is forever remembered for his rescue from the icy Ohio of the colored woman immortalized as Eliza in *Uncle Tom's Cabin.*

It was while Lyss was home from Ripley for Christmas vacation that the notion of attending West Point first loomed in his life. The Georgetown version, which differs somewhat from others, holds that the plot started when Hannah sent him over to the Bailey house for milk. The Baileys kept cows and the Grants got their daily supply of milk from them.

While waiting at the rear door of the house for his pail to be filled, Lyss overheard Mrs. Bailey tearfully confiding to a friend in another room that word had just come that their son Bart, a cadet at West Point, was having trouble with his studies and was being dismissed. Dr. Bailey, proud and sensitive, would be very hard on the boy, she feared.

It so happened that some time before this, Jesse had surprised his son by bringing up the possibility of his attending the Hudson River military academy. Ever alert that Lyss should have "advantages," Jesse spoke about the four boys who already had gone from Georgetown and its neighborhood to the Point. Bart was one of them, but of course the Grants knew nothing of his difficulties.

Startled at first by his father's suggestion, Lyss had been thinking it over. He was seventeen and the one thing he knew was that he didn't want to stay in a tannery all his life. He had traveled as far as Maysville, his uncle's home, but he longed to see more of the world. Maybe the Point wasn't such a bad idea after all.

The boy hurried home from the Baileys, deposited the pail of milk and walked quickly around the corner to call on Hamer, who by this time was a U.S. Congressman. Lyss knew he had the privilege of nominating candidates from his district to West Point.

Hamer, lifelong Democrat, and argumentative Jesse, a Whig, once devoted cronies, had fallen out over politics and were not speaking to each other. Lyss knew this. Nevertheless, he summoned courage and blurted out his request to Congressman Hamer: If a vacancy for West Point should occur in this county, could he please be considered!

Hamer, unaware of what was happening to young Bailey, felt another appointment from his bailiwick unlikely. But he wanted to be friendly to Jesse's boy—by now he was heartily sick of that foolish quarrel. So Hamer said yes.

A few days later the slow mails brought the news about Bart, and Hamer kept his word to Lyss. The Congressman was about to leave for Washington and he was obliged to prepare his new appointee's papers hastily. Inadvertently he wrote the boy's name "Ulysses Simpson Grant," influenced, probably subconsciously, by the fact that Simpson kin, at the moment, were staying with the Grants.

When Lyss got to West Point he tried to have the error in his name corrected, but soon gave up. It would take an act of Congress, he decided, to change the name. So the initials "H.U.G.," for Hiram Ulysses Grant, as he had been christened, which his family so proudly had lettered on his trunk, he painted over, and in the space blocked out boldly: U. S. Grant.

Embarrassed to approach Hamer, some say Jesse had applied secretly for his boy's consideration to Thomas Morris, Senator from this district. Morris, in turn, according to this story, sent the letter to Hamer, who, ready to close the old breach with Jesse, quickly put Lyss's name through.

Whichever way the appointment came about, it restored the former warm relationship between Jesse Grant and the Congressman. Further, it seemed in no way to interfere with the Bailey-Grant friendship. Lucinda, Bart's attractive younger sister, Georgetown claims, was a one-time flame of Lyss. At any rate, when U. S. Grant became President of the United States he appointed her village postmistress.

While still in "pinafores," which little boys wore, Lyss showed his passion for horses. This stayed with him for life. At that early age, Jesse, with fatherly pride in his man-child, would lift him to the backs of his team on the way to the creek for water.

At seven or eight he began driving the horses himself, hauling lumber and oak bark to the tannery.

"When eleven I was strong enough to hold a plow," he wrote in his memoirs, adding, "in my early days everyone labored more or less." He evidently never questioned the work Jesse exacted of him. The father was generous, too, supplying him with spirited horses and seeing to it he had good clothes, better than what most of his playmates wore.

Neighbors noted other characteristics which made "that Grant boy" different. In a frontier society, where firearms were always at hand, he did not enjoy hunting. He hated to kill. Sight of blood made him ill. But he liked to shoot at targets and he was a good marksman. He never as much as blinked if a gun went off suddenly beside him, which happened one time when he was three or four.

He could not endure the sound of a band or fife and drums. Even in church he fidgeted until the hymns were done. Something about his ears was responsible for this aversion to all music, he explained many times.

While Jesse was ambitious, he was not extravagant. He built his house small at first, with only two rooms down and two up. As more children came, and his means improved, he added to the house, front and back.

Here Lyss grew up. It was his home from babyhood until a month after his seventeenth birthday, when he took the stage for Ripley on his way to West Point, which seemed a great distance away. He went by Ohio River steamer as far as Pittsburgh, glorying in the river traffic and in the passengers who boarded and debarked at every wharf. He chose the slow canal packet to Harrisburg. It was cheaper than the railroad, and anyway he could see more of the country from open decks as boats were towed leisurely past lush Pennsylvania farmlands . . . and finally steam cars to the Point.

According to Ulysses Grant, his father "from my earliest recollections [was] in comfortable circumstances." In addition to his thriving Georgetown tannery, Jesse "tilled considerable land" and cut lumber on a five-acre timber stand he owned outside the village. Before the outbreak of the war, during an interval when Ulysses was out of the army, his father was prosperous enough to establish him and his two brothers in a leather shop in Galena, Illinois.

Jesse was able to travel in his old age. He liked to visit haunts of his youth. Back when he was a carefree bachelor he had accepted the promising offer of a partnership in a tannery in Ravenna. Local tradition here records his love affair with one Prudence Hall. The two planned to marry. Jesse was stricken with malaria fever which persisted so long that he was bankrupt.

It was at this point that he left for southern Ohio for a fresh start. The wedding was postponed until Jesse's prospects improved. Both promised to write to each other and later insisted they did. Neither, however, received any letters from the other. Versions differ as to who jilted whom, but in Point Pleasant Jesse married Hannah Simpson, and Prudence married a Ravenna man.

On one of Jesse's tours, in his late seventies, when Lyss was in the White House, he stopped off in Ravenna to see Prudence, now widow Coe and a grandmother. Prudence boasted of her children's accomplishments. Old Jesse interrupted her: "Anyway, you can't claim a son who is President of the United States," he slyly reminded her. "You could have, you know, if you had married me."

U. S. Grant's longest association with Ohio, that so boastfully claims him, was in the Georgetown house. Yet it carries no sign to indicate the fact.

Cherished by its owner as a historic landmark, the building has been restored to the way it was in Grant's day, except for the addition of an out-of-character front porch. World visitors come to the Point Pleasant birthplace. Many also travel to Georgetown to look at the officially designated Grant schoolhouse. But few ever see the house on Grant Avenue in which he began his book learning, or the one further along the same street where he spent his youth.

They also miss the monument to Lyss in Confidence Cemetery on the edge of town. It is a large granite slab with a cannon mounted on it. A bronze plaque tells the story of the stone.

Lyss, fourteen, and sturdy for his age, was working for a man erecting a new house in the center of Georgetown. The builder wanted a broad stone for a doorstep. Lyss knew just the one. It lay in White Oak Creek, but its size was formidable.

He was advised not to tackle it. When he persevered he was laughed at. He went ahead, manipulated it with stout chains and underslung it beneath his wagon. He hauled it to town and installed it where his employer wanted it.

Years later this house was demolished to make way for the town's Public Building. Someone remembered the history of the stone just in time and it was moved to its present location.

Georgetown thinks it is a memorial to General Grant more meaningful than even his impressive tomb on New York City's Riverside Drive.

Robert G. Ingersoll

Bob Ingersoll, age six, and his brother Clark, a couple of years older, between them fondled a languid rooster with a dirty, blood-stained bandage around its neck.

The boys were sitting on the steps of Tappan Hall. Four stories of fresh red brick, plus cupola, it soared proudly above tree stumps and mud at "God's College," Oberlin Collegiate Institute, in northern Ohio.

Bob and Clark, whose first name was Ebon but who seldom was called that, were tired and lonesome. They wished their father would come.

Soon, a tall man with the physique of an athlete and the unmistakable mien of a preacher turned in at the board walk.

"Well, sons, what do you think of Oberlin?" Reverend John Ingersoll's solemn face lighted with a faint smile for his children.

"We haven't seen any Indians," Bob ventured in the aggrieved tone of one denied a promised treat.

"No, unfortunately no," agreed his father. "But there are other souls to be saved, my son."

Bob, who would grow up to be Royal Bob, the Great Agnostic, sensed, if he did not entirely understand, his father's disappointment. The Easterner, who expected to find Ohio a wilderness dotted with Indian encampments, had talked to his boys about them and his expectations of bringing salvation to these "heathen."

The section around Oberlin had, indeed, been a wilderness when the "colonists" felled its virgin trees for the Institute's founding in 1833, only six years before. But there were no Indians.

Despite his dedicated fundamentalism, John Ingersoll never was retained long by his congregations, and at the moment was without a charge. With his friend and mentor, Charles Grandison Finney, noted evangelist, now a professor of theology at this young college, he hoped there might be an opportunity for him here. And, perhaps at the same time, he could fulfill his longing to minister to the native tribes.

The trip from his last church in northern New York State to this western outpost had been strenuous and tedious, with many stops. He and his boys traveled on the Erie Canal to Buffalo, from there to Cleveland on an uncomfortable lake voyage, thence by stage via Elyria to Oberlin, the road growing rougher with each mile.

While their canal packet was moored at a lock waiting its turn to proceed, John Ingersoll, in mounting disapproval, watched a cockfight in progress beside the towpath. One bird, cruelly mauled, fell prostrate. He could ignore the affair no longer. Leaping to the wharf he stopped the contest. The annoyed promoter, with a blistering oath, thrust the injured fowl at him, and the dignified preacher was forced to return to the deck clutching a limp and bleeding chicken. His boys welcomed it and nursed it the rest of the way.

One bright spot on the journey had been an overnight stay at the fabulous Franklin House on lower Superior Street in Cleveland. It claimed to be the first three-floor frame building in the Western Reserve and was the change center for all stage lines coming in and out of town.

Tavern Proprietor Philo Scovill was undismayed by the presence of a rooster. He was accustomed to oddities. Trained animal troupers and theatrical entertainers, attracted by Mrs. Scovill's famed cooking, put up here and staged acts for their board. Scovill often had a knowing orangutan, a "Fire Eater," or maybe Siamese Twins on his hands. He also operated his own "museum of curiosities" that included "quadrupeds, fish, birds and minerals." Admission was a shilling, children half price. The Ingersoll boys never had seen anything like its wonders.

When Bob and Clark, youngest of five children, were little more than babies their mother died. The brothers were inseparable companions and the "Parson Priest" loved them in his stern way. He took them everywhere he went, even on this arduous trek to Oberlin.

John Ingersoll had been a disciple of Finney since the latter first attained prominence in his foray for Christ through the Mohawk Valley, where, at the time, the peripatetic Ingersoll was going from pastorate to pastorate. He had many opportunities to hear the handsome giant as he thundered Hell and damnation at his hearers, then wooed them with dulcet promises of salvation. Ingersoll fell under his spell, as did other New York State ministers. These men were referred to as "Finney's Prayer Band."

When Finney moved to New York City he asked some of the group, Ingersoll among them, to come to the city to work with him as he lured thousands into his Broadway Tabernacle. Ingersoll preached there in the 1830s for almost a year.

From the beginning, Finney and those in his camp, took an aggressive stand against slavery and viewed its eradication as a Christian's God-directed duty. John Ingersoll became an impassioned abolitionist. His son Bob, though he would reject his father's religious doctrines, agreed with his stand on Negro freedom.

In 1833, before Ingersoll went to the Tabernacle, he occupied a pulpit in Dresden, on Lake Seneca, New York. Here, that year, Bob was born and baptized Robert Green Ingersoll.

His first name was for one of his mother's ancestral connections. The middle name, his father's selection, was in honor of Reverend Beriah Green, orthodox divine and himself a fiery antislavery champion like Ingersoll.

Later, when Robert G. Ingersoll commanded national attention as the Eloquent Skeptic, his detractors liked to say the "G" stood for "Godlessness." It was a great satisfaction to the unregenerated Robert that Green, whose name he bore, in his later years adopted a gentler religious attitude that stressed deeds rather than creeds.

But Green was firm in the faith of Calvin when Bob was born. That year he was appointed head of Oneida Institute in Whitesboro, not far from Utica. John Ingersoll knew and approved the school, which endorsed Christian education and the manual labor concept, a combination of the "plough, the shovel, the axe . . . and Virgil, Cicero, Euclid. . . ."

Ingersoll and Green, both "Finneyites," met first as students at Middlebury College, where, Robert Ingersoll quipped, his father had been trained "in the rudiments of ignorance."

Green came to Oneida from Western Reserve College, established seven years before, in 1826, in Hudson, Ohio. He had vacated the chair of sacred literature, intolerant of the college's espousal of gradual freedom and African colonization for the Negro instead of immediate emancipation, to which he was committed.

These opposing points of view, current in many abolition circles, tore asunder the college as well as the village of Hudson. Owen Brown, father of the militant John, a supporter of the Hudson college, transferred his allegiance to Oberlin, thirty-five miles away. His daughter, Florella, later Mrs. Samuel Adair, a missionary to Osawatomie, Kansas, had graduated from the second class of the Ladies' Course at Oberlin. That commencement took place a few weeks after the Ingersolls' arrival in 1839. Florella received no degree, since Oberlin did not grant degrees to women until 1841.

A further historical coincidence was Green's and Ingersoll's friendship with Gerrit Smith, devout philanthropist and northern New York State landowner. Through the far-flung and all-embracing influence of Finney, Smith gave generously to Oberlin and later was one of John Brown's principal backers.

Oberlin, conceived "to supply the world with the best means of grace," sprouted from Upper New York State evangelism. That Christian renaissance surged into Ohio seeking new souls for the Lord as an integral part of the western push for new lands. Oberlin's founder, John Jay Shipherd, was from that New York State region, a missionary who had felt Finney's inspiration and had known Ingersoll and Green.

Oneida Institute contributed its share to Oberlin, which accepted Green's radical discarding of "pagan" classics for strictly Biblical languages, as well as Oneida's labor plan. In Finney's wake in the East there was much talk about the ambitious Oberlin colony and school, into which he was breathing the breath of life.

Such crosscurrents of interests and wide acquaintanceship caught up John Ingersoll, earnest but without a pulpit, and lighted his eyes with the vision of fair, far pastures. In this virgin land of Ohio, with its college flowering under the masterful Finney, he hoped there would be a place where he might serve his God and establish a home for his motherless boys and girls.

For little Bob, unaware of his father's entanglements with the past and dreams of the future, the Ohio interlude just coming up would shape the pattern of his life and help mold him as the Great Agnostic.

Finney had a house ready for the Ingersolls. This probably was taken as a good omen by the newcomer, for there were not many houses as yet in the colony that was so closely knit with the college.

Along with his academic obligations, Finney was also the local minister. However, he was often away barnstorming for friends and funds for Oberlin. Ingersoll acted as substitute preacher for him on several occasions. These were trial appearances that might lead, presumably, to a permanent post in the growing community.

A large room in Tappan, and sometimes in Ladies' Hall, accommodated worshipers in lieu of a church or campus chapel. In summer the Big Tent, pitched in Tappan Square, covered three hundred feet of ground and could seat two to three thousand. It was the gift of some of Finney's New York State admirers and was intended for revival meetings around Ohio. Over its top, like a gay circus banner, fluttered a blue-and-white pennant proclaiming to the breezes: "Holiness unto the Lord." Around this canvas, hoisted in Heaven's name, hogs and chickens ran unconfined, and tasseled corn grew tall in Tappan Square.

Ingersoll, thoroughly grounded in Biblical Greek and Hebrew, solid in scripture, sound in dogma, trimmed sermons as well as delivery after Finney. He was there to save souls and he pleaded for repentance, warned of eternal fires awaiting the wicked, and quoted chapter and verse to back his argument. He punctuated it with denunciations of slavery as bitter as any of Beriah Green's. His audience was given full measure with exhortations of two to three hours at one standing—and never any abbreviating of prayers.

Despite such consecration—or maybe because of it—Oberlin hearers, like others before them, failed to respond. The wave of conservatism washing over abolition groups elsewhere was affecting Oberlin, stronghold of antislavery though it was. In fact, when some years before the idea was first announced of admitting Negroes to the new campus, it roused a storm of opposition, much to the surprise of Shipherd and associates.

Ingersoll's emancipation views did nothing to gain adherents. The churched of Oberlin, whether on this score or not, did not care for the few sample discourses he offered them.

In May, 1841, he left for Ashtabula, Ohio, to become minister of the First Presbyterian Church. Bob and Clark were with him. The older children, who had joined him in Oberlin, remained to attend the academy and college.

After a year in Ashtabula, Ingersoll went to North Madison, and then to Rome, all northeastern Ohio towns only a few miles apart. Though he labored tirelessly, parishioners let him go as readily as before. For the father those years were disillusioning and discouraging. For the son, who would become one of his generation's prominent men, it was a time of awakening. He turned keen, boyish, appraising eyes on the gloomy parental teachings—and shied away!

Many tales about Robert Ingersoll's Ohio boyhood are based on reminiscent remarks he made during a visit to Ashtabula in 1896, three years before his death. He came to deliver a lecture, one on his regular schedule. He stayed on to see more of the town, "where I lived 55 years ago," as he reported to his daughter in a letter from Cleveland a few days later. He "saw the old church where father preached—the house where I went to school—the old Baptist Church where I recited 'I remember, I remember'—the old house in which we lived . . ."

He added that he had had a good audience in an engagement in Cleveland. "The new lecture: 'Why I am an Agnostic' was well received."

An example of his magic hold on the public was the incident of the toothless old country woman in poke bonnet and outlandish clothes who traveled from a distant farm by wagon and by train to hear him in Ashtabula. The next morning she was at the local depot bright and early to wait half the day to see her idol once more when he and his wife would come to take the train for Cleveland.

At this time Colonel Ingersoll—the title won as a cavalry leader in the Civil War—was at the height of his reputation as a trial lawyer, a force in national politics, and as an orator of the cadenced phrase, unsurpassed in his era.

Most of all he was known for the controversial religious topics he spoke and wrote about. Wherever he went he made headlines. Though he insisted he was not an atheist nor an infidel, but an agnostic seeking truth rationally, he was hounded by churchmen of all denominations.

In the vanguard of nineteenth-century effort to reconcile entrenched Christian concepts with the new science, Ingersoll magnified the issue with such platform titles as "Some Mistakes of Moses," "Myth and Miracle," "Superstition," "The Holy Bible"—in which he asserted he was trying to assay the truth about the book—and "The Devil," wherein he wondered if the Devil were to die whether God would create another.

It fell to the role of Royal Bob to nominate James G. Blaine for the presidency, extolling him as "the plumed knight." This imperishable phrase brought renown to Colonel Ingersoll and kept

Blaine's name alive, though he lost the nomination. Rutherford B. Hayes of Fremont, Ohio, gained the convention's nod instead and Ingersoll campaigned for him—as he did for James A. Garfield and William McKinley, both Ohioans like Hayes. All three, though stanch and articulate churchmen, were friends of Heretic Ingersoll and grateful for his support. The devout Mrs. Garfield, writing from Lawnfield, her Mentor home, could not help but insert: "Though your theology may not be able to give me much comfort, your magnificent friendship does; and I thank you for every word you uttered. General Garfield joins me in admiration and gratitude . . ."

The following July Garfield was shot by a disgruntled office seeker, Charles J. Guiteau. Oddly, this same man, in a burst of fanaticism, had threatened Ingersoll some years before as he was delivering a lecture.

It was Garfield, when President-elect, who, meeting Ingersoll in Washington, called him Royal Bob.

The Ingersoll home was on Main Street near the site of the present-day Hotel Ashtabula. Next door lived John Robertson, church elder. Robertson had a cow. Young Bob, though only eight, was held responsible for most of the care of the large vegetable garden at the rear of the parsonage.

One day the boy straightened up from weeding a row of beans to see Robertson's cow charging toward him, trampling through the peas and potatoes as she came. He knew his father would whip him if the vegetables were ruined—they were important to a pastor receiving only $200 per annum.

Bob was as terrified of the cow as of his father's punishment. He heaved a clump of earth at the animal. It was a good aim. The cow wheeled, pranced off, and disappeared over the bank at the end of the garden. The boy ran to the cliff, sure he would see the creature dashed to pieces in the river below!

How to face Mr. Robertson, a church elder! But the cow, he found, had slid down the slope and landed safely on all four feet well away from the river. The tale was one he liked best to tell about his Ohio years.

Elder Robertson and Bob became good friends. The boy was often seen in the Robertson store sitting on bales and boxes, swinging his legs as the two chatted together. Robertson, attempting to instill tidiness in Bob, who was habitually slovenly, brushed one of his muddy shoes to mirror shininess, then, handing it back to the boy, suggested he treat the other likewise. But Bob was indifferent, content to wear one polished and one dirty shoe.

Reverend Ingersoll, in his zealous attempt to do his duty and raise his children as Christians, used the strap to enforce righteousness. The result was that his boys and girls were afraid of him. When the clergyman came in the front door, they slipped quietly out the back door. The woodshed adjoining the house was a place of torment. Ingersoll recounted one beating he received there for a misdemeanor he did not commit and which he denied. But the more denials, the harder the thrashing. Eventually his father, greatly chagrined, discovered another was guilty.

That episode stayed with the boy, suggested lectures and articles on tyrant parents and inspired the kindly regime followed with his own girls. His daughters worshiped him. The atmosphere of his home, the evident love between husband and wife and parents and children, struck all who came within its walls.

A visitor once said that to step over the threshold of Royal Bob's home was to enter paradise.

One day in his childhood Bob wandered into a Methodist revival meeting in Ashtabula. The minister, catching sight of him as he stood in the aisle, threw searching questions at him: "Do you know you're a sinner?" and "Do you want to be a Christian?" To the divine's consternation, Bob answered, "No," both times. The final admonition that he surely was headed for Hell sent him scurrying from the hall. For days he lived in fear the evangelist might relay his apostasy to his father, and Bob knew only too well, if this happened, what the consequences would be for him.

One of young Bob's pastimes was loitering in the graveyard near the church. He would "speculate on what had become of those people lying there who once were alive, as I was," he recounted years later.

His recital of the "I remember, I remember" verses in the "old Baptist Church" was not altogether a star performance. It was Christmas time and fragrant pine branches decorated the auditorium. Bob, recognized at an early age as an elocutionist, was on the program. He had learned the Thomas Hood poem thoroughly, but when he turned to face the people sitting expectantly before him, the words left him and his tongue was stilled. Three times he tried, running shamefaced, after each failure, to the back of the room. The third time he plunged through the whole of it. He vowed he would never speak again in public!

In North Madison Bob's father took charge of the Bell Church, so called for its steepled bell, one of few thereabouts. In its site today stands the Community Church that also boasts a bell.

Though Oberlin had not welcomed Preacher Ingersoll warmly, he kept in touch with the village. On June 20, 1842, a month after settling his children in North Madison, he returned to Oberlin and was married to one Esther Gates.

Pastor Ingersoll, it would appear, gave out little information about his bride. In North Madison annals she remains unidentified as to name or origin. In records of the Ashtabula Church she is referred to merely as a widow with several children. Local lore also has it that the marriage was not a happy one. The trouble stemmed from her cooking—"Her apple dumplings are heavy enough to shoot a dog with!" her husband was said to have exclaimed.

However, it seems to have been more than apple dumplings that tripped her up. Her food was too elaborate for the clergyman. During his first stay in Oberlin he embraced Sylvester Graham's diet theories, then in full force on campus and colonists' tables. Pious adherents allowed themselves only the simplest food and in small amounts. Money thus saved went to the church.

Whole bolted wheat, known as "graham flour," vegetables, and fruit were eaten. Butter was labeled a luxury. Meat, fish, tea, coffee, and, of course, hard liquor and wine were taboo. Along with "soft" water, a permissible table beverage was "graham coffee," concocted from crusts of stale brown bread soaked in water.

The new Mrs. Ingersoll did not care for such abstemious fare. In this she doubtless was supported by young Bob who always appreciated good meals, as his later girth testified. Perhaps the father's notions on diet made Robert Ingersoll a gourmet in the same way that parental ideas of divinity turned him to agnosticism.

While Graham had his apostles throughout the Western Reserve, there were scoffers like Mrs. Ingersoll who claimed "you can always tell a Grahamite by his lean and hungry look." Finney eventually abandoned the system for Oberlin students as offering inadequate nourishment.

Whether divorce or death terminated Mrs. Ingersoll's career is not known. In a well-rooted tradition, the minister and one Squire Brown were overheard discussing the subject of divorce in the abstract one afternoon when the parsonage parlor door inadvertently was left ajar. Whatever the significance for the second Mrs. Ingersoll in that rumor, the fact is in 1852 John Ingersoll married Miss Frances Willard, former schoolteacher. The family was living in Illinois.

On more than one count the years in North Madison were unpleasant. Ingersoll continued to mix with sermonizing his radical antislavery sentiments. A local and powerfully built blacksmith, critical of his stand on Negro freedom, bullied him practically every Sunday after service. One day Ingersoll lost his temper. He, too, was a strong man and he soundly trounced his foe. His antagonism cooling as suddenly as it had flared, Ingersoll realized it was the Sabbath! He was overwhelmed thus to have desecrated the holy day.

Church members up to now indifferent attenders, the following Sunday filled the pews, for they admired their cleric's just anger and forensic skill as they never had his preaching. Nevertheless, they did not importune him to remain in their midst. Soon he was installed in Rome, in charge of a beautiful steepled church that still stands.

Some present-day communicants recall hearing grandparents speak of John Ingersoll, strict in doctrine and in discipline of his boys, Bob and Clark. The older children were away at school most of the time.

The two boys, always together, endured the ordeal of their father's Sundays: church all morning with interminable prayers and sermons; a quick, frugal meal and back to the meetinghouse for more of the same. Once the prayers were over, the father walked his boys to the parsonage, one on each side of him, holding them firmly by hand lest they skip or run in their relief and so violate the day.

In the decade the Ingersolls spent in Ohio, Bob's education as well as Clark's suffered from the shiftings from one village school to another. Reading matter for them, in addition to the Bible, was confined to their father's shelves, heavy with writings of Calvin, Jonathan Edwards, Foxe's *Book of Martyrs,* and Bunyan's *Pilgrim's Progress.*

Bob decided "God so loved the world that he made up his mind to damn a majority of the human race," as he said in one of his most quoted lectures, "Why I am an Agnostic." He asserted he could not remember when he "believed in the Bible doctrine of eternal punishment," and he had a "dim recollection of always hating Jehovah."

In his maturity, a mellow and benevolent Pagan Prophet, he insisted his iconoclastic beliefs were not in revolt from his father's orthodoxy and, therefore, if he had fallen from grace, his father could not be held responsible.

Clark absorbed his brother's agnostic point of view. The two were law partners in Peoria, Illinois. They had a wide and lucrative practice, until Clark, elected to Congress, left for Washington, and Robert for war service.

Returning to Peoria, Colonel Ingersoll resumed his legal career, which was to continue for forty-four years and involve him in hundreds of cases in many parts of the country.

He appeared so often before the Supreme Court that he moved to Washington. Here he and Clark opened a law office. His intimates were those in top echelons of government and celebrities of such varied stripe as Mark Twain, Walt Whitman, Andrew Carnegie, and General William T. Sherman.

Though a force among Republicans, his outspoken liberalism stunted his political rise. He was denied nomination as Illinois governor when he told an inquiring delegation he "would not smother one religious idea to be emperor of the round globe." His creed was happiness here and now through making others happy. He "believed hands that help holier than lips that pray," C. H. Cramer writes in his biography, *Royal Bob.*

Ingersoll, who had learned of war in a courageous encounter at Shiloh, hated it. It solved no problems, he contended, and he could never forget the widows and orphans it made. His writings and speeches, that were popular well into this century, are little read now, since what the forward-looking Ingersoll pleaded for is blended in today's thinking.

The sudden death of Ebon Clark, at forty-eight years of age, was "the deepest tragedy of my life," Robert Ingersoll wrote. "My poor brother lies asleep in that silent chamber that has no window to the East."

In fulfillment of a compact made years before, that whoever died first would have his funeral conducted by the other, Robert Ingersoll gave the oration, closing it with the following lines repeated at many funerals of "believers":

Life is a narrow vale between the cold and barren peaks of two eternities. We strive in vain to look beyond the heights; we cry aloud, but the only answer is the echo of our cry. From the voiceless lips of the unreplying dead there comes no word; but in the night of death Hope sees a star, and listening Love can hear the rustle of a wing.

Annie Oakley

ANNIE OAKLEY fired her first gun when she was ten. It was a cap and ball Kentucky rifle, taller than she.

The incident was the start of her fabulous career that crowned her the world's trigger queen. Her scarcely believable marksmanship lifted her—and her family—from desperate poverty in the western Ohio wilderness to exhibition matches in European capitals, where she shot a cigarette from the lips of the future Kaiser of Germany and outscored a duke from the Czar's court.

She starred in the Wild West Show of Buffalo Bill (William F. Cody) and thereby re-created the historical American frontier. She lives today in perennial, though often inaccurate, *Annie Get Your Gun* stage and film versions of her story.

Her gun wizardry, afoot or on horseback, coupled with her shy gentlewoman personality, makes her a national legend. In her native Darke County, Ohio, to which she returned again and again between triumphs, and to die, she is well remembered—and very real. This is, indeed, the Annie Oakley country. It attracts so many tourists that guide signs have been erected throughout the area.

Annie was born in 1860, twenty miles north of Greenville, near the tiny village of North Star, not far from the Indiana line. A monument erected by her friends on the north-south highway points to the site of her birthplace, a one-room cabin no longer standing.

She is buried a few miles away, in a small, rural cemetery at Brock. Under a simple tombstone her ashes repose in a silver urn presented to her by the people of France. Beside her lies her husband, Frank Butler, her companion in their make-believe, as well as in their real-life, drama.

In the Darke County Museum at Greenville, high points in her life are revealed in an exhibit of Annie Oakley memorabilia, real Americana, record of the Old West. School children of the county, reared on tales about her, pooled their pennies with a civic leader's contribution to purchase the collection from her relatives.

She was christened Phoebe Ann Moses but was always known by her stage name, Annie Oakley. Her birth date frequently is recorded later than it was because press agents habitually undercounted her years. She did not gainsay the practice. Content to be forever young, to the end of life she was "Missie," Cody's pet name for her, darling of the tanbark. She, in turn, called Butler Jimmie. Missie and Jimmie were together fifty years.

In the crowded home of her girlhood a yawning primitive fireplace supplied heat and cooking needs. Over it hung the rifle that changed her life. No one had been allowed to touch it since her father had put it there a few days before he died.

Secretly she had longed to get her hands on the musket. The opportunity came one day when she was left alone in the cabin. She pushed forward a bench, climbed up, and reached for the weapon. It was heavier than she expected. But she had no trouble loading it, managing the powder horn and shot adroitly, as she had watched her father handle it many times.

Quickly she was outdoors, across her family's fields, and into the forest that circled close. She was at ease in these woods, never afraid, though a wildcat once had leaped on her father's horse and sometimes wolves were heard howling at night.

Straggling bands of Indians had lingered hereabouts long after General "Mad" Anthony Wayne's treaty at Fort Green Ville—the original Greenville—officially disbarred them from this land. Children, frightened by oldsters' tales of those days, were wary of encountering a stray warrior behind a big tree. But not Annie. She knew all the Indians had left. Besides, she didn't scare easily.

Annie had been home only a few days after two terrible years as a "bound girl." When Mrs. Moses's husband died, she was forced to place some of her six children in temporary homes, as she was unable to support them with her irregular nursing jobs. Annie, unbeknownst to her mother, was treated virtually as a slave by the farm couple who took her.

Finally the child ran away, to be lovingly received on her return home. She found her two older sisters married and gone. But the family was still in dire straits. Often there was not enough to eat.

Annie's tragic experience, which would make her for the rest of her life alert to unfortunate children, had matured her beyond her years. She immediately set out to provide for her loved ones with her gun.

Her bare feet trod silently through the bush. An unsuspecting rabbit appeared, sensed danger, and hopped off. But not quite soon enough. Annie lifted her rifle—she never aimed—and fired. The rabbit fell. Before long she stopped a second cottontail. Now her mother could fix a good dinner!

The little girl fairly sang as she balanced her gun with one hand and, with the other, carried her still warm booty back to the cabin.

After this Annie went out every day. Wild life of all kinds was plentiful: pheasant, woodcock, turkey, grouse, wild geese, and quail. She was bagging more game than her family could consume. She was trapping some, too. It occurred to her she might sell the surplus.

In a day or two she "ketched a ride" with a neighbor driving his wagon to Greenville. There Annie called on a storekeeper from whom she bought shot when she had a little money and could get into town.

Falteringly, she asked the merchant: Would he buy her game? The man had heard about the struggles of the family. Annie seemed such a little girl . . . He could not refuse to help. Cautiously he agreed to take a small quantity on trial. He gave her an extra amount of ammunition on credit against what quarry she would bring him.

Annie's problem of getting her produce to the store while fresh was solved, too. Her father had been in charge of the district mail route. His successor, moved by the girl's pluck and her family's need, volunteered to take her birds to market.

After the first few lots the storekeeper ordered more. Her produce came neatly dressed and moist, carefully wrapped in swamp grasses. The flesh was never riddled or torn, for she had mastered the trick of shooting game through the head, leaving the meaty parts whole.

The Greenville merchant put her in touch with a friend, manager of a fine hotel in Cincinnati, eighty miles away. Shortly, the two were taking all that she could bag. She also sold pelts to an old-time French fur trader who lived in a hut on the outskirts of Greenville. He liked the girl, especially for the way she prepared the skins.

By the time she reached her early teens, Annie had a going

business. She was able to help her mother substantially with finances.

With some of her first earnings she planted an apple orchard. She loved apple blossoms and during the long years of her stardom she tried to be at home, if only briefly when the trees were in bloom.

When Annie had been with the family who treated her so shamefully, she was allowed to attend a country school for a few terms. At recess one day a boy teasingly called to her: "Annie Moses-Poses, Moses-Poses!" Other children, seeing it annoyed her, took up the chant, repeating it whenever she appeared.

Ridiculing of her name rankled and she came to hate it. She began calling herself "Mozee." It was the way the French fur trader pronounced Moses, which she dropped forthwith. As the years went by she used it only once again, on her marriage certificate. Mozee appeared on all other future documents. She went so far as to have Moses removed from family gravestones and Mozee incised in its place. Though some clung to Moses, eventually Annie persuaded all her kin to her way of thinking, except her brother. He was John Moses to the day he died.

When Annie was fifteen, an older sister, married and living in Cincinnati, invited her to the city as a treat. The sister's husband and the manager of the hotel where Annie's game was served, belonged to a trapshooting club. An exhibition match was staged for Thanksgiving Day, favorite time for such events.

The challenger was one Frank Butler who was appearing entr'actes in marksmanship demonstrations at a downtown theater. There was a fifty-dollar prize for the winner. Annie's brother-in-law, who had been boasting about her cleverness, listed her in the event. Annie was doubtful, but she was tempted by the award.

She had brought her father's gun with her to Cincinnati. For the trip she had discarded her usual calico and made herself a gingham dress, pink, with a bonnet to match. Her brown hair in two thick braids, tied with pink ribbons, hung to her waist.

In this costume she arrived at the shooting grounds. When she saw the crowd she was terrified and wanted to leave. The suave Butler, in well-cut city clothes, with a shiny, slim rifle held gracefully in hand, stepped forward.

He laughed when his opponent was pointed out. The slight,

oddly garbed girl looked even younger than her age, and her awkward muzzle-loader seemed too big for her. But Butler was a kindly person and sensing her discomfort smiled at her encouragingly. She felt reassured at once—and she never forgot that smile.

Butler, confident and relaxed, shot first, marking the clay pigeon neatly. Annie stood beside him trembling—until she snuggled her gun on her shoulder. Directing it in the seemingly casual fashion that was her uncanny technique, she fired squarely at her pigeon.

Then Frank, then Annie, one after another. Each hit the mark. Butler's final turn. He missed. The onlookers were breathless. .No one moved. Annie seemed completely calm. In a quick gesture she pushed off her bonnet and it dangled from its ties at her back. *Crack!* She hit her target!

The audience let go in wild applause, the kind she was to hear continually in the years ahead. The money handed her was the largest sum she ever had earned in so short a time. It was a fortune to her.

The astonished Butler, instead of resenting his defeat, was over·whelmed with admiration for the girl, ten years his junior. He gave her and her relatives tickets to the play scheduled for that night. It was *Uncle Tom's Cabin.* Annie was excited. She never had been inside a theater. Her family could not afford such luxury and, besides, from religious convictions they disapproved of the stage.

Feeling a bit wicked, she took in the entertainment. She loved the play, but even more the fancy shooting put on by Butler and his partner. In a "William Tell" number they smashed an apple resting on the head of Butler's white poodle, George.

When the program was over, Annie went backstage, wide-eyed at the whole affair. Butler held George by a tight leash, watching him closely, for the dog hated women and was known to bite them. Suddenly freeing himself from his master, the animal bounded up to Annie, wagging his tail to be petted and fondled.

George's appraisal confirmed Frank's. The man was drawn by the girl's simple dignity and natural charm, which were destined to win so many to her in the future.

Before long Butler was to ask Annie to be his wife. Annie's mother was poor, but she was firm. No daughter of hers would marry an actor.

With Annie on his side, Butler soon convinced the mother. Her only stipulation was that Annie must be sixteen before she could marry.

The wedding duly took place in the little home, clear now of its mortgage. Two small rooms had been added to the house, paid for by Annie's gun. For the ceremony her dress was pink gingham, a copy of the one she wore when she outshot Frank.

The couple agreed that the bride should resume her schooling, for she could scarcely read or write. But this plan was not to work. A few nights after the wedding, when the theater was already filled, Frank's partner became ill and could not do his part.

Annie volunteered to take his place. A rehearsal was out of the question. Nevertheless, the program went off without a hitch. George seemed to sense the emergency and stood particularly still when Annie aimed at the apple. She shot a cork from a wine bottle her husband held in his hand. As she finished with a flourish, she left the stage with a little kicking step that would become her trademark at every finale.

From that night on, Frank had a new partner, his wife. They billed themselves at first as Butler and Butler, but soon changed to Butler and Oakley. They picked the name for her out of the blue.

Annie could not relinquish the idea of an education. Classroom attendance was impractical. So her husband, an avid reader, turned schoolteacher in their off hours. He opened a magic world to her, using as textbooks daily newspapers and what books were at hand: a biography of Daniel Webster; *Tom Sawyer*, recently published; *Robinson Crusoe*, and *Oliver Twist*, which brought tears to Annie, always affected by childhood ills.

The partnership before the footlights and their husband-wife devotion were as much part of contemporary theatrical lore as Annie's fantastic feats.

It was not long before Frank realized the lead attraction in their program was his slim, girlish wife with her quick smile and sure shot. He promptly withdrew to become her manager and helper.

It was not a minor role. He handled all practical details, improvised new acts, was tireless and constant in promotion of Annie and unfailingly proud of her.

They booked with Forepaugh and Sells Circus. Annie found it a different kind of experience to shoot under canvas. She was drawn to the horses, the first she had encountered since her Ohio childhood. Neither Frank nor the management had known she was an accomplished equestrian.

She dashed around the arena on horseback, shattering crystal balls, as many as six at a throw, clipping pennies held up by Butler, stooping for one gun, firing it, galloping on to grab another . . .

Buffalo Bill witnessed a performance and signed up the couple for his Wild West Show. Annie became a celebrity, billed as the World's Champion shot. But she was outshining the great Cody himself. This piqued him.

The Butlers moved to Pawnee Bill's Frontier Exposition. However, they soon were back with Cody, now welcoming them warmly.

Missie and Jimmie rounded out seventeen years' association with Buffalo Bill, appearing in major cities in this country and abroad, before untold thousands. Annie, slight and feminine, was the most talked about woman of the decade.

The dramatic Cody, impeccably groomed in white, on a handsome white charger, lived well and saw to it that his company did also. He marshaled his exuberant cast like a close-knit clan. Among them were many Indians, including Chief Sitting Bull and his Sioux. They were often discontented and troublesome. But they had an understanding ally in Annie, from frontier Ohio, where Indians were not yet quite forgotten.

She watched fascinated as they played their parts, realistically waylaying mail stage and prairie schooner. It was almost more than she could bear to sit through Sitting Bull's faithful re-enactment of the terrible battle of the Little Big Horn when, under his command, General George Armstrong Custer and his regiment were wiped out to a man. The Montana battle had occurred in 1876, the year Annie was married. Like all Americans she had been greatly upset at the time.

Custer, an Ohioan too, was born in New Rumley. He was a major general at twenty-five, youngest in the Union Army. It was to him Robert E. Lee handed the white flag of truce at the conclusion of the Civil War, when Annie was five.

Later Annie met Custer's widow. The two became friends, Annie sympathizing deeply with Mrs. Custer, admiring her efforts in her books and speeches to vindicate the general's stand at the Big Horn.

Despite Sitting Bull's bloody record, the big lumbering chief and the dainty Annie Oakley liked each other. The first time he saw her shoot, he was astonished that a woman, and white at that, could be as good with a gun as he was. To honor her, he asked to adopt her into his tribe to take the place of a daughter who had died. After the adoption ritual, he kept her photograph always before him, calling her Little Sure Shot, a name that stuck.

Buffalo Bill moved his company to New York City, where the

entire populace, it seemed, emptied into the streets for the miles-long parade. At Madison Square Garden Annie rode a spirited pony and starred anew. She fired at glass balls and sometimes eggs, with a pistol held upside down, or backward over her shoulder.

How could she reach a target she could not see? She felt it with her whole being, she tried to explain to mystified onlookers. With Butler holding playing cards fifty feet away, she shot through the spots. From this trick, complimentary theater and sports event tickets, customarily punched with holes, came to be known in entertainment parlance as "Annie Oakleys."

Butler and his wife were keenly interested in children. Cody gave the two permission to arrange a free show in the Garden for orphans and other underprivileged youngsters. Annie bought ice cream for her guests. The affair proved an excellent advertisement for the Wild West Show, though this had not been in anyone's mind.

They stirred up more publicity, and again unintentionally. One snowy day Annie and Frank, in a spirit of fun, hitched Jerry, the show's tame moose, to a cutter, for a drive through the streets of New York City. They did not go far. Jerry spied a sidewalk vendor and a pushcart loaded with big red apples. He made a dive for the fruit, spilling what he did not eat. Jerry was huge and hungry. Frank, helpless to control the beast, paid for the damage. Finally he got the big fellow back to his corral. Next morning the city's newspapers carried page-one stories about Missie and the Moose.

The great of the land streamed through the turnstiles, personages like the Reverend Henry Ward Beecher, General William Tecumseh Sherman, General Philip Sheridan, and Mark Twain. The last, always an enthusiastic traveler, suggested to Cody that he take his show to Europe.

The Butlers, thrilled at the prospect of going abroad, hurried to North Star for farewells. Annie's mother, at such homecomings, took care of her famous daughter's wardrobe. It was an extensive one, for Annie had dozens of costume changes. Her mother, a clever needlewoman, created new outfits, mended and remodeled the old. In the days before ready access to dry cleaners, she hung the renovated garments on her clothesline to flap and freshen in the clean air of a country spring.

The long lines of gay attire hanging in the dooryard, like in-residence flags over a royal castle, signaled to neighbors that Annie was home—and they arrived en masse. The Butlers put on special matches for them, inviting all who cared to come. Frank liked to wander about North Star, visiting with villagers, who welcomed him as one of their own.

Thanks to Annie's generosity, the homestead was larger and really comfortable. But the old-style high beds still were in use. On them were straw mattresses, fragrant and inviting. Annie's mother was a meticulous housekeeper.

By April, 1887, Missie and Jimmie were back in New York to board a chartered steamer, *The State of Nebraska*, a happy choice, for Cody was a Nebraskan.

The voyage was stormy and a tremendous undertaking for such an assemblage. The varied personnel counted over one hundred Indians, dozens of rough riders, cowboys, scores of ponies and show horses, buffalo, deer, elk . . . and Jerry the moose. Few among them, humans or beasts, ever had been on an ocean ship.

They landed in England when the country was celebrating Queen Victoria's golden jubilee. The festival spirit in the air was conducive to a warm reception for this strange contingent, the first genuine American western aggregation ever to cross the sea. It captivated Britishers, commoner and titled alike.

The Prince of Wales, destined fourteen years later to be King Edward VII, was so taken with the show he urged his mother, Queen Victoria, to view it, too. At a royal command performance ox-driven caravans of settlers beat off an Indian attack, rodeo actors lassoed their steers and ponies, and Custer's cavalry was wiped out. Finally, Little Sure Shot leaped into the arena. She rode at breakneck speed, shooting coins and balls continually tossed into the air by Frank on a horse at her side.

After the band sounded the last curtain, Queen Victoria sent for Annie. The young American, so sure of herself in the ring, stood at the royal box tongue-tied before the old Queen, so dowdy and yet so regal in her widow's black.

"You are a very clever girl," said the Queen. "I want to give you this as a souvenir for the pleasure you have given me." She handed Annie the pearl-and-gold opera glasses through which she had followed the acts. These opera glasses now are part of the Annie Oakley collection in the Greenville museum.

The London press the following day was full of the Queen's recognition, and more gifts came to Annie—jewelry, the first of any value she had owned, and so many flowers that she distributed bouquets daily to the city's hospitals.

The Butlers were guests for weekend hunts on English estates and they made lasting friendships among the gentry. When they returned to play in later years in England they said it was like coming home.

Buffalo Bill took his company abroad again two years later, this time landing in France. After six months in Paris, their schedule took them on the proverbial Grand Tour. The girl from the Ohio backwoods, billed as twenty and looking not one whit older, though she was nearing thirty, was seeing the Old World.

In Barcelona and Madrid, Spanish bullfighting shocked her. In Rome the whole cast attended the anniversary of the ordination of Pope Leo XIII. Everyone dressed in his best. The Indians added special paint for the occasion and were restrained, only by Annie's pleading, from letting go with war whoops in the Vatican.

The Butlers staged special shoots before "Mad" King Ludwig of Bavaria at his regent's request. In Austria they hunted with the emperor in his game preserve, where Annie couldn't bear to raise her rifle against the gentle-eyed deer.

Crown Prince Wilhelm saw the performance in Berlin. Annie described to Ohio relatives how she accepted his dare and shot a cigarette from his lips. During the war which he loosed on the world when he was Kaiser Wilhelm, Annie staged benefit matches for the American Red Cross. But when Annie first met him there was no hint of conflict.

The Wild Westerners stayed three and a half years in Europe. They returned to the U.S.A. to be headlined at the World's Fair in Chicago.

During an interval in the East, Jimmie and Missie were asked to come to West Orange, New Jersey, to visit the laboratory of their friend Thomas A. Edison. While the couple acted out a silent pantomime, Edison turned a crank in a strange machine to make what Frank called a "peep show." It was one of the first motion pictures.

There followed strenuous years, crisscrossing the country on itineraries that stretched from the Gulf to New England and into Canada. In 1901, when the long circus train was heading north from Charlotte, North Carolina, as the season was ending, a southbound freight train missed a signal and the two locomotives crashed head on. Frank pushed through the debris in their crushed sleeping coach to find his wife. He carried her out, badly injured.

Over one hundred animals, many of them horses Annie and

Frank had ridden, and knew by name and loved, shrieked and stomped in agony and had to be shot.

It was a year before Annie could handle a gun. The shock and suffering turned her brown hair snow-white. But when her hair was dyed and she discarded crutch and cane, she became Missie again, young enough to star in *The Western Girl*. This play, written for her, made her the symbol of the girl of the golden west.

Fred Stone, dramatizing *The Wizard of Oz*, later was to win fame in *The Red Mill*. Annie loved the plays and saw them many times. Stone and his wife and the Butlers were congenial and often were together. Will Rogers, crony of all of them, taught Annie rope tricks.

The Butlers tried to retire. They never had lived extravagantly and did not need money. But trouping was in their blood. The Road called. Annie Oakley's name was in lights once more!

However, Missie began to tire easily. She came back to Greenville to rest. She settled herself in the home of a friend. A sister arrived to nurse her. Jimmie was frail. He had a persistent cough that worried Annie. They had vacationed frequently in Florida. Annie insisted he must go south to escape the Ohio winter. She usually had her way and he planned to go.

But before he could start south, Annie died in her sleep. Butler seemed to stop living. Eighteen days later they dug a grave for him beside Missie's fresh one. It was 1926, the year of their golden wedding.

After all her wanderings she was back in Darke County. This was the place she always thought of as she listened night after night to the band playing "Home Sweet Home," the show's final curtain.

Woodrow Wilson

CHILLICOTHE's fashionable Paint Street, where the Thomas Woodrows lived, was gay that summer evening of 1881. Carriages deposited laughing, smartly groomed young people at the Woodrows' handsome doorway. Lights twinkled late up and down the row of stately houses built close to the crisscrossed brick sidewalk.

The old central Ohio city was founded by Virginia aristocrats, many of them friends of the early U.S. presidents from their state, including Washington himself. Those settlers left a legacy of architectural elegance and culture that has been cherished through the generations. An air of the Old South continues to hover over this one-time state capital, noted today as in the past for its gracious way of life and its hospitality.

When this little-known chapter in American annals opens, the Woodrows' talented daughter, Harriet, had just returned from a year at the Cincinnati Conservatory of Music, having won many honors there. A series of parties and formal balls was under way in recognition of the attractive young lady, who was soon to celebrate her twenty-first birthday.

Harriet's cousin, Tommy Wilson, arrived from Wilmington, North Carolina, for the fun—but, more particularly, to see Harriet. He planned to remain for the rest of the summer.

Tommy was named Thomas Woodrow Wilson for his mother's adored brother, Harriet's father. After this present trip—perhaps in memory of it—he dropped the Thomas and adopted the shorter, more euphonious Woodrow Wilson. But he always was addressed as Tommy by his kinfolk, not excepting when he was President of the United States!

The previous winter, poor health had forced him to leave the

University of Virginia, where he was enrolled in the law school. He wrote to former classmates in discouragement while pursuing his studies alone at home, "My doctor found my digestive organs seriously out of gear," and "How can a man with a weak body ever arrive anywhere?"

Uncle Thomas and his wife thought a change would be beneficial and this summer had invited him for a prolonged stay. Members of the Woodrow and Wilson families, close-knit and deeply affectionate, saw a great deal of each other. Young Wilson felt at home in Chillicothe, for he had been here on numerous occasions since babyhood.

This visit of Tommy's, however, was different. He bounded up the high flight of steps at the entrance as if he could hardly wait to be inside. The tall, rather delicate-appearing young man, who would be twenty-five in December, was very much in love.

The Woodrow house, now the Philip Butler residence, happily spared remodeling, retains its good design, including such details as its original hand-wrought iron embellishments. The Greek Revival house looks much as it did to Tommy on that warm August evening.

The nation was scanning anxiously every report from the sickbed of President James A. Garfield, Ohioan, who was fighting for his life from an assassin's bullet in Washington. Young Wilson, already seriously interested in politics and government, had criticized Garfield's nomination the previous year, labeling the American convention system "the country's curse." An ardent Democrat, he caviled at the Republican party, Garfield's party, as "disintegrating" and "doomed to speedy death."

But at this moment, hurrying to his uncle's door, Tommy was giving little attention to the dying Garfield. Certainly he could not guess that thirty-two years later he would follow in the footsteps of the twentieth president when he himself took office as the twenty-eighth. Tommy was concentrating on his romance with Harriet.

She is described as beautiful, with gold-brown hair, flower-petal complexion, and the bright blue eyes of her Scottish forebears—the same "Woodrow eyes" that Tommy had. As the two were growing up, they often were together, for their families, in that day of difficult journeying, made long stays in each other's homes, once arrived.

Harriet's father, Thomas Woodrow, a successful Chillicothe merchant, was looked to as head of the clan. His big house, which was the birthplace of his eldest child, Harriet, in 1860, was the gathering place for the connections.

Born in Scotland, he came to this side as a boy, one of eight children. Exhausted from the turbulent, two-month voyage on a crowded packet, his mother died shortly after landing. The father, also Thomas Woodrow, a learned Presbyterian minister who read his Bible in Hebrew and Greek, was appointed minister of the First Presbyterian Church in Chillicothe.

Young Thomas, while in his teens, clerked in a local clothing store and before long became a partner in the business. His father married again and four more children were born.

The junior Thomas left the crowded manse, setting up a separate home for himself and two of his sisters, Jessie, who became the mother of Woodrow Wilson, and Marion, later Mrs. James Bones. Though only a few years older than his sisters, he cared for them like a father, sending them to boarding school and lavishing fine clothes and expensive gifts on them. The three were devoted to each other throughout their lives.

Because of these ties and his responsibilities, Thomas did not marry until both girls were in homes of their own. Then, at thirty-six, he chose as his wife a charming Chillicothean, Helen Sill, just half his age.

Sister Jessie attended the wedding, which took place early in 1860. With her came Tommy, not yet four, and her husband, Reverend Joseph R. Wilson, then pastor of a Presbyterian church in Augusta, Georgia.

The North-South breach was widening. Civil War was coming closer. In Augusta, destined to be a Confederate industrial center, Tommy's father in a couple of years would dismiss his congregation one Sabbath that they might hurry to the former U.S. arsenal, now in Southern hands, to make desperately needed ammunition. His church became a hospital for wounded and dying Confederate soldiers. Like all the others in the town, the Wilsons suffered from a food shortage.

At the war's end, Tommy, with his parents and the populace, greeted the sad Robert E. Lee. He never forgot the event and he made Lee one of his heroes . . . Tommy's father, born in the north, with relatives in the Union Army, though not a violent Southern sympathizer, was loyal to his flock . . .

But the Civil War had not yet broken out when Thomas Woodrow was married and everything was serene and happy in Chillicothe for the wedding. One and all, the Woodrows and the Wilsons took the girlish bride to their hearts. Little Tommy capitulated on sight. She was always his "dear Aunt Helen."

The Woodrows christened their first son James Wilson, honoring Tommy's father, and the boy was known as Wilson. The record, then, is confronted with a Wilson Woodrow and a Woodrow Wilson!

Through the years Tommy and Hattie took each other for granted —until his senior year (1878–79) at Princeton University. Harriet was at Augusta Female Seminary, later Mary Baldwin Seminary, in Staunton, Virginia. Several other young cousins also were there, as well as Tommy's sister, Jessie, named for their mother.

The Wilsons had moved to Wilmington, where Dr. Wilson was in charge of the Presbyterian church. The North Carolina home was not too far from Staunton and Harriet was a welcome guest whenever school sessions permitted.

Tommy, returning to the parental roof from college during one of these interludes, took a new look at this Ohio cousin with the brown curls and bright blue eyes. He liked what he saw. Hattie suddenly had become a young lady—and an accomplished one. She excelled in French, had a sweet, well-trained voice and played the piano and organ.

The sober-minded Princeton senior, never what might be called a sociable person, was attracted to the vivacious girl. She in turn apparently saw him in something more than a cousinly role.

In the fall of 1879 Tommy entered the University of Virginia and Harriet enrolled for another year at the Seminary. There was good railroad service on a direct route over the Blue Ridge connecting Charlottesville and Staunton. The distance of forty miles was not enough to daunt a lover.

Staunton was Tommy's birthplace, as is proudly proclaimed on every Virginia map today. The Seminary was housed in the former Presbyterian church, whose pulpit Tommy's father had occupied and where Tommy was baptized.

Though the Wilsons left the town when Tommy was a year old, it was familiar territory to him. Most conveniently for him, and for Harriet, another uncle-aunt team, the peripatetic Boneses, lived here at the time.

Harriet spent the Christmas holidays at the Bones home. Tommy came across the mountains from the University for his vacation. The Bones's daughter, another Jessie, younger than her cousins and a jolly tomboy when they all were children, made a congenial third.

However, Harriet and Tommy managed to have a good deal of time to themselves. Harriet had made great progress, especially in music. Indeed, before the year was out she would receive three gold medals, all the Seminary awarded annually.

Tommy listened by the hour as she played and sang for him in the Bones's parlor—Presbyterian hymns, Mendelssohn's "Spring Song," the "Brook" by Pape, and "The Last Rose of Summer." He thought her voice as exquisite as Adelina Patti's.

He wanted her to teach him to sing so they might perform duets together. It would help him in his "elocution" drill. Already he had attained a reputation as a public speaker, prelude to the brilliant oratory that marked his career.

A few weeks later, in mid-January, 1880, James Bones wrote Tommy's mother about the holiday guests:

> We had a quiet, but very pleasant Christmas and our chief enjoyment was in having dear Tommie with us for a week. He capivated all our hearts most completely, being such a manly, sensible, affectionate fellow . . . We hope to see him frequently as he can easily run over Saturday afternoon and return by early Monday morning train in time for his (University) lecture. He has promised to come often. Hattie spent the week with us and she and Jessie and Tommy had nice times together.

Tommy apparently kept the promise Uncle James referred to. He spent many a weekend in the Bones home—not entirely to see the Boneses. He was in the audience one evening for a concert at the Seminary, and when Harriet finished her number his applause was so long and loud she was embarrassed.

He assured her repeatedly that the admiration he expressed for her singing and playing was sincere and in no sense flattery . . . Her father sent a barrel of apples from his Ohio orchard to Staunton and bade Hattie share the fruit with Tommy and the Bones family.

Came the day for Harriet's graduation concert. The Woodrows arrived from Chillicothe. Likewise Tommy from his parents' home in Wilmington, where he resolutely was pursuing his lawbooks and trying to build up a body that tended always to be somewhat frail.

Harriet was not alone a winner of scholastic kudos. Before leaving the University, Tommy, too, distinguished himself, recognized as a writer and debater, particularly in his speech on John Bright, a contemporary English orator whom he admired. So felicitations were in order for him from his fond relatives, as well as for Harriet. Her performance topped all others, Tommy insisted, pointing out that it had aroused the longest and most enthusiastic ovation.

That fall Harriet sought further musical training in the more exacting precincts of the Cincinnati Conservatory. She and Tommy, still working out his law destiny by himself, were more widely separated. They had been writing to each other and now the correspondence was stepped up. During a period of two years many letters were exchanged, ardent love letters, judging by the nine from Tommy which survived.

Though she had married another, Harriet preserved these letters in a little bundle carefully tied with a blue satin ribbon. After her death her daughter, Helen Welles Thackwell, found them amidst Harriet's treasures in a rosewood and copper box, later depositing them in the Princeton University Library.

In an article published in the autumn, 1950, University Library Chronicle, Mrs. Thackwell summarizes the letters and recounts details of this courtship which has had relatively little attention from Wilson biographers.

Writing while still at Charlottesville, Tommy gives vivid glimpses of campus life, his pleasure in his fraternity and literary and debating societies. Harriet is his "Sweet Rosalind." Later, at home and discouraged by his lack of health and the lonely academic schedule, he emphasizes how much he is cheered by word from her. Since they cannot see each other often, they must make it up by mail.

Both are working hard. He is perfecting himself in every way he can, that he may be "a commanding influence in the councils of my country." He sent her a book of Longfellow's poems which he knew she admired, but he did not. The binding he considered better than the volume's content.

On Decoration Day—May 10 in the South—he watched as the Ladies Memorial Association decorated graves of Confederate soldiers. To him this seems "an empty ceremony," calculated to keep alive the war's bitterness. He decries the day's oratory and the parades as sentimentality.

Wishing that Hattie might come to Wilmington, but realizing this is impossible, he tries to content himself with prospects of his visit to Chillicothe in the summer. That seems far in the future, but by then he will have wound up his law studies and be prepared for the bar.

There is every evidence that the attachment between the gifted Woodrow daughter and the highly regarded Wilson son, despite the unusual cousinly status, had the sanction of both sets of parents, and of all the relatives. Harriet, on the other hand, was developing some very real misgivings.

Her mother and father, totally unaware of her growing disquietude, were genuinely glad to see Tommy and greeted him with their usual warmth. Jessie Bones also arrived and it was a merry family gathering.

Elite youth of Chillicothe and some from out of town crowded the Woodrow ballroom for the first of the several entertainments arranged. Tommy and Hattie were partners as often as he could contrive it. During a dance halfway through the evening he suddenly stopped. Holding her firmly, he insisted in a tense whisper that she leave the floor with him. Harriet hesitated at first, but, not wanting to make a scene, slipped away with him.

Tommy escorted her down the winding stairway and out into the garden. In the quiet darkness he told her what he said he was sure she realized: that he loved her and could not imagine life without her. He wanted her to marry him without delay, adding "your parents approve of me, and mine of you—you know they would be happy to see us married!"

He could support her, he went on, for he was ready now to practice law. He was aware she did not especially like life in the South, so he offered to settle in any northern city of her choosing. There he would open a law office—if she would be his wife. Otherwise, he declared, he would give up law after a few years' experience in it. Furthermore, he would turn to teaching, the profession he really wanted to follow.

They walked arm in arm as they talked, their footsteps crunching over the gravel path that was bordered with fragrant flowers and shrubs. The night air was refreshingly cool after Chillicothe's midsummer daytime heat. Curbside lampposts glowed softly under the canopy of fine old trees. A horse and buggy could be heard going by now and then. Music filtered down to them from the dance . . .

Tommy, who had been pressing his suit earnestly, stopped as if for breath. Harriet, too, was silent. After some minutes she spoke so softly he had to strain to catch her words.

She had the deepest affection and admiration for him—and always would have. But she did not love him, not in the way he was talking about. She had been worrying about this for some time . . . She was sure it was wrong for cousins to marry . . . Young Wilson argued his case eloquently. Harriet, close to tears, held her point.

After a bit he led her back to the gay revelers and excused himself.

Going to the room he so often had occupied as guest in the Woodrow home, he packed his bag and went to the hotel. Having pleaded with him in vain to stay, Harriet rejoined her friends, hoping none would suspect how upset she was.

Next morning she received an agitated message from him, scribbled on a torn scrap of yellow paper . . . She must reconsider . . . He had not slept . . . He was plunged into despair . . . She must see him.

The two had a long session later that day. But Tommy could not change Harriet's mind.

That afternoon he left for home, despite the Woodrows' urging that he stay, as he had planned. All of them, including Hattie, were dismayed and sad at this turn of events. Hattie's brother, Wilson, drove him to the railroad station. There they encountered Edward Freeman Welles, just arrived from Marietta to attend the festivities at the Woodrows' home. Tommy was immediately suspicious of the Marietta youth.

His presentiments were sound. Ultimately Harriet became Mrs. Welles.

Not one to give up easily, Tommy was sure Hattie loved him . . . it was the cousin matter that blocked her, something he felt of no importance . . . Would she grant him one favor: be photographed, for him, in the pink frock she had worn that last morning they were together, no hat, her hair arranged exactly as it was then, a profile view?

In Rome, Georgia, two years later the two met once more in the home of the Boneses, now located there. Woodrow was a fledgling attorney in Atlanta.

At this time he first became acquainted with Ellen Louise Axson. Accounts differ as to how this meeting came about. Mrs. Thackwell states that Hattie introduced them when the family was assembled in Rome for the funeral of Marion Bones. Tommy was reluctant about seeing the unknown Elly-Lou. But Hattie insisted, sure the two would like each other. She was right, for in a couple of years they were married.

The other version of how Miss Axson came into his life, is that Wilson, in Rome on legal business, saw Ellen while attending services in her father's church. It was a Presbyterian church, of course. That glimpse was practically love at first sight for him.

The Woodrows and the Wilsons at once were attracted to Ellen.

On her part, as Mrs. Woodrow Wilson, she received her husband's many relatives frequently and cordially—in the President's House at Princeton University, the New Jersey Governor's Mansion—and in the White House!

For the first inaugural in 1913, Wilson Woodrow, in proper Prince Albert coat, marshaled the kinfolk. A private reception was staged for the family connections, who turned out en masse to honor "Tommy." They occupied the Presidential box for the inaugural parade and all ceremonies. At the formal dinner in the Executive Mansion, Harriet, long since Mrs. Welles, was seated at the President's right. It was her place on numerous other occasions when she visited at the White House. On state tours in the West, President Wilson stopped whenever possible at the Welles home, then in Denver, Colorado. Harriet and he were always on the friendliest of terms.

She often said that had she not rejected Tommy, he never would have been President. Instead of becoming the northern lawyer, as he had offered Harriet if she would marry him, he soon gave up his Atlanta office and prepared himself for college teaching, with graduate study at Johns Hopkins University. There followed appointments at Bryn Mawr College, Connecticut Wesleyan University, and lastly Princeton, springboard for what he termed his "public spirited statesmanship."

Through it all, the Woodrow and Wilson links remained. Another wedding carried on the tradition. Harriet's grandson, Donald Wilson Thackwell, married President Wilson's granddaughter, Faith Wilson McAdoo . . . A nice footnote, this, to the Tommy-Hattie story.

Isaac M. Wise

AFTER SIXTY-THREE DAYS AT SEA, most of them stormy, the little ship shuddered to rest in the port of New York. A Bohemian rabbi, Isaac M. Wise, and his girl-wife, with their baby in her arms, picked their way down the steep gangplank into the heat of a July day in 1846.

They were exhausted from the gales' tossings, foul air in the crowded steerage, and lack of food. What food they had brought had spoiled before the long voyage ended.

None of this mattered. The frail, scholarly man felt an upsurge of happiness. He and his dear ones at last were in their dream country.

Nothing about the twenty-seven-year-old-man, in poor, rumpled clothes, set him apart from the other bewildered immigrants who were fumbling through Castle Garden's red tape. Nevertheless, Isaac Wise, fifty-four years later, at life's end in 1900 in Cincinnati, Ohio, would be mourned as one of the country's outstanding religious leaders.

History would niche him among the distinguished and influential American Jewish personalities of the nineteenth century.

Within four years of reaching these shores, before he was naturalized, his reputation was such that he dined with Daniel Webster, chatted with President Zachary Taylor in the White House, and had discussed the Missouri Compromise with William H. Seward, then U.S. Senator.

The theater of his lifework was to be Cincinnati, where he was a rabbi for almost fifty years. Here is Hebrew Union College, which he founded, his monument, the first permanent rabbinical seminary for American Jews.

Only a few Jews landed in New York at the time he came. Jewish immigration was as yet sparse. Those early arrivals had uprooted themselves from European countries, as he from his native Bohemia, to escape discrimination, persecution, and ghetto life. They were political and religious pilgrims.

And so was Wise. But he had advanced ahead of them.

Standing beside his wife and baby, surrounded by bulging boxes and roughly tied bundles, he might not look different from other newcomers milling on the dock. Yet he was one apart. He was already Americanized to a real degree.

In a secondhand bookstore in Prague he had come upon a shelf of American publications. These included the complete works of James Fenimore Cooper and the writings of the Revolutionary liberal, Richard Henry Lee, advocate of the Bill of Rights. Wise bought the entire collection and read each volume and pamphlet avidly: "with the heart more perhaps than the head," he afterwards declared. The reading improved his meager knowledge of English and gave further form and impetus to his democratic leanings.

Back in Bohemia Wise had been a rabbi at Radnitz. Rebelling against humiliation of Jews under bigoted Hapsburg domination of the country, he sought also to break through the rigid patterns set up within Judaism itself. He preached in German, a daring innovation not acceptable to a congregation accustomed to Hebrew, language of the synagogue.

Restrictions of everyday life seemed increasingly intolerable. America beckoned the visionary, youthful rabbi. He had heard a new note in Abraham's old message. It was directed especially at him: "Get thee out of thy country and from thy kindred and from thy father's house into the land where I shall show you."

Now he had come to the land the patriarch of his people had showed him, this land of freedom, of opportunity, and of brotherhood.

Disillusionment overtook him almost at once. Expenses for the hard journey had been more than anticipated. His cash assets in New York consisted of two one-dollar bills—all he had received at the exchange counter for his diminished kreutzers.

Summoning a hack from the pier, Wise loaded his family and the cumbersome baggage. Assuming the immigrant knew no English, the driver spoke to him in German demanding six dollars for the short trip to an East Side address on a card Wise handed him. However, the young rabbi had read the tariff notice posted in English and gave the man the prescribed $1, refusing to pay more.

Caught in his gouging, the expressman unceremoniously dumped his passengers, letting loose a barrage of anti-Jewish invectives, worse than the worst Wise had ever heard across the sea.

Further disappointment was ahead. New York City appeared to him, as he recorded it in later years in his autobiography, "like a large shop where everyone buys or sells, cheats or is cheated."

This refined son of the Old World "had never known a city so bare of all art and every trace of good taste; likewise, I never witnessed such rushing, hurrying . . ." He was shocked by the noises of fishmongers, milkmen, newsboys . . . "Everything seemed small and paltry . . . and New York like a lost station by the sea."

The Promised Land was promising little to his fellow Jews, he discovered. He himself had brought letters of introduction to a couple of Jewish doctors and lawyers in New York. They urged him to give up all idea of taking a post as a rabbi. Instead, they advised him to apprentice himself to some trade, or take up peddling—even become a Christian! Prospects were poor for Jews in this country, they insisted.

Wise soon realized why his coreligionists were downhearted. American Jews were living in self-imposed isolation, each group clinging to customs and languages of their European origins. They had made the difficult trek to these shores to free themselves from domination of one sort, yet were not attempting to learn America's mores or its language.

Their Judaism, Wise saw, followed the same lines. It was virtually bound to the homeland, each nationality practicing its own variety. Many had strayed entirely from the synagogue. Others were uncompromisingly orthodox.

The result was congregations walled against each other. Judaism carried on in unrelated segments, "a veritable Babel of Confusion," in Wise's words.

Young and newly come as he was, Wise was fired with two great goals: he would Americanize the Jew and Judaism and he would unite all divisions of American Jewry. He would strengthen Jewry, liberate Jews from their European bonds "so that they might be warmly responsive to changing needs and the splendid future" he saw ahead for Jewish life in the United States.

He was a reformer and he met the usual opposition that all reformers meet. Nonetheless, he succeeded.

America's twentieth-century Jews, whose number is estimated today at five million, honor his contribution. His leadership is recognized not alone by the million Reform Jews who are his followers, but also by the Conservative and Orthodox Jews, as well, who differ with his theology.

Wise thought of himself as called to organize all Jews in this New World to which he had come. If this seems a large ambition, it must be remembered the Jews in those days were few in number, a scattering of them in cities and towns along the coast and a lesser number settled inland.

In the entire country there were only three ordained rabbis, two in New York City and one in Charleston, South Carolina. The other congregations were directed by ministers and sometimes laymen conforming to no consistent ritual. It was not until after the Civil War that the Jewish census in the United States attained any significance.

An Albany, New York, synagogue called him as rabbi. He went from New York City by boat, admiring every mile of the beauty and grandeur unfolding in Hudson River scenery. Nearly thirty years later he wrote that he could recall nothing in his experience that impressed him so much:

> The steamer seemed a floating palace, the people higher beings, and the river a second Chideqel flowing out of the Garden of Eden. The lofty walls and rocks seemed to shut off the Old World and the steep heights in the vicinity of West Point were for me a mighty door, the grand opening into the New World . . . I could have embraced every mountain, every rock.

Thus did America move this adopted son.

With enthusiasm and dedication he took up his new duties. He stated that since he knew nothing about living costs or salary scales in this country, he would leave remuneration to the congregation to decide. They voted him $250 a year and $9 for each pupil in the school he was to manage. He had to meet all expenses of the school, but undertook the teaching gladly.

Education was a passion with Wise. Within a week after landing in New York he had organized a night school in his rooms, to teach English to recently arrived immigrants in the neighborhood.

In Albany he found the Jew, as everywhere, an alien by self-imposed barriers. He denied himself the benefits of full citizenship and human rights that this wonderland offered. Wise, never noted for caution or patience, set about in whirlwind fashion to change all that.

He preached in English, the language of the land, before hearers who could not understand, because they were accustomed to Hebrew-German services. He opened pews to women who heretofore were either non-attenders at the synagogues or relegated to out-of-sight benches in the gallery.

In a day when Jews and Gentiles alike considered even a pitch pipe in a religious service an intrusion of the devil, Wise, who loved music, trained a mixed choir and introduced violin accompaniments.

He had gone ahead too fast in his effort to "reconcile his people with the spirit of the age in their new fatherland." A storm broke over his head, spewing acrimonious accusations of apostasy at him and relieving him of his charge. Loyal supporters of his religious program split off into a new synagogue, made him their rabbi.

It was his first conflict and his first victory. He launched the reform movement in Albany only four years after coming to this country. He stayed long enough to see this second congregation take over and remodel as a synagogue a former Baptist church with a thousand-seat capacity.

Meanwhile he was proclaiming his ideas in Jewish journals, winning both adherents and violent detractors, all of this focusing attention on him. Praise came his way from two vaunted non-Jewish American intellectuals, Boston's Unitarian preacher Theodore Parker, and the New York *Tribune's* Horace Greeley. They were impressed and wrote to tell him so following publication of his 600-page *History of the Israelitish Nation,* the first such history in English and certainly a feat in this language for its author.

His reputation traveled farther—to Cincinnati, Queen City of the West. Even back in Bohemia, Wise had heard of the culture and progressive spirit of this early settlement on the Ohio River, where, from the beginning, no anti-Semitic prejudice existed. Jew and Gentile mingled in business and civic affairs since the first Jews had come. The early Jews came from England, soon followed by Germans from Bavaria imbued with the new philosophies of political and religious freedom then surfacing in Germany.

In Cincinnati the progressive Bene Jeshurum congregation was without a rabbi. They selected Isaac Wise and offered him the post for life, an unusual contract detail.

He was thirty-five when he brought his wife and family, now numbering four children, into Ohio. They came in April, when "all the peach, plum and cherry trees were in full blossom . . . the fields dotted everywhere with flocks of sheep and playful lambs. It was a charming picture. My children shouted with glee."

He was not at all sure he would make as good an impression on his congregation as Ohio was making on him. After the strain of his Albany pastorates—"I was thin," according to his own description, "my face pale, my lips colorless and my figure bent and insignificant."

There were four thousand Jews in Cincinnati and two synagogues. The one Wise was called to head was made up largely of German Jews who had broken away from the older temple of English Jews. Wise was confronted with vestiges of strong Orthodoxy.

However, there were many young and forward-looking men in his audience who soon went along with him in his reforms and Americanization of the service, including the innovation of non-Jews as members of the choir. The older English group, being without a rabbi, asked him to preach to them as well. At this time the young, delicate-appearing Wise was the only rabbi preaching in Cincinnati.

As was his lot all his life, Wise stirred an army of very vocal critics who labeled him a dangerous radical, bent on destruction of ancient dogma. Yet his audiences increased steadily. He had many friends among non-Jews and he served in nonreligious capacities, such as that of trustee of the University of Cincinnati and member of the public school board.

He had been in Ohio only a short time when he established two publications, *The Israelite,* in English, and *Die Deborah,* in German. While preaching in two temples, the prodigious worker was editor and contributor of both.

The journals were potent tools in spreading his life aims: United States citizenship participated in by all Jews and a seat of learning for Jews, with a seminary to train an English-speaking rabbinate dedicated to an American ministry. Such a scholastic setup would meet a wide need.

Jewish youth wishing advanced schooling faced a problem. Secondary education was largely in private academies under Christian domination. Colleges and universities likewise were church oriented, often clergy-training centers, narrowly sectarian. This academic environment was unacceptable to Jews.

Wise lost no time in starting a school. The class met in a small room in the basement of his temple. Seventeen teen-agers enrolled, only four to study, the others to resist instruction. One was an eleven-year-old girl who cared not a whit about irregular Hebrew verbs.

The young man Wise hired as teacher had trouble with discipline and continually appealed to him for help in keeping order. The library was locked up every night in a two-and-a-half-foot tin box, not for fear of thieves, but to protect the few precious books from mice.

Gradually a change came over American education, gaining force after the Civil War. Nonreligious public high schools were taking the place of academies, and colleges were becoming secularized. These trends of growing liberalism and democracy were welcomed generally, especially by Jews.

As a result, Wise's students were now young men with leanings toward the rabbinate. It was apparent the new emphasis among Jews should be on a school of theology.

Two abortive attempts on Wise's part to create such a seminary convinced him an institution like this could succeed only with all congregations united to support it. For the next twenty-five years he bent his energies to this end, speaking on the subject of union before Jewish communities in all parts of the country, preaching it from his pulpit, and writing about it.

Setbacks and disappointments seemed only to urge him on. His charm, his persistence and eloquence, in short, his genius for organization, triumphed. In 1873 delegates from thirty-four congregations met in Cincinnati and solemnly proclaimed a Union of American Hebrew Congregations.

Out of it grew Hebrew Union College from which more than 1,000 rabbis have gone forth. Wise was its first president, an honor he considered greater "than a seat in the Senate or the office of Chief Justice." Until a couple of days before he died he taught a class. His students he regarded as sons, and they reciprocated with affection and admiration.

The college rose in Cincinnati, though New York had ten times as many Jews. But in that metropolis Reform and Orthodox refused to work together. In Ohio, Wise was able to steer between the two. Gradually, however, college policy veered toward Reform philosophy.

Hebrew Union College opened first with a half dozen students in the vestry of a Cincinnati temple. It was moved after several years to a renovated residence, and after Wise's death to the eighteen-acre campus near the University of Cincinnati.

All this would delight the man who conceived and nursed along the school from its precarious infancy. Even more, he would rejoice at a later expansion, its consolidation with the Jewish Institute of Religion in New York, which was founded by Rabbi Stephen S. Wise, no relation. And there is an outpost on the West Coast, in Los Angeles. Isaac Wise's practical idealism and daring imagination have spread a scholarly network, as all-American as he could wish.

The library on the Cincinnati campus, inaugurated by gifts of rare volumes from Rabbi Wise, is one of the most distinguished and extensive Jewish libraries in the world. In the files is a formidable array of work by Wise, including fiction interspersed with serious articles he wrote for his two weekly newspapers.

A rich body of anecdote has been handed down in Cincinnati about the little Bohemian immigrant whose indomitable spirit and persistence brought the school into being. He was a familiar figure all his life on the streets of Cincinnati, a stooped man in black, who walked with a slight limp, often trailed by a string of students, like Socrates moving through the agora at Athens.

While extolling piety, Wise was not one to think it demanded constant turning of the other cheek. When the Catholic bishop John B. Purcell announced that none of his parishioners could sing in Wise's synagogue choir, as one of them had been doing, Wise retaliated. He advised Jews not to employ Catholics or trade with Catholic merchants. The bishop withdrew his edict. He and the rabbi became best of friends after that.

While he declared he saw no connection between eating and religion, Wise was careful that foods forbidden by Orthodox dietary laws did not come into his home. At his insistence meals were kept simple, but he enjoyed company and there was usually an extra place or two set for unexpected guests.

Orthodox food restrictions wrought havoc for Wise on an occasion when he most wished to avoid dissension. The largest body of Jews ever assembled in this country met in Cincinnati in 1883 for a session of the Union and to witness the first graduation of rabbis from the college, which, also, was the first ordination of rabbis in America. Delegates represented 128 Reform and Orthodox synagogues throughout the country.

It was an event Wise had labored years to bring about. A large banquet was planned following the exercises. A qualified Jewish caterer was put in charge. The big dinning room was brilliantly lighted, tables beautifully set. The invocation was pronounced and the first course was brought in.

Suddenly rabbis throughout the room rose from their tables and dashed out. Shrimp, outlawed by the dietary laws of the Orthodox, by some misadventure had been served. Wise's antagonists seized upon the incident as an intentional insult, called it heresy on his part and withdrew their support of the union and of the college. Repercussions were long-lasting and undid a great deal of Wise's careful work of harmonizing the extreme elements of Jewry. Wise, however, was too buoyant to give up, too accustomed to problems to be discouraged.

One phase of Judaism he never endorsed was Zionism. With his strong conviction that Jews should consider themselves citizens of the country where they live, the idea of divided loyalty to another homeland was out of the question for him. Jews in the United States, for example, were Americans whose religion happened to be Judaism, just as other Americans were Methodists or Catholics . . . Further, Wise had imbibed the nineteenth-century philosophy of universal brotherhood and civil liberty. Mankind's golden age had dawned when persecution of the Jews was ending. They were citizens of the world. There was no need for a refuge in a homeland of their own, he contended.

Dying at the turn of the century, Wise was secure in that ideology. Not yet on the horizon were the disruptions of World War I or the Hitler devastation to sharpen focus on an autonomous Jewish state.

Isaac Wise was vigorous to the last. After his Saturday morning sermon delivered in his beautiful Plum Street Temple, he taught his regular afternoon class at Hebrew Union College. As he dismissed "his boys," he collapsed.

His funeral took place a few days later, on his eighty-first birthday, March 29, 1900, a date still observed at the college he created. For his final rites crowds jammed the temple he had made famous throughout the land. Other hundreds stood in tribute outside, though the day was rainy.

This crusading American had lived to see all his goals fulfilled.

And Isaac Wise, first president of Hebrew Union College, would be particularly gratified by the achievements of his successor, the present president, Dr. Nelson Glueck, world-renowned archaeologist. His explorations in eastern Palestine have verified passages and entire books of the Old Testament and have quickened interest in the birth land of Judaism.

Thomas Alva Edison

SNOW HAD FALLEN all through the night. Dr. Lehman Galpin, homeward bound, waded through deep drifts. For years he had been ministering to the sick and introducing babies to the world in Milan, northern Ohio village. Yet, seldom had he felt greater satisfaction than on this blustery morning, February 11, 1847.

After all the tragedies that had been her lot, Nancy Edison was safely delivered of a son. God willing, she might raise this one, her seventh child. To be sure, the baby was not too husky and his abnormally large head worried the doctor.

Dr. Galpin's thoughts turned to the pleasant scene he had just left. Nancy and her husband, Big Sam, were discussing a name for the new mite snuggled against his mother. Sam wanted Thomas, after his brother, while Nancy favored Alva, for their good friend Alva Bradley, a young lake captain.

They compromised on Thomas Alva. His father called him Tom, his mother Alva, and he was Al to his playmates and to all of Milan . . . Thomas Alva Edison.

Galpin was weary. It had been a long night at the Edison cottage . . . the cottage that would become a national shrine as the birthplace of this baby. Gusts rattled shutters and beat the whirling snow into a curtain against the single window in the tiny first-floor bedroom. Sam faithfully fought the cold, feeding thick locust logs to the fire that crackled cheerily on the broad hearth of the adjoining sitting room. Between times he was kept busy supplying Galpin with tins of hot water from the kitchen below.

The brick house Sam had built on the hogback overlooking the lively canal basin was all too familiar to the doctor. Sickness and death had called him there many times during the past few years.

Six-year-old Carlisle Edison and his brother Samuel, not quite a year, died one after the other. Nancy's niece, gentle Ann Dutton, who lived with the Edisons and taught village school, faded away before their eyes and succumbed to consumption. Now the Edisons' little Eliza, three, and constantly ailing, was growing daily more delicate. Galpin, trying not to, feared the very doom that carried her off a short time later.

The three older children seemed healthy enough: Marion, eighteen, William Pitt, fifteen, and Harriet Ann, fourteen. This wee newborn might make it, too, Galpin hoped, and, in his precise hand, wrote the date in his ledger.

Not until World War I was this entry discovered. This was when Thomas A. Edison, full of honors and years, giving the United States Navy the benefit of his inventive mind, needed a birth certificate.

The doctor was dead, but his son William obligingly went through his father's files. Beside the sought-for notation, Dr. Galpin had recorded his fee at the birth of America's Most Useful Citizen. It was two dollars.

Despite such modest charges, Galpin prospered. The previous year he took possession of his dignified new home up the street from Edison's. Houses like his and others more pretentious, many of good Greek Revival design, were taking shape all over the village. This was Milan's Golden Age.

In the 1840s, the village, though some ten miles from Lake Erie, was the busiest harbor on the Great Lakes. In the year of Edison's birth, for example, nearly a million bushels of grain, not to mention other commodities, were shipped from here. Bills of lading substantiated the Ohio community's boast that it was second only to Odessa, Russia, as a world fresh water grain port.

All this was due to a three-mile canal laid from Milan to the navigable part of the crooked Huron River. The village thus secured an outlet on Lake Erie, site of the town of Huron. The short waterway, dug at a cost of $75,000, linked Milan with Europe through transshipment of cargoes across the lake to the ocean via the Welland Canal and St. Lawrence River. Ships often carried barrel staves from Ohio oak forests to be bartered in England for iron and machinery needed in new industries along Lake Erie.

After years of frustrating delays, the canal was opened July 4, 1839, when the first boat, the 150-ton *Kewaunee,* dropped anchor in the basin. The event was celebrated with fireworks and florid oratory before milling, cheering bystanders. Among the throng was Big Sam Edison.

Thirty-five, more than six feet tall, and with muscles of iron, Sam was in Ohio as a fugitive. Sometime before, he had left the tavern he owned in Vienna, Ontario, to participate in an abortive insurrection aimed (like the American Revolution) at Canadian independence from Britain. It was called the Papineau Rebellion for its French-speaking leader, Louis Joseph Papineau—also the Patriots' War, by a contingent of sympathizing "freedom fighters" from Ohio.

Canada considered those who had taken part were traitors, and Sam was in trouble. He was as hotheaded and restless as his forebears, who had pioneered one hundred years before in New Jersey. Involved in political upheavals of the Revolution, they were exiled to Nova Scotia. Unlike Sam they were Tories. Some of them, including his family, eventually moved into the wilds of Ontario.

With the Canadian uprising quelled and dominion militia on his trail, Sam prudently left Nancy and their children in Vienna while he sought safety and a livelihood across the border. He had heard of Milan from Captain Bradley, whose barges plied between Ontario and Ohio shores, and who foresaw the village's future as thriving from its canal trade.

Sam had tried his hand at many crafts, including lumbering and carpentry. Looking around the burgeoning community, he decided it would be fertile ground for his skills. Needing money to move his family, he took whatever jobs he could find, including strenuous work on the first plank road hereabouts. It netted him fifty dollars and stock.

Returning to Vienna, he eluded authorities and packed up his family for Ohio. They crossed, some say, in Brother Thomas's ship, the *Digby,* named for their native Nova Scotia village. Or, they may have sailed in Captain Bradley's sloop.

After the Edisons were settled in Milan, Captain Bradley boarded with them while his ship, the *South American,* was in port. Soon word got about that he and the lovely Ann Dutton were betrothed. Bradley's maritime operations were expanding, and after Ann's death he went to Cleveland, where the Bradley name figured prominently.

Sam first installed his family in rented rooms above C. B. Choate's tin shop on Milan's Front Street. It was the birthplace of little Samuel, destined for so short a life. Carlisle died here in 1841.

That year the Edisons paid $220 for a lot, part of original holdings of Ebenezer Merry, one of the founders of the village. The deed was taken out in Nancy's name on what was then Choate's Lane—called Seminary Street for a period, after a local academy, and now Edison Drive.

Like everyone else, Sam was realizing quick success from the spiraling economy. Within a year he could afford a fairly commodious brick-and-frame house which he erected practically single-handed. Sam was evidently a master builder with a good sense of design. The house stands today, sturdy and of simple, well-proportioned lines.

Hugging the bluff, its seven rooms, small for the most part, are on three levels: under the eaves the well-nigh windowless sleeping rooms which Alva shared with his brother Pitt and their sisters; street-floor living quarters, and down thirteen steep, narrow steps, the kitchen. A woman-killer by today's standards, that must have made housekeeping arduous, but it reflects domestic arrangements Nancy knew in Canada.

Actually, once reached, it is an attractive sunny room with a hospitable fireplace that took care of both heating and cooking needs. An outside door opens to what in Al's day was a thrifty orchard and a sloping garden. Nancy had a green thumb and raised all manner of flowers—pansies, purple heliotrope, and yellow roses particularly. She planted them, too, in boxes that Sam made for the broad stone window sills.

What a spot, this, and all of Milan, for that matter, for a boy like Al Edison! In the dooryard, within earshot of his mother at her kitchen duties, he could see the procession of vessels arriving and departing. Sails glistening white and wind-filled, the regatta of commerce united Milan with far places. On the basin, where the canal widened to six hundred feet, the boy might count twenty boats at a time. Canvas furled, their bare masts rose like clumps of naked trees as the fleets waited for their freight.

Today it seems incredible that ships touched here, the village's veritable back yard. Through obscuring, rank tree growth one can glimpse only ruins in the lowlands. A weed-tangled swamp marks the basin's location. The old canal bed and muddy river are vaguely outlined amidst encroaching underbrush.

No sign remains of Sam Edison's shingle mill and lumberyard that sprawled at the foot of the hill within easy view of his house. As soon as Al could toddle he followed the path to it to play with discarded chips and watch for Uncle Thomas's ship. It pulled up at the wharf laden with shingle bolts, which were three-foot lengths of good Canadian timber. Handsawed, deftly split and shaved, each bolt yielded two nearly indestructible shingles.

Recognized for excellent workmanship, Sam's roofing was in demand for most of the building mushrooming along the water fronts. The sound of hammer and saw, brick on brick, was the song of village and valley. The boom was in full swing. Newcomers streamed in.

Almost overnight, industries sprang into being: iron foundries, distilleries, linseed oil and soap factories, tanneries and slaughterhouses. Grain elevators could be seen against the skyline. Flour, carding, and filling mills flourished. Smithies' fires glowed from dawn into night, shoeing horses and oxen. Barrel shops clamored for lumber. Wagon makers, saddlers, and tinsmiths had all the business they could manage.

Half a dozen dry docks operated in the basin, another under the master shipmaker, William Raynor, working for Valentine Fries at Fries Landing. The canal, only thirteen feet deep, limited ship draughts. Nevertheless, more than a hundred lake schooners and brigs slid off the ways during Milan's heyday. Included, too, were six revenue cutters for the federal government. A 749-ton schooner was christened the Marion Edison Page for Alva Edison's sister, now the wife of a local farmer, Homer Page.

Boyhood's most exciting memories, as later described by Edison, were the oft-repeated scenes beside his home when "the hogback would be filled with what seemed to be the entire population of the town who came to witness the launching of new boats in the (Merry and) Gay shipyard below us."

Firsthand entertainment also was offered by lines of bulging "prairie schooners" that fanned into Milan from a radius of 100 to 150 miles distant. From 300 to 600 wagons a day discharged as many as 50,000 bushels of grain. Six-horse hitches were necessary since rural roads were mud-choked and most streams, bridged inadequately or totally unspanned, had to be forded. In this parade now and then patient oxen plodded through the streets hauling their creaking loads to the docks.

Drivers, expecting to be a long time en route, came prepared. Frequently accompanied by wives and children, they camped in boisterous groups on the outskirts or along congested village streets. Resigned to long delay for their turns to unload in this churning bottleneck, they laughed loud and joked roughly. It was romantic pageantry to fascinate any youngster.

Canal packet hands staged another kind of real-life drama. Tough and jolly, they bellowed lusty, strong-worded chanteys as they guided their mules over towpaths. One day when Al was no more than five, properly reared Nancy discovered to her dismay her little son could lisp verse after bawdy verse about "trips on the Can-awl."

Such stir and commotion, difficult to picture as the background of today's serene and somnolent village, made the environment of Al's boyhood and he didn't miss a bit of it. He was the kind of boy who "got into things" and obviously there were plenty of "things" for him to get into.

In one of his earliest escapades he came near to drowning. He stumbled, rolled all the way down the incline beside his home, and fell into the canal. Someone pulled him out dripping, frightened, but unharmed. Another time he came within minutes of smothering while enjoying a forbidden ride atop a car full of wheat. As it was shunting from weighing scales to warehouse bin, he lost his footing and plunged into the load. His cries attracted a workman who frantically shoveled him free as he was sinking under the grain.

There is the story of the blaze he started in a shed at his father's mill "to see what would happen." What did was an almost disastrous spread of flames, which his father extinguished in the nick of time. Shortly afterward, coming upon Al playing in the square, Sam whipped him then and there, indifferent to onlookers' strongly voiced disapproval of such public chastisement.

Sam did not spare the rod on this son, whose behavior baffled him and whom he sometimes labeled stupid. Father and son were far from congenial. Al, on the other hand, was close to his mother—"who was the making of me," he often avowed. Nancy kept a birch rod handily behind a clock shelf for Al "was a handful" and she, too, believed in discipline. But she sensed the unusual promise in the boy and fostered it.

Feeling Al not robust enough for daily attendance at school, Nancy revived her classroom training and determined to educate him at home. Careful search by the late Neil Jones, superintendent of the Milan school system, revealed that Al never was enrolled in a local school though names of other Edison children are duly listed.

As a result, there was ample free time for his "investigations." He had a habit of disappearing, and in the rich Edisonian lore of the locale there are many tales of family and townspeople combing highways and byways searching for him.

A frequent jaunt took him to the farm near Fries Landing, where his sister Marion started housekeeping. She and Homer Page were married in the living room of the Edison home when Al was two. Marion and her husband were devoted to the boy, and he to them.

One day Al was missing for many hours and anxiety mounted. Finally Marion came upon him behind her barn, where he had been all the time, he said. He was sitting motionless on some duck eggs. If the Pages' hens could produce chicks by sitting on hen eggs, why could he not get ducklings from duck eggs by the same technique? He chose duck eggs, he explained, because he liked ducks better than chickens. Edison himself, at the height of fame, stopping briefly with the Pages, pointed out the spot where this experiment of his was interrupted.

Marion Page liked to talk about the brother whom she loved dearly and who became so renowned. Her stories have been handed down by her granddaughter, Mrs. Marion Wheeler, who inherited another Page farm on the edge of town, where she has lived for years, and who herself remembers her distinguished relative.

"Grandmother," said Mrs. Wheeler, "used to tell us that Uncle Al, even when he played, seemed bent on some serious purpose. Once he showed her pieces of wood and iron he found on the farm. 'Marion,' he explained, 'I'm going to make wood and iron talk.' Grandmother always insisted this was his genius asserting itself, anticipating his invention of the phonograph, which he never called anything but a 'talking machine.'"

Edison is said to have referred to this incident when he sent the Pages one of his first phonographs. Several of his early models repose in the Page-Wheeler homestead, a pleasant farmhouse, tranquil and content behind its white picket fence.

Reminders of the great man hover in every room. Walls are hung with pictures of him; an intense-eyed boy of fourteen, a world figure receiving high acclaim, a white-haired venerable relaxing with his cronies, Harvey S. Firestone and Henry Ford.

Milan has become a repository of Edisonia. Any spot connected with him is noteworthy—like the site of the Star Mill. It was a steam-powered flour mill owned by Thomas and Samuel Winchester. Al was drawn to it as if by a magnet. He would stand tiptoe at a rear window, his face flattened against the glass, gazing by the hour at what was going on inside. His father more than once punished him for hanging around the place, for Sam Winchester was known as the Mad Miller of Milan.

However, Al could not stay away. The miller, he learned, was making a balloon that would take passengers aloft. One evening when Winchester was filling the bag with hydrogen something went wrong and he set fire to his mill.

Al was not the only one intrigued with the balloon idea. George and Ralph Lockwood, early settlers and prominent merchants, lent Mad Sam money for his project. The Lockwoods had backed other local enterprises, including the canal, which they pushed to completion against all opposition.

George Lockwood built Milan's most remarkable building, a big brick affair dubbed Lockwood's Temple. He was a hardheaded businessman until he accepted the Millerite religious tenet of the world's imminent destruction. On the Day of Judgment the good would be ushered bodily into heaven, he believed. To aid their ascent he raised a dais, and above it a convenient trap door and a glass cupola in the roof of the Temple, which was cleverly constructed without inside supports. He presented his faith in a series of articles in the Milan *Tribune*, and planned his temple to be big enough for the congregation of converts he anticipated.

Winchester's passenger-bearing balloon did not seem impossible to a man like Millerite Lockwood—nor to little Al, either. And the balloon worked. Winchester demonstrated the fact September 18, 1855. Al was lucky enough to have been a spectator.

By this date Milan's decline had set in. Canal-minded citizenry had refused a right-of-way for a railroad, the Lake Shore and Michigan Southern. It by-passed the village, and the tracks were laid instead to Norwalk. Soon Milan's waterway, the community's life line, was losing out, unable to compete with the more expeditious handling of freight and passengers by "steam cars."

Sam Edison's business, like that of his neighbors, fell off. There was another Edison uprooting, this time, in 1854, to Port Huron, Michigan.

The next year Al, always welcome at the Pages', spent a good part of the summer at their farm, and he was visiting there in September when Winchester staged his exciting balloon test.

Winchester dragged the big bag with its basket dangling from it to Milan's public square. It was a bare area then, marked by hitching posts, without today's fine stand of trees. The "bag had 623 yards of silk, dress silk, and was the largest balloon bag ever made in the United States," according to a precious letter from Winchester's daughter, Jane, inviting her cousin, Olive, to "come see Pa's ascension."

Pa left Milan in the fragile basket under the big bag at 3:40 in the afternoon. Al was in the crowd looking skyward as the balloon was borne up and off, westward at first. Winchester was carried almost to Fremont, then veered southeast until his contraption caught in a "tall white ash." Gingerly he got himself to the ground and found he was in Hudson! It was 5:28. He had stayed aloft an hour and forty-eight minutes and estimated his journey at 135 miles. Direct by road the distance between Milan and Hudson is about 65 miles.

Winchester recounted in detail what he termed "the first voyage through the regions of space." The clouds were very low. He could make out Sandusky and the bay, the streets of Huron, boats at Vermilion.

"The ball increased in size as it went higher. The mercury fell to five degrees below zero." Winchester put on his overcoat. His "ears were assailed by a cracking sensation and respiration was difficult." The balloon began to drop too rapidly. He "opened an escape valve and tried to throw out ballast, but it was frozen . . ." He had reached a height of 25,396 feet, he said. But, as he had no altimeter, his claim can be neither confirmed nor contested.

Next, Winchester made plans to take daughter Jane and her mother aloft. But authorities forbade it. So he went up alone early in October. This time he started from what was called Benedict's Pasture, in Norwalk.

News of the previous flight had got around and a tremendous throng was on hand for this one. A brass band and the cannon on the courthouse grounds were in readiness. Winchester took his place in the basket. Ropes were cut, the balloon started up, cannon let go a resounding volley. The brass band sounded with all its might. The lone balloonist leaned far out and waved an American flag to the spectators. Women fluttered handkerchiefs in response as long as they could see the soaring craft. Some cried.

Well they might, for Winchester was never seen nor heard from again. Surmise was he went down in Lake Erie—or perhaps the Atlantic Ocean!

Al missed the second ascension for he was in Port Huron when it took place. But he heard all about it from his relatives. It was the sensation of the area, and of course he never forgot seeing Winchester go up from Milan.

He decided to do some testing of buoyancy himself. His father had a young helper named Mike Oates in his woodworking shop in Port Huron. He was good-natured and gullible and a slave to Al's whims. Al induced him to drink quantities of the effervescent purgative, Seidlitz powder water, cup after cup of the fizzy stuff.

Mike, violently ill, told on the culprit. Edison's mother switched her son soundly, mystified the while, until he tearfully explained: he merely wanted to inflate Mike to find out if he could fly like Mr. Winchester, but without a balloon.

Winchester had lived in a house with a history. It was built by Zenas King, pioneer bridge builder, who moved to Cleveland and from there erected spans throughout the country.

During Al's babyhood the modest house had a third occupant destined for fame, Jeptha Homer Wade. He was a telegrapher. One of the first west of the Alleghenies, his wire service was greatly relied on by shippers and warehouse owners for market quotations and fluctuating grain prices.

Like Bradley and King, Wade established himself in Cleveland. He was in the vanguard of the telegraph industry, eventually affecting mergers of widely scattered independent lines to form Western Union Telegraph Co., and to become its president in 1866.

Wade and Edison had no contact at the time. Baby Al was too young to be aware of the new wizardry clicking over the wires. Telegraphy, however, was one of Edison's earliest concerns. He was tinkering with it when other boys were content to spin tops. Before he was eleven he had evolved his own set of instruments, put together from scrap metal, wire, and brass pieces cadged from junkyards.

His first real job, at sixteen, was as telegrapher in Port Huron, taking the place of a man with the Union ranks at Gettysburg. Three years later, Edison, a "tramp" telegrapher, moving from place to place, was operator in Louisville, a small cog in the telegraph network Wade then headed.

Milan today, quiet and peaceful after its exciting Edison era, is like an inviting museum, harboring treasured relics of other days. Along shady streets the prosperous past lingers everywhere, brought into focus by well-cared-for homes, eloquent of the best in early Western Reserve architecture.

As in those hearty, booming days of long ago, the world still streams in. Tens of thousands annually find their way here, no longer by ship or rail, but by motorcar. They come to visit the Edison birthplace on the hogback. It is a public museum maintained by an association headed by the inventor's daughter, Mrs. John E. Sloane of West Orange, New Jersey.

Near-by is Dr. Galpin's home, headquarters of the local Historical Museum. Tourists walk to it from the famous birthplace, as Galpin himself did on that winter morning in 1847.

The baby, considered so frail by his mother and doctor, lived to be eighty-four. When he died in 1931, electric lights throughout the nation were dimmed in symbolic homage to Milan's Miracle Man who had brought light—and so much else—to the whole world.

Harman Blennerhassett

NO ONE COULD UNDERSTAND why the sophisticated Irish aristocrats Harman Blennerhassett and his beautiful young wife, Margaret, secluded themselves on the island wilderness in the Ohio River.

The denouement came years later, after intrigues of Aaron Burr, former Vice-President of the United States, wrecked their frontier paradise. Their heartbreak chronicle flickered out in fresh mystery on another island, Guernsey, in the English Channel, thousands of miles away.

There was no hint of the tragedies ahead when the handsome pair first landed at the Ohio country's infant hamlet of Marietta. A dozen settlers, curious and hospitable, hurried to the wharf as the strangers' keelboat neared. Harman leaped ashore. With a flourish he gave his arm to his wife, who gathered her long skirts about her and nimbly stepped after him.

The newcomers were in fine form that warm August day in 1797. They had floated down the Ohio from Pittsburgh, the very route Marietta's forty-eight founding fathers had followed nine years before. The Blennerhassetts had enjoyed every mile "through the solitude," where deer browsed beside densely wooded shore lines, the wail of the wolf echoed from far hills, and here and there smoke curled above treetops to indicate a lonely inland habitation.

Marietta's welcome delighted the travelers. They were surprised at the culture of this remote community so imaginatively placed at the confluence of the Muskingum and Ohio rivers. It was the first settlement in the vast Northwest Territory. From this would be carved the states of Ohio, Indiana, Illinois, Michigan, Wisconsin, and part of Minnesota.

Many among the founders were college graduates. Also, they were veterans of the Revolutionary War, officers and enlisted men. Superintendent of the colony was General Rufus Putnam, who had been a member of General Washington's staff. He had built the fort at West Point. In Boston he had helped organize the Ohio Company of Associates that took title to 1,500,000 acres in this promiseful western world.

Dignified Scottish-born, General Arthur St. Clair, also a former member of Washington's staff, was governor of the Territory and administered it from here, making it an important, busy outpost. Most of the pioneers were personal friends of Washington, who had given the colony his blessing.

The Blennerhassetts brought tidings from the first President just at the time when he was about to relinquish the office to John Adams. They carried letters of introduction to leading families along the seaboard, where they had been visiting since coming to America. They had reached Philadelphia too late to attend one of Washington's levees, to which they were invited. They described to his interested Marietta friends just how he had looked as they sat in the pew next to his during a Sunday service.

Marietta opened its heart and its log houses to the fetching two—he in his early thirties, and she not quite twenty. It was not every day that such delightful emissaries from the outer world made their way here.

Homespun-clad citizens, so long separated from the elegances of the East, found even the couple's clothes a treat: the genteel, English-style dress of Blennerhassett and his wife's fashionable, fine-textured costumes.

Like everyone in the New West, the arrivals were seeking land. They were on their way to investigate Kentucky, which had been made a state some years before. Then, they would go on to Tennessee, admitted to the Union the previous year, aided by Burr, a Senator and already studying the Mississippi country.

Burr's dreams of western empire would be the undoing of the Blennerhassetts. But they were free and safe from his corroding contact . . .

After a pleasant stopover in Marietta, Harman and Margaret continued exploring. In a few months they were back—they had seen nothing they liked as well as Marietta. Their new-found acquaintances vied in pointing out available acres.

The Blennerhassetts were desirable prospective buyers for Ohio

Company officials alert to real-estate sales. Putnam and surveyors like Return Jonathan Meigs, a future Ohio governor, took them about by oxcart and horseback to Duck Creek, where the state's first mills were going up; to Harmar Hill, below which stretched the panorama of Marietta's clustered cabins and the two stately rivers cutting through forested banks. But no spot met the Blennerhassetts' fancy. They could afford to be choosy. As was apparent, they had ample funds.

Harman Blennerhassett, youngest son of a wealthy Irish family, was born in England during his mother's temporary stay there. He was educated in law at Dublin's Trinity College. The deaths of two older brothers made him heir to the family holdings near Killorglin, compact town not far from Killarney.

In this same lovely County Kerry, on Tralee Bay, is another seat of this family. It is known as Ballyseedy Castle, currently the home of Miss Hilda Blennerhassett, a collateral descendant. It is an estate Harman knew well. There are numerous Blennerhassetts hereabouts, several families of this name living in the town of Tralee, all of the same ancestral tree.

The clan traces lineage to England's King John. The first of them in Ireland took title to several thousand acres. The domain was the gift of Elizabeth I whose munificence with Irish lands, to which she had no right, planted the Irish-Anglo animosity that still persists so vigorously.

Harman, not pressed to make a living, had traveled extensively, particularly in France. On one such trip he heard from his sister, wife of Robert Agnew, crown-governor of the Isle of Man. Would he be willing to chaperon her daughter Margaret, as she returned from school on the continent? He complied readily. But, when the two reached the Agnew manor house on the Isle of Man, they were man and wife.

Relatives were scandalized at the elopmement—the bride was disinherited and both were ostracized. They determined to escape the opprobrium leveled against them and start anew in America, where their incestuous marriage would not be known.

Blennerhassett liquidated his properties to his cousin, later Lord Ventry, for $160,000. In London he and his bride purchased furniture, silver plate, books, and expensive scientific apparatus. Soon they were on their way to America's aboriginal northwest.

So well did they keep the secret of their irregular union, no one —not even their children—suspected it until both Harman and

Margaret had been dead more than sixty years. Then, a distant relative, Therese Blennerhassett-Adams, writing in *The Century* magazine in 1901, disclosed the relationship.

With nothing to suggest the sinister chapter in their background, the two burst on the isolated frontier settlement as glamorous beings from afar. Animated raconteurs, they shared their colorful experiences across the sea—save one—and always had an eager audience. As winter closed in, making land search difficult, much good talk flowed around friendly hearths and cozy blockhouses in Campus Martius.

This Latin name was given by the erudite settlers to the fortification thrown up against possible Indian attack. Within its spacious precincts were log homes of leaders like General Putnam. His cabin is still intact within the Campus Martius State Museum. Here, too, was Governor St. Clair's house, presided over by his lively daughter, Louisa, beloved by the cultured Indian chief Joseph Brant. The buckskin-attired Louisa and the urbane Margaret Blennerhassett were about the same age.

Commodore Abraham Whipple, Revolutionary War naval hero, listened understandingly to Blennerhasset's account of their stormy, seventy-three-day voyage from England. Their sailing vessel, alternately becalmed and driven off course, covered 10,000 miles. The traveler reckoned the distance with his sextant and chronometer. Blennerhassett discussed familiarly the turbulent happenings in France, of intense interest to the colonists, who had named their settlement for Marie Antoinette.

Marietta's abundant and mystifying remains of the original inhabitants—the Mound Builders—were designated with classic names: Sacra Via, for the earth-walled thoroughfare leading from the Muskingum to elevated squares that, in turn, were Quadrannou. A conical mound, thought to be a burial place of the vanished race, became Conus, and the pivot of their own cemetery. Eventually laid to rest around it were twenty-four officers of the Revolution, more than anywhere else in the country.

The ancient earthworks, then distinct, now blurred by time's onrush and the encroaching city, whetted Blennerhassett's scholarly inquisitiveness and he spent many hours examining them. The more he saw of this country, the surer he was it was where he wished to put down his roots.

Spring comes earlier along the Ohio than at the Lake Erie end of the state. Ice blocks in the river were breaking to pieces against each other and willow branches, dipping toward the water, were turning yellow-green.

The Blennerhassetts resumed their quest. They were poled downstream by two hardy young pioneers in a pirogue, rough adaptation of a canoe. It was a mild March day in 1798. At Belpre, twelve miles away, they inspected Farmer's Castle, a stockade like Campus Martius. Though three years before, General "Mad" Anthony Wayne had forced a "peace" treaty on the Indians, remnants of the tribes lingered in their ancestral valley and the white interlopers maintained their vigilance.

Opposite Belpre sprawled a big island three and a half miles long. Harman and Margaret knew at once it was what they wanted! Its giant trees towered skyward, intertwined in almost tropic profusion with vines and luxuriant undergrowth breaking into bud. Except for a blockhouse erected as a lookout against Indians, civilization had not touched this land mass midstream in the Ohio.

First noted by George Croghan, early explorer, and, five years later, in 1770, by George Washington himself on his surveying mission in these waters, it was mapped as "a cluster of islands." In the intervening years recurring floods filled in dividing channels to amalgamate the islands into a whole.

Blennerhassett bought 170 acres of the island's 500, selecting the end nearest Belpre. He paid the owner, Elijah Backus, $4,500, which seems an extraordinarily large sum. But to Harman money did not mean much—until the time which was to come, when extravagance and the Burr fiasco drained his treasury.

Known as Buckus Island, and sometimes Bacchus for the Roman god of revelry, the new owners chistened it Isle de Beau Pré, Island of Beautiful Meadow. But it became and remains Blennerhassett Island, scene of a historic drama more fantastic than fiction could invent.

Immediately construction of the mansion was begun. Harman and Margaret occupied the blockhouse as best they could. They were fortunate to have at hand a boat and church builder, Joseph Barker, also a "housewright," sufficiently skilled to warrant the title of architect. He lived on the Muskingum at Wiseman's Bottom, his property fronting on both sides of the river, a grant for daring deeds in the Indian Wars of a few years back.

When Barker first homesteaded here, red men still lurked in the hazel thickets. "Upriver" from him Wyandott and Delaware warriors had massacred a dozen intrepid frontiersmen who had gone there from Marietta. Barker claimed he cleared the forests on his farm and planted fruit trees with one hand while holding his scalp on with the other!

Barker was operating a dry dock, converting the wonderful oaks at his waterside into river boats, and building ocean-going vessels as well. It was one of several shipbuilding operations thriving here until Jefferson's Embargo Act of 1808, interdicting foreign trade, destroyed the industry.

First task on the island was felling the trees grown to tremendous girth in the fertile soil. Barker laid down landings for a little flotilla of work boats, mostly from his own shipyard. Stone for the house's foundation was transported from Virginia. It was of good quality and plentiful enough for the entire structure. But, Blennerhassett preferred a frame house, believing it was less likely of damage by earthquakes, which he feared in the New World.

He bought ten Negro slaves, first of the considerably larger staff he later owned. Since the island lay within jurisdiction of Virginia (now West Virginia) slavery was permitted, though outlawed in Ohio and the entire Northwest Territory.

It was two years before the house was completed. The two-story main section of ten spacious rooms was flanked by large wings radiating from it. One formed the servants' quarters, the other the master's library and laboratory, with its valuable instruments. The entire front extended over 200 feet. The imposing house, painted pure white, created an impressive scene against its backdrop of magnificent trees. These were leveled at designated points for unobstructed views up and down the river.

Decorative materials, hardware, and "glazed window glass" from eastern shops came by oxcart over the mountains and down the Ohio by flatboat direct to island docks. Interior walls and ceilings bore elaborate plaster motifs and soft-tone designs. Rooms were embellished with velvet and brocade draperies, original paintings, and gold-leaf mirrors. Carpets, silver, porcelains, and furniture, much of it imported from Britain, gave it royal splendor.

Most frequently commented on was the dining room, setting for formal entertaining. It resembled another Blennerhassett dining room—one this writer knows—the one at Ballyseedy Castle, that today is probably little changed from Harman's time. In it an intricate carved oak chest bears the date 1656 incised in mother-of-pearl. Soft patinaed old Irish silver is arrayed on a sideboard of mellow mahogany fashioned from wood washed in at the Bay of

Tralee. Here, from earliest times, the family had salvage rights to shipwrecked flotsam . . .

The Ohio island grounds were landscaped like an Irish country gentleman's, with gravel walks and carriage ways winding between ornamental gates, past lines of clipped hedges. Garden walls supported espaliered peaches, plums, and pears ripening in the sunshine. Bowers and grottoes were festooned with fragrant eglantine and purple wisteria. Serpentine paths led through acres of exotic and native flowers and shrubs. Well-groomed kitchen gardens and a hundred-acre farm produced rich harvests. Blennerhassett is said to have spent $40,000 on the house and $20,000 on the grounds of this enchanted realm in the rough frontier.

He busied himself with hobbies. He studied the heavens through his telescope and toyed with electricity, craze of the day. He dabbled in a chemical formula to produce whale oil for illumination by submerging sides of beef in the river. But the prolific schools of fish ate the meat . . . There was time to play his fine bass viol and cello, and for composing for these instruments. He had time to read Latin and Greek in the original. It was said he could recite pages of Homer from memory. Informed on pharmacology, he often administered drugs and medicines during illnesses of his family and mainland friends.

Mrs. Blennerhassett, well educated in French and Italian, quickly adjusted to her frontier environment and learned to supervise her unusual household, where everything had to be produced on the place. Social functions were the couple's joy. House parties bringing prominent persons from the Virginia and Ohio shores lasted days at a time. Their hospitality was a topic talked about up and down the river.

For such occasions, following many-course banquets, there were musical programs by Harman. His wife gave spirited readings from Shakespeare, sometimes staging entire plays in the large drawing room, distributing handwritten parts to each guest.

Host and hostess dressed in silks and satins which they continued to import from Europe. His usual costume for home social functions was scarlet satin breeches, fancy waistcoat under a blue broadcloth tailed coat with ruffled neckpiece, silk stockings, and silver buckle slippers.

An expert horsewoman, Mrs. Blennerhassett made a dashing picture in the saddle. On trips to Marietta, "metropolis of the valley," she eschewed the usual water route by pirogue as too tedious. Instead, she had her Negro servant Ransom, who always accompanied her, row her across the river the short distance to Belpre, where she mounted one of the horses from their stable here. She was a fast rider and the Negro was hard pressed to keep up. She rode sidesaddle, resplendent in full-skirted red velvet or broadcloth, bedecked with gold braid and buttons. Her hat was a wide-brimmed white beaver from which a long ostrich plume dangled. The *clippity-clop* of her horse was a signal to Marietta friends, who hurried to gateposts to wave her down for a chat.

The country was developing rapidly. Colonel Barker was building houses for Marietta customers, and he may have built Aaron Putnam's good house overlooking the river at Belpre. Putnam organized a library as early as 1796, the first subscription library in Ohio. It was known as the Farmers' Library, as he was living in Farmers' Castle at the time. He moved his books into his new home, storing them in a bushel basket. Margaret used to borrow from the collection, selecting such volumes as *Natural History of the Bible* and Locke's *Essay concerning Human Understanding*.

At the Putnam housewarming festivities in their ballroom, Margaret scratched her initials on a windowpane with her diamond ring. This talisman of a bygone era can be deciphered today in the house, which is owned by a Putnam descendant.

When catastrophe overtook the island, the Putnams rescued some exquisite pieces of Blennerhassett furniture. Many of these are now on display at Campus Martius Museum in Marietta.

No ill omen hovered in the breezes as monarch and mistress set up their Shangri-La. The two were complements of each other. Harman was six feet tall, inclined to stoop, his nearsightedness and reticence giving him a withdrawn air. He was dreamy and impractical, easily depressed. His wife, nearly his height, carried herself as straight-backed as an Indian and met life with vivacity, a cheerful, self-confident young woman.

Courageous and undismayed, she faced the birth of their first child, Dominick, while living in makeshift quarters in the island's blockhouse. Their second son, Harman, Jr., was born two years later in the mansion.

When the boys were mere babes, she undertook the difficult trip to New York City to have them inoculated with smallpox vaccine, Jenner's discovery of only a few years before and as yet not widely trusted. She brought back vaccine and successfully administered it to riverside friends.

Early years in the idyllic retreat passed in a gay, carefree round of pleasure and satisfying intellectual pursuits. Gradually Harman's imprudence and excessive spending began to undermine his assets. He entered into partnership with Dudley Woodbridge, respected Marietta merchant. The firm sent to London for a $14,000 consignment of pewter, linen, tools, and luxuries like fans and silk and satin dress goods. The speculation proved unprofitable. Blennerhassett's financial situation declined. Frontier sharpsters and clever swindlers took advantage of his generosity and gullibility. Woodbridge, who retained an affection for him, was to say later he possessed every sense but common sense.

To retrieve his fortune, Blennerhassett now toyed with the notion of moving on to fresh fields. Also, fear increasingly haunted husband and wife lest their marriage secret might be divulged. Travelers from the British Isles were more numerous. There always was the chance one from home might turn up . . .

Such a setting was ready-made for Burr to enter the scene and spin his ensnaring web. He came down the Ohio, covering the same course the Blennerhassetts had, in what he described to his daughter as a "floating house." It was a river boat "60 feet long, with a dining room, kitchen and fireplace and two bedrooms." He bought it in Pittsburgh for $133—and "how it can be made for that amount passes my comprehension," he expostulated.

This was 1805, in early May, when the Ohio Valley was resplendent in its loveliest attire of spring, unsmirched by grime and smoke and racket of progress. Docking at Marietta, Burr found the city "prospering, having about 80 houses, some that would be called handsome in any village on the continent."

He was much taken, also, with "its works of unknown antiquity." He had not come into the Ohio country to savor spring or relics, however, but to recoup resources and his reputation. He was on his way to the Gulf of Mexico, his intentions and his actions now, more than a century and a half later, still disputed. Ohio was the main arena of his so-called conspiracy and many of its prominent citizens were participants—among them, Harman Blennerhassett.

Four years before, Burr had tied with Thomas Jefferson for the presidency. Each had received seventy-three votes, the House breaking the deadlock by electing Burr vice-president. He had finished that term a bare two months before under a terrible cloud. While still vice-president, but certain he would not be renominated, he entered the lists for the New York State governorship, and was defeated. The campaign was bitter. For the venomous remarks against him by Alexander Hamilton, Burr challenged him to a duel.

In an era when political passions boiled over, dueling was the accepted answer. Hamilton's son had fallen in one. Duels or challenges had settled differences for men like DeWitt Clinton, Andrew Jackson, Henry Clay. The gesture flung out was: pistols or swords for two, coffee for one. In this case it was pistols at ten paces and coffee for Burr. Hamilton was mortally wounded.

His death shocked the public. Dueling was condemned. Hamilton became a martyr, Burr a murderer. Burr was forty-nine, short and dapper, with a scintillating mind and all the social graces.

Burr's lineage was as notable as Blennerhassett's. Burr's father, Aaron, was a founder and the first president of the College of New Jersey, later Princeton; his mother, the daughter of Jonathan Edwards, a preacher New Englanders rated as the very voice of God. Aaron, Jr., a prodigy, at thirteen was ready for college but underage for matriculation at Princeton. Ultimately he was graduated with high honors. At nineteen his daring gained him a captaincy in the army at the bloody siege of Quebec against the British. Promoted to major, General Washington swore him in as staff member. But before long the general came to dislike him.

A top-flight lawyer in New York City, a power in politics, he was a senator from New York State when he was pitted against Jefferson for the presidency. Jefferson never forgot this close call to his political ascendancy, and so was born his everlasting enmity for Burr.

The duel brought down on Burr's head indictments for murder in New Jersey, where the affair took place, and in New York. Charges against him were quashed. But he was thousands of dollars in debt, dead politically, and, all in all, beached like a boat at ebb tide.

Rescue lay in the southwest, which had fascinated him for years and which he looked into on his recent flight. That whole section currently was in the forefront of the news.

The Louisiana Purchase added to the area of the United States more than 800,000 square miles. The lower Mississippi had been closed by Spain as suzerain of Mexican border territory, thereby strangling commerce of the states west of the Alleghenies. War with Spain loomed as inevitable. Burr had listened sympathetically to the states' complaints to Congress and also had given ear to their mounting talk of secession—it was not uncommon for states to consider leaving the young republic.

As he started west, Burr's aims were expressed intentionally in the vaguest terms. Whether he was patriot or traitor remains an unresolved question. His advocates in history argue his purpose was to lead a filibustering thrust against Spain's Mexican holdings for annexation to the United States, greatly to this country's advantage. His critics insist that any foreign possessions he might have controlled, he expected to organize as nucleus of a sovereign principality to be united with western states he would separate by force from the Union. In other words, he plotted a treasonable attack on his country. It was on such a charge he later was tried—and acquitted.

Marietta, stronghold of Federalists (Hamilton's party), at first was cool to Burr. A helpful contact, however, was Meigs, son of a comrade-in-arms at Quebec and newly appointed judge of upper Louisiana.

Resuming his floating house, Burr could scarcely credit his senses as he came within sight of Blennerhassett Island. The gleaming white mansion rose out of the river mists like a fairy castle, incongruous in the untamed country.

He tied up at the pier. Not one to break with etiquette, he waited for an invitation to call. Soon a Negro servant brought a summons. Suave and charming, Burr was recognized as of the gentry class, like the Blennerhassetts, and was welcomed.

During polite dinner-table conversation about literature and music, the guest dropped adroit references to his enterprise. He sensed that Blennerhassett yearned for financial betterment and was not unwilling to listen.

Burr took his leave and drifted on to New Orleans. By fall he was back, returning by horseback to save time. Blennerhassett was away from home. However, in December, when Burr was in the East, he received a letter from the "Lord of the Fabulous Island." Blennerhassett wanted to take part in the venture!

With the opening of Mississippi ports, threat of war with Spain vanished. Likewise, Burr's excuse for attack on that country's Mexican territory disappeared. He turned to Louisiana, took title to 400,000 acres, part of a grant outside the Purchase. It would serve as springboard for an invasion of Mexico, an idea he appears not to have relinquished.

As a convenient blind for such an operation, he promoted the holdings as a grand colony for refined and superior persons. This and Burr's entire prospectus attracted such luminaries as Jackson,

Clay, and New Jersey Senator Jonathan Dayton, owner of an Ohio tract encompassing today's city of Dayton. Burr's son-in-law, Joseph Alston, and Blennerhassett eloquently demonstrated their faith in the chimerical business. They supplied most of the $5,000 Burr paid for the Louisiana acres. Alston was a planter of South Carolina, subsequently governor.

The scheme's luster was enhanced for Blennerhassett and his ambitious wife when Burr delicately let drop a notion of making Harman ambassador to England from the "empire" that he himself would head as Emperor Aaron!

Naive Blennerhassett, capitulating completely to Burr's spell, was ready to risk his all for the promise of great riches and a life at court. Margaret was even more enthusiastic. Everything was falling into place beyond Burr's rosiest hopes. By mid-August of the next year, 1806, preparations for the ill-defined and improbable adventure were under way in earnest.

Burr and his beloved daughter, Theodosia Alston, arrived at Marietta, where Burr rode with Meigs in the annual militia muster, his soldierly finesse with troops and his magnetic personality winning the hitherto indifferent populace. At a ball that evening the courtly father and his gracious, accomplished daughter were toasts of everyone. Many young pioneers signed up for his expedition, which he outlined in nebulous but alluring terms.

Blennerhassett put his name to a promissory note to Colonel Barker for fifteen boats to be built at his Muskingum dry dock. Ten were to measure forty feet in length, the others fifty, all pointed at bow and stern for easy rowing up- or downstream. One, outfitted with fireplace, partitioned rooms, and "glaze windows" was for the comfort of the Blennerhassett family. Barker's bill was $1,319.

The island, as headquarters for supplies and equipment, hummed with the business. Several hundred barrels were filled with corn meal prepared on the grounds in home-made emergency ovens. Quantities of flour, pork, and whisky, to the tune of $2,000, were assembled. Capable Margaret Blennerhassett dedicated herself to the challenging project with whirlwind energy.

Burr and daughter Theodosia stayed at the mansion. Alston was a regular visitor. Balls and banquets varied the serious program. Burr came and went, recruiting men and money. In Cincinnati he called on John Smith, his former confrere in the Senate.

Though innocent of involvement, Smith's political future was ruined by his friendship with Burr, once "the plot" was exposed. Smith and Thomas Worthington were Ohio's first senators.

In Chillicothe, Ohio's capital, Burr stopped at Adena, Worthington's remarkable mansion designed by Benjamin Latrobe, one of the architects of the White House. The senator was not there. Mrs. Worthington entertained Burr, who afterward sent her a consignment of rare shrubs and flowers for her garden. Here he saw Governor Edward Tiffin. The meeting was friendly, unshadowed by the clamor the governor later would raise against him.

Burr journeyed on to Lexington, Kentucky, to stay with Clay, and to Nashville, Tennessee, to confer with Jackson at his estate, the Hermitage, and was feted with banquets at both places. Jackson agreed to be responsible for five additional vessels and considerable material. Burr gave him $3,500 on account. "Old Hickory," as everyone knew the Tennesseean, announced he and his friends had lined up seventy-five recruits.

Burr had reason to rejoice. All was going according to plan. But time pressed. It was November, with winter at the threshold. Orders went out to speed up schedules at the island and at Barker's dry dock. The feverishly advancing program gave substance to disquieting rumors rumbling through the Ohio valley. Blennerhassett, writing in the Ohio *Gazette* under the signature "Querist," added to the growing suspicions by his strangely injudicious statements regarding advantages of certain states withdrawing from the Union. The series of articles drew vigorous counterfire from the Ohio press and intensified the tension.

Citizens of Wood County, on the Virginia side of the river, reacted with mass meetings, hysterically organized to attack Blennerhassett Island.

Jefferson dispatched John Graham, representative of the State Department, to Ohio to investigate. He interviewed Blennerhassett and then went on to Chillicothe to inform Tiffin of the barge construction. He reported back to the President he could find nothing illegal about what was going on. Blennerhassett grew apprehensive, nevertheless. He returned from a hurried rendezvous with Burr at Lexington, disturbed particularly about danger to his island from the Virginians. However, he was reassured by Colonel Hugh Phelps, of that state's militia, that no harm would befall his estate.

The finale, nonetheless, was shaping rapidly. The true villain in the cast, General James Wilkinson, of the U.S. Army, at this juncture played his hand. His long and checkered history had culminated in his appointment as a commissioner of Louisiana and commander of American forces on the Spanish border. Burr relied on his co-operation from the start, and, in fact, may have been inspired by him originally with the possibilities in the southwest.

What Burr did not know was that Wilkinson for years was well paid by Spain as its Spy No. 13. Already false to his native country, Wilkinson doubled in disloyalty by turning over to Jefferson a letter-in-cipher written to him by Burr. He decoded it for the President, making translations and omissions to his own advantage, as it came out later in Burr's trial.

Jefferson, ignorant of Wilkinson's treachery, considered he at last had tangible evidence against his old foe, Aaron Burr. He was quick to press the advantage. On November 27 he issued a proclamation warning of a "military expedition against the dominion of Spain . . . fitting out and arming vessels in the western waters . . . engaging in criminal enterprises . . . the President orders all participants to cease," etc. . . . No word of treason appeared in the document.

Tiffin, nudged into action by the proclamation, informed Ohio lawmakers of "a hostile expedition afoot inimical to the peace of the United States." Legislators responded on December 6, 1806, by voting the governor power to call out the militia if necessary to suppress an uprising, appropriating $1,000 for the purpose.

Tiffin's orders continued in a flurry of high-sounding letters and messages. He posted the constabulary at strategic river stations: called up volunteer companies of "officers, privates and musicians" and directed "the batteaux of the Muskingum flotilla be seized."

Reading the florid dispatches one would assume Ohio and the entire country were in dire danger. Mariettians and folk up and down the river on the Ohio side refused to take any of it seriously. Blennerhassett was well known and well liked. They were cordially inclined to Burr, a familiar figure in their midst. All this to-do about such men being enemies of the government was nonsense. They mocked it all with pranks against the militia, waggish rhymesters recording the fun.

But Blennerhassett was downhearted. Completion of the boats lagged, blocking the entire procedure. In the slow communication exchange of the day, he had no real knowledge of what was transpiring. Each hearsay tale reaching him was more alarming than the last. Sensing collapse of the whole project, he was ready to withdraw.

At this low point in his spirit, one of Burr's recruits sailed in from Pittsburgh with four boats in tow carrying twenty men bent on colonizing in Louisiana. Egged on by his wife, Blennerhassett finally went off with them at midnight on December 10. Slipping silently into the swift and freezing current, they headed for the mouth of the Cumberland to meet Burr. None of the sentries waiting along the river banks spied them. The explanation probably is in a verse of the pioneer's ballad "Battle of the Muskingum":

> The band so bold, the night being cold
> And a blacksmith's shop being handy;
> Around the forge they drink and gorge
> On whiskey and peach brandy.

Mrs. Blennerhassett departed for Marietta next day to procure the boat prepared for her and her boys, her plan being to join her husband and Burr. During her absence a detachment of Virginia militia landed on the island, raided the mansion's wine cellar and in a drunken orgy looted the beautiful home. The island's mistress returned to find draperies ripped to the floor, mirrors smashed, furniture chopped for firewood, shots fired wantonly into walls, and windows used as targets.

With winter settling in in earnest and ice beginning to coat the river, she and the boys were glad to escape on December 17 with another boatload of Burr "colonists" that arrived from the East uninformed of the turn of events. In January, after a voyage of much hardship, she and her sons met Blennerhassett in Natchez.

The bubble had burst, though Burr was unaware of the fact. As he placidly drifted down the bucolic Mississippi with his little fleet of houseboats, frenzied stories circulated about "the approach of gunboats" while protective cannon were mounted on vessels in the river. On the shore soldiers marched and countermarched.

Burr and Blennerhassett were arrested in Natchez. The latter was discharged and left at once for his Ohio island. Burr was released, but on bail, and, realizing this meant prosecution, escaped in disguise. He was captured, taken to Richmond, Virginia, and tried for treason. Blennerhassett had got as far as Lexington when he heard a charge of treason was directed also at him. He submitted at once to arrest. Clay acted as his counsel.

The trial, one of the most famous in American jurisprudence, dragged through the summer of 1807. Crowds in holiday mood streamed into the sweltering Virginia capital, tipped up foaming tankards at the inns, camped in covered wagons by the roadside, pitched tents as close as possible to the courthouse. Andrew Jackson was there to proclaim Burr's innocence in fiery polemics to anyone who would listen.

Fortunately for justice and for Burr, the presiding judge was Chief Justice of the United States, John Marshall, outspoken antagonist of Jefferson. The jurist's scrupulous regard for legality was assurance against presidential political prejudice creeping into the docket. Counsel on both sides were strikingly able men. Burr, a stately little figure in powdered wig and black silk, was his own advocate.

After an opinion three hours in delivery, Marshall's verdict was that no treason had been proved against Burr, or Blennerhassett, viewed as the lesser culprit. Both were free—and outcasts—their dazzling aspirations turned to dust.

Blennerhassett demanded that Burr reimburse him $50,000 for notes he had endorsed in Burr's favor, for loss by creditors' forced sale of his household goods, and for destruction of his property.

Burr could not have repaid a farthing. Poverty and calamity pursued him. The pride of his life, his grandson, Aaron Burr Alston, died. Theodosia was lost at sea on a ship that disappeared in a storm between South Carolina and New York.

He failed in numerous artful attempts to regain wealth, lived in England for a time, practiced law in New York City, and there married the notorious, wealthy widow of Stephen Jumel.

In 1836, when Texas independence from Mexico was assured by Sam Houston's defeat of the Mexican general Santa Anna, Burr quipped:

"There! You see I was right!! I was 30 years too soon. What was treason on my part then, is patriotism now!"

A few months later he died. On that very day he learned his wife's divorce decree from him became final. He was eulogized by his alma mater, Princeton, and buried with full military honors in the college cemetery.

Burr and Blennerhassett had parted at Richmond, never to meet again. Blennerhasset was able to gather enough remnants of his patrimony to buy a thousand acres in Mississippi as a cotton plantation, calling it La Cache, the Hiding Place. After twelve years, through collapse of the cotton market and pressure from debts, he was forced to sell. He received $27,000 for the estate, which included twenty-two Negroes.

While living here the second of two daughters died and their last child, John Lewis, was born. During this period, in 1811, Harman learned that his Ohio island home, where he had tenants, had burned to the ground when a hemp crop drying in the basement was accidentally set on fire.

There ensued a succession of flittings to New York City, to Montreal, to England, seeking in vain to re-establish himself. Tragedy was compounded by the dissipation of the two older boys. Blennerhassett's sister, Avice, took Harman and wife into her home in Bath, England. From there the couple went to Jersey Island in the English Channel and lastly to the neighboring island, Guernsey. Blennerhassett suffered a series of strokes, dying February 2, 1831.

His widow, who survived him eleven years, came to America in 1842, with her son, John Lewis, to press claim for damages to the Ohio island by the militia. As a $10,000 settlement was in sight through a bill introduced in the Senate by the ever-loyal Clay, Margaret Blennerhassett died in New York City. The oldest son, Dominick, was found wandering in New Orleans, destitute, his ultimate fate unknown. Harman, an artist, died of cholera, an alcoholic in a New York City almshouse. John Lewis, located on a government section of land in Missouri, practiced law there, but left no descendants.

The whereabouts of Margaret Blennerhassett during the decade of widowhood was conjecture until 1956 when this writer, while a resident of Guernsey Island, discovered Harman's will. It disclosed that Margaret spent those missing eleven years in St. Peterport, the island's only city, living with "Mistress Mary Nelbern, Milliner," mystery woman in Blennerhassett's life. Margaret's income was largely rent money from the house in Bath, inherited at Avice's death.

Harman's testament, found in the Greffe (records office) of the Royal Court, a kind of Whitehall and Parliament combined, revealed a hitherto unknown chapter in the Blennerhassett saga. It parted the curtains of time for a poignant glimpse of Harman on the edge of death.

"Bury me at night and limit funeral expenses to no more than for an ordinary laboring man," ordered Blennerhassett, who had lived like a prince.

He directed that Margaret "take in Mrs. Nelbern, soon to become a destitute widow, and also her orphan child, [named] Avice," presumably for Avice Blennerhassett. Margaret was also told to "share with Mistress Nelbern her income" and, moreover, give her one third of the household furnishings and silver plate. In the event Margaret did not live with the widow, "though I so earnestly desire it," Mistress Nelbern was to receive a sixth of his bank deposit, equivalent to $1,800.

"Mistress Nelbern," the document continues, "hath saved my life and that of my sister on more than one occasion and I am mainly beholden to her . . . not only for my family's subsistence, but for the very property I am now disposing."

Who was Mary Nelbern? And what service did she render Blennerhassett to make him so eternally grateful? And how did the once high-spirited Margaret take to the idea of living with the lady and her child, sharing money and furniture with her? History supplies no answers.

In Her Majesty's Ecclesiastical Court, Harman Blennerhassett's burial place was recorded as in Le Cimetière des Étrangères (cemetery for foreigners). During a recent restoration of the cemetery, tombstones were moved about so that the exact location of many graves, including Blennerhassett's, is lost.

After so much tribulation, Harman Blennerhassett sleeps far from his lavish Ohio island home, on another island, leaving behind unsolved the mystery of the milliner.

Marshall Field

MARSHALL FIELD was twenty-seven and shy. In the six years since he had left his native Massachusetts to clerk in a dry goods store in raw and booming Chicago, he seldom wasted energy on social functions.

Born in 1835 on an impoverished New England farm, he had known only work, hard work, from the age of four, when he tended his father's cows. In the intervening years there had been no place nor inclination for play.

However, in the winter of 1862 he was persuaded to accompany a friend, a young man of his age, to a Chicago home to a party. This party that was to change his life took place when the country was being ravaged by the Civil War.

Before he knew it, Field was drawn into a most enjoyable tête-à-tête with one of the guests, twenty-three-year-old Nannie Scott, vivacious and very pretty. She had been in Chicago a couple of weeks, she told Field, visiting a former classmate from Emma Willard's School in Troy, New York.

On the morrow she was to leave for her home at Mount Vernon Furnace, Ohio. The town, she explained, was named for the iron foundry her father operated there, center and sole industry of the community. It was a few miles north of Ironton on the Ohio River.

Field knew nothing about ironmaking, nor of the Ohio district that Nannie referred to as the Hanging Rock Iron Region. The young dry goods merchant listened spellbound to the girl's description of the southern Ohio counties threaded with veins of iron ore and of the many other smelting industries sprung up in the wake of the ore seam.

Why the odd name Hanging Rock, Field wanted to know. Nannie had the answer. At Ironton, thriving "iron" town, an enormous rock rose from the river bank, and over this convenient projection boatmen hung their vessels' ropes when they went ashore. Another tradition attributed the name to a huge rock outcropping hanging over the roadway in the palisaded shore line. You could take your choice of explanations, Nannie stated with an engaging smile.

But she did not do all the talking. Adroitly she managed to draw out this diffident new acquaintance. Soon Marshall, who usually had very little to say, was deep in details of his role in the retail establishment of Cooley, Farwell and Company, where, two years before, he had been made a junior partner. Probably he did not divulge to her that he had borrowed $100,000 to buy that partnership and was financially handicapped because of payments due or being made on that loan.

He did confide to the flatteringly attentive Miss Scott some of his innovations, such as a sound money policy against too-easy customer credit and merchandising geared to the conviction that the war would bring a business upswing. Whether or not Nannie was interested in dry matters of retailing, she, nonetheless, gave Field the notion she was.

The two sat out several dances. Nannie was attracted to Field. The sheer drama of being singled out by this serious stranger appealed to her, for Nannie was said to have been romantic until the day she died.

On his part, Field, back in his comfortable bachelor quarters in a Chicago hotel, could not keep his mind off the lively Ohio girl. The following day he acted on an impulse, the first and only instance in his life, an action, it is claimed, he regretted.

Nannie, he knew, was departing at noon. He hurried to the railroad station, arriving as the cars were pulling out. Leaping aboard the moving train, he quickly located the young woman he sought. He dropped into the seat beside her and there and then proposed.

Startled at the sudden appearance of the breathless Field, and more so by his words, Nannie composed herself. She sat quietly as he went through his impassioned plea—and accepted him. There was time only for a hasty embrace, and for Marshall's promise to fulfill Victorian proprieties—he would come to Ohio as soon as possible to present himself to Nannie's father. Everything was settled in a few minutes and Field got off the train at the next station.

True to his word, Marshall Field soon arrived at Mount Vernon Furnace. He traveled as Nannie had, by "steam cars" to Cincinnati, thence by Ohio River passenger packet to Ironton, "metropolis" of the Hanging Rock Iron Region. There, Nannie's father, Ironmaster Robert Scott, sent the family carriage for him. Otherwise he could have taken the Iron Road, a thirteen-mile spur of the railroad laid to aid iron furnaces of the district, with Ironton its terminus.

Scott, who had established himself here sometime after 1833, when the valley's pioneer ironmaster, John Campbell, founded Ironton, liked Nannie's suitor. He was impressed with the earnest Chicagoan's ambitions and solid commercial viewpoint. The practical Scott did not miss the implication that, young as he was, he already was launched toward substantial success.

Field, in turn, was fascinated by the unusual community that he found clustered about the furnace. It was like nothing in his experience. He was full of eager inquiries. Scott, delighted, showed him over his domain and described its operations.

The foundry was at peak production, meeting war orders for Northern troops. Ohio River settlements on the border between North and South, often professed Copperhead leanings. But at the time Lawrence County, where Scott's foundry was located, was pushing enlistments for the Union and collecting clothing and hospital supplies. That Field, of military age, was not in the army seemed of no moment to his future father-in-law.

The ironmaster's authority and responsibility were like a feudal lord's. His holdings encompassed a few thousand acres. Through this land the valuable "limestone ore" wound its way, a narrow strip, its shallow overburden of clay making for easy mining. Limestone rock, everywhere abundant, supplied lime for smelting. Luxuriant stands of giant hardwoods, largely virgin timber, were ruthlessly felled for the needed charcoal. By the turn of the century this kind of wasteful handling exhausted forest resources and, along with discovery of rich Mesabi ore deposits in the northwest, closed most of Hanging Rock's foundries.

Field, however, saw Scott's foundry in its heyday. The workers, numbering a hundred or more, included smelting experts, wood choppers, charcoal burners, ore and limestone diggers, stone crushers, teamsters, and a couple of blacksmiths. A corps of skilled artisans turned out pots and pans, doorstops, bootjacks, heavy iron kettles for making apple butter and rendering lard, tools, stoves, lamps and lighting equipment, as well as cast-iron mantelpieces molded in classic, often charming, design.

These household items, manufactured at the furnace since its start, now were giving way to metal for the Civil War. Pig iron was shipped to armament and munitions factories, particularly in the Pittsburgh area. Transportation, most of the way by river barge, was direct and cheap. Some of the metal was used closer to home, at small gun shops like the one at Portsmouth, Ohio.

Hanging Rock's "pig," recognized for its exceptional strength, qualified for heavy ordnance and fieldpieces. The cannon, christened the "Swamp Angel," participating in the siege of Charleston, South Carolina, was cast from iron originating at Hecla Furnace in Jackson County to the north. In the same county Jefferson Furnace produced iron for plate on the turret gunboat, U.S.S. *Monitor,* which stopped the Confederate *Virginia,* formerly U.S.S. *Merrimac.* The battle near Hampton Roads, said to be the first naval engagement between ironclads, occurred in March, 1862, shortly after Nannie and Marshall's betrothal.

Typical of furnace neighborhoods, Mount Vernon was self-sufficient and more or less isolated. Scott, as ironmaster, was both employer and paterfamilias. His labor force depended on him not only for income, but for care and help in sickness and adversity. His men and their families lived in management-built and controlled split-log cabins, each with a neatly fenced-in dooryard garden plot. Cows, sheep, and pigs grazed in a common pasture.

Workers' pay was in scrip, each furnace printing its own, negotiable solely within its precincts. Scott maintained a widely stocked general store, where his personnel were forced to trade, for their paper money was redeemable only there.

Scott's furnace pioneered in placing boilers and hot blast over the tunnel head to utilize waste gases, an innovation soon adopted by other Hanging Rock iron foundries. Mount Vernon Furnace was built into the side of a rise, its site marked today by tumbled stones from the stack. Slag, charcoal, and ore dumps lie about, overgrown by wild grass and weeds.

A tiny hamlet, on the map now as Vernon, survives. To reach it one travels over a road the state highway department forgot, an uninterrupted series of chuckholes. It climbs over the knobs (southern Ohio for hilltops) through empty country, only an occasional power line reminding one of the civilization left behind.

The small cabins of old-time workers remain, trimly painted white, occupied for the most part by newcomers who know little of the story of the furnace. Only one house, it is apparent, could have been Scott's. A mansion in its era, as befitted the ironmaster's position, an air of elegance clings to it, despite years of neglect. A sturdy brick, well proportioned, its interior retains some original embellishments, like the handsome iron mantels made in Scott's furnace. Lonely, but proud, the old house sits aloof from the humbler dwellings of the one-time furnace employees.

During Field's preliminary visit here he and Nannie set their wedding for the coming June 19 (1862). Nannie's sister Jennie, acclaimed the prettiest of the several Scott daughters and acknowledged belle of the Hanging Rock region, was selected maid of honor.

As mid-June approached, the district buzzed with news of the wedding preparations. Furnace proprietors, largely Virginians, maintained hospitable traditions of the South. The ironmaster's home was a center of social doings. The Scotts, accustomed to entertaining the elite of the Valley from as far away as Cincinnati and Kentucky, were setting the stage for an elaborate event. An orchestra and caterers from Ironton were engaged. Guests coming by river packet were to be met by carriages. A bevy of Nannie's school chums was expected from the East.

The marriage day fell on Thursday. On the preceding Monday all was festive and gay in the Scotts' big house. Jennie, after helping Nannie, was packing her own trunks. The girls had been inseparable since childhood and Jennie was to accompany the bridal couple to Chicago, where Field had bought a fine new house on Michigan Avenue.

Tea was announced. Jennie hurried down the long stairway to summon Field and her father, who were visiting together in the parlor. She passed under a handsome crystal and brass chandelier hanging in the wide central hall. A servant had just lighted it with his long taper after filling it with camphine.

Suddenly a terrifying crash and a young woman's screams tore through the house. The fixture's moorings in the high ceiling had let go as Jennie walked beneath it. Flaming fuel saturated her clothes, turning the girl into a torch.

In an instant her father and Field were at her side, as well as others in the house. Several, including Field, were burned as they attempted to smother the blaze. Jennie had every available medical aid, but she died the following day, Tuesday. The floor of that house still bears the burn marks.

Instead of Nannie and Marshall's wedding on Thursday, Jennie's funeral took place. Because of the slow communication means of the day, wedding guests could not be notified in time and they arrived. Many disembarking from river steamers at Ironton's wharf were met by messengers relaying the tragic turn of events.

The wedding ceremony was postponed to January 8, 1863, and then was solemnized as a strictly family affair. The prenuptial calamity was a bad omen. Once he had installed his bride in the new house on Michigan Avenue, Field turned with renewed concentration to his store and Nannie was left more and more alone.

Union armies reeled under Confederate blows at the Second Bull Run; Maryland was invaded and Antietam shocked both sides with its casualties. All day and all night recruiting drums rolled in Chicago. Patriotic crowds milled about the courthouse chanting "The Battle Hymn of the Republic" and "John Brown's Body," while young men signed up to save the Union. Field and many another young merchant sponsored rallies, gave liberally to drives for war needs, but did not enlist, nor were they criticized for not doing so.

The war boom which Field had anticipated materialized with a steadily rising demand for scarce goods of all sorts. At the news of Appomattox, when Field was not quite thirty, his interest in the firm amounted to $260,000 and he had paid off his entire loan.

In Chicago's disastrous fire of 1871, quick-acting Field moved quantities of stock to an empty car barn, made generous free distributions to fire victims and realized a "handsome profit of $125,000" from the sale of his salvaged merchandise.

Making money engrossed him to the exclusion of family life. His courtship had not prepared Nannie for his subsequent austerity and exclusive concern with business. Husband and wife grew apart. She and their two children spent most of each year abroad. Field saw his wife at long-spaced intervals, usually in Paris. Nannie died in Nice in 1896. Field gave himself to amassing a fortune that reached $150,000,000.

In September, 1905, when he was seventy and looked ten years younger, he married fifty-year-old Mrs. Arthur Caton, widowed the previous year. He and the Catons had been neighbors and friends over a long period. Though it was rumored that Field had been in love with her secretly for years, she and he conducted themselves with such dignity that no whisper of impropriety ever was bandied about in regard to them. The marriage took place in London with U.S. Ambassador Whitelaw Reid, native Ohioan, Field's close friend, in attendance. The wedding breakfast was an exclusive affair at Claridge's. The groom's gift to the bride included a collection of tiaras, necklaces, and rings set with priceless diamonds, pearls, and rubies.

Burne-Jones, celebrated English artist, once described the new Mrs. Field as possessing "the sweetest smile I have ever seen." Field's friends exclaimed they never had known him to be so happy.

Two months later, in November, his son, Marshall II, died, generally conceded a suicide, a tragedy from which the father never fully recovered.

In January, Field played golf, the only recreation he ever indulged in. Robert Todd Lincoln was in the foursome at a Chicago country club. They used red balls, for they played over a snow-covered course. Field became ill and pneumonia developed. On January 17, 1906, a little more than four months after his second marriage, Marshall Field died. Chicago mourned him as it never before had mourned another notable, not even a United States President.

He was buried in a simple stone vault in Graceland Cemetery near the grave of Nannie, gentle, disappointed daughter of the Ohio ironmaster.

Katharine Wright

ROMANCE CAME to Katharine Wright at fifty-two. And she was afraid to tell her brother Orville. It would have been different had Wilbur been alive.

As a teen-ager she was backing and encouraging "the boys," both older than she, long before they made history at Kitty Hawk in man's first machine-powered flight. She had been their companion in their play, in their disappointing early struggles, in their successful years. Wilbur had been dead fourteen years. From then on Orville and she were together constantly.

Katharine's suitor was her age, a widower, Henry J. Haskell, highly regarded editor of *The Kansas City Star.* She had known him from their undergraduate days at Oberlin College. On several occasions he was a guest at the Wrights' home in Oakwood, a Dayton, Ohio, suburb. Orville liked him—but not as a brother-in-law.

For a while Katharine and the editor kept their engagement to themselves. In the meantime Haskell joined Orville and his sister for a summer outing at Georgian Bay, a part of the country Orville loved.

"We will tell him up there where all is peace and quiet and Orv will be in a happy mood," they decided. But neither found courage to divulge their secret.

It was months before they dared set the date for the wedding—November 20, 1926. Orville was alternately furious and inconsolable. Katharine was abandoning him, he declared.

The ceremony took place, not in Dayton in what had been Katharine's home for many years, but in Oberlin, at the home of Louis E. Lord, Oberlin College professor. Dr. and Mrs. Lord were classmates and close friends of both bride and groom. President

Henry Churchill King, president of the college, officiated. Orville did not attend.

The Haskells took up residence in Kansas City. Brother and sister did not see each other until Katharine was on her deathbed, not quite three years later.

Orville was alone now in the big house they called Hawthorne Hill. The three of them had planned it—Wilbur and Orville and Katharine. But before it was built, Willbur, age forty-five, died of typhoid fever and overwork and the strain of patent litigations.

From the very beginning, their conquest of the air had been a joint achievement. Without Wilbur, Orville was crushed. Katharine had devoted herself to him from then on.

Now Orville had only his memories of her. He recalled how, following their mother's death, when Katharine was fifteen, she had taken charge of their first little Dayton house, at 7 Hawthorne Street, where she and Orville were born. Here the boys had begun their experiments with flying, after their father, benign and perceptive Milton Wright, Bishop of the United Brethren Church, gave them a toy helicopter. It had two propellers and it flew. They promptly took it apart to see how it rose in the air. Then satisfied, they discarded it, but not what it taught them.

Katharine, "baby" of the family, born in 1874, was three years to the day younger than Orville, and seven years younger than Wilbur. Two older brothers, Reuchlin and Lorin, in due time, left for homes of their own. The three junior Wrights, however, "the boys" and their sister, seem to have had no thought of matrimony—until Katharine was claimed by the man from Kansas City.

Wilbur and Orville, inseparable from childhood, shared their toys, their bicycle repair business, their passion for aviation. As boys they would stop their play to lie side by side on a summer day, watching birds wheeling above, the wing dip, balance, and turn in mid-air. They had a common bank account, each using it without need to consult the other.

Katharine was a background partner, a cheery booster when luck ran low. As the boys' experiments in the back yard of their bicycle shop progressed from gliders to problems of an engine for a flying machine, they were put down as visionary cranks, or worse. Even the broad-minded bishop had his misgivings, questioning whether man, created without wings, was meant to have dominion over the air. Katharine's faith through it all never wavered in her brothers' final triumph.

After graduating from Oberlin College, she taught Latin at Dayton's Steele High School. At the same time she managed the house with the aid of Carrie Grumbach, a tiny person so long in the Wrights' employ she seemed like one of the family. It was a happy household, each member following individual pursuits.

The boys were absorbed in mathematical calculations, in perplexing quirks in their machine and reports of other continually discouraging efforts by flying enthusiasts like Chanute, Lilienthal, Langley . . .

Enlisted as helper, Katharine cut material for covering the first wings, carefully following the pattern laid down, then stitching yards of the stuff on her mother's old treadle sewing machine.

Katharine writes in 1900 to her father, off on a church mission: "We don't hear anything but flying machines and engines from morning to night. I'll be glad when school begins and I can escape." And again, in 1902: "The flying machine is in the process of making now . . . There is no place in the house to live. But I'll be lonesome enough this time next week to wish I could have their racket around."

Wilbur and Orville were getting ready for another trip to the sand dunes of Kitty Hawk, South Carolina, where periodically they had been making practical tests of flight theories and experiments. The area had been recommended to them by the U.S. Weather Bureau for its steady winds and low hills.

Katharine was eager for them to get away from Dayton: "Will is thin and nervous, and so is Orv . . . Salt breezes will do them good."

While there, they camped, doing their own housekeeping. Katharine worried about their food. Will tried to reassure her. They took turns at cooking. Orv always served bread and butter and meat three times a day, he reported. Will made hash of Orv's leftover meat the first half of his week, then fixed eggs and sweet potatoes the rest of the time—the same for all meals.

By September of 1903 they finished their invention, a contraption with an engine and propellers that they were convinced was IT! It would carry a man aloft! This was in their shop in Dayton.

They packed it tenderly and went off to Kitty Hawk to try it out. Performance there would spell either success or failure. In the lonely dunes weeks followed weeks of reassembling, checking, repairing, and adjusting parts. There were frustrations of many sorts —not the least, bad weather.

December came. Will and Orv still were in South Carolina. Katharine and the bishop grew anxious—would the boys be home for Christmas? Only Wilbur could stuff the turkey . . .

Supper was on the table one Thursday evening at the Hawthorne Street home. Lorin had dropped in. The doorbell rang. Carrie answered and brought in a yellow envelope, a telegram. Katharine tore it open and read its message aloud:

> Success four flights Thursday morning all against 21 mile wind started from level with engine power average speed through air 31 miles longest 57 seconds [it should have read 59 seconds] inform press home for Christmas.

This was December 17, 1903, forever after one of mankind's memorable dates.

Bishop Wright, relieved that the family would be united for the holidays, thought maybe the Dayton newspapers might be interested in the boys' flight, and suggested that Lorin go to one of them with the news. No hurry about it . . . "after you finish supper."

The editor was bored and skeptical: "If your brothers had stayed up fifty-seven minutes, it might make a news item."

Next morning *The Dayton Journal* noted that the Wright brothers would be home for Christmas. A few newspapers elsewhere carried brief announcements of the flight . . . on inside pages. Most ignored the event that was to set a new course for history.

Katharine Wright alone seems to have comprehended the significance of this first power flight. She immediately wired the brilliant French-born aeronautical authority, Octave Chanute, in Chicago. He had been sympathetic from the first with her brothers' project, had visited them in Dayton and at Kitty Hawk.

Next day Miss Wright had difficulty keeping her mind on her pupils' translations of Cicero's orations. Reward had come at last for the boys' endless hard work, for the days and nights they had pored over technical details. No one knew better than she what had gone into that pioneer airship. She had been in on all of it—some of the brain work, some of the brawn. And there were those who claimed that at crucial moments her teacher's salary helped plug holes in her brothers' budget.

Orville, on the other hand, denied such stories. In a statement issued through his secretary shortly before his death, it was reported he said: his "sister was his and his brother's closest confidant and comrade, but it was without foundation that she contributed to their success scientifically or financially."

Katharine is fondly remembered by many Oberlin friends, who point out that Orville's discounting of her aid came after her marriage had embittered him; that Wilbur, on the other hand, at his death left her $50,000, possibly an admission of her material support as well as expression of his brotherly love.

Recognition of the Wrights' achievement came slowly in the United States. Europe, contrariwise, more alert and experienced as regards aviation, hailed them. Letters, cablegrams, deputations arrived at the Wright Cycle Shop.

Katharine resigned from schoolteaching to give all her attention to her brothers and their home—until her marriage more than twenty years later. Wilbur and Orville now went abroad frequently, Katharine often accompanying them.

In France in 1908, after demonstrations at Le Mans, Wilbur moved south to Pau for a long awaited reunion with Orville and their sister. Their coming was delayed by a bad accident to Orville's plane near Washington, D.C., when his passenger, Lieutenant Thomas Selfridge, was killed and Orville seriously injured. Katharine sat by his bed for weeks after the smashup.

In Pau she went aloft for the first time, one of the first women in all the world to leave the ground in a heavier-than-air machine. She sat amidst struts and wires in an open cockpit. To keep her skirts from billowing immodestly, Wilbur tied them with a rope securely about her knees. French dress designers shortly introduced the hobble skirt.

Hundreds flocked to Pau to see the flights, among them King Edward VII and entourage, Lord Arthur Balfour, Spain's King Alfonso and Lord Northcliffe. In Rome, King Victor Emmanuel, J. P. Morgan, and Railroad Tycoon J. J. Hill were enthusiastic onlookers. The Kaiser and Crown Prince Friedrich Wilhelm invited the Wrights to Berlin and were personally attentive. Katharine hobnobbed with them all, gracious and unperturbed, as if crowned heads and potentates were everyday acquaintances.

Home, after all this, they found that Dayton, at last awakened to the importance of their citizens, the Wright brothers, was putting on a city-wide celebration. It was a prelude to what lay ahead. Applause and prosperity were arriving, if tardily, nonetheless surely, on wings of their invention. Before long it seemed that all the world, America too, was knocking at their door.

Katharine and the boys had need of the big comfortable house they planned for the wooded tract they called Hawthorne Hill. Wilbur, drawing the plan of his bedroom, stipulated it must have a southern exposure. But he was never to live in it. Katharine and Orville went ahead with the house after his death and Orville carried through as best he could with the growing demands of the air age he and Wilbur had inaugurated. His heart was in none of it. With his brother gone, the interplay, the creative spark, was stilled. He depended more and more on Katharine.

Prominent people of two continents called to pay respects to Orville and to the memory of Wilbur. Katharine was a delightful hostess, enjoying the visitors and in turn putting them at ease. A writer in an Oberlin alumni magazine comments that in the Wright home "one might encounter European aeronautic experts, publishers like Collier and Page, authors like Percy Mackaye and Hamlin Garland, explorers like Ackley and Stefansson—and editors like Haskell—all feeling very much at home."

Described by associates as "gay," "fun loving," "radiant," one who made friends and kept them, Katharine was a great contrast to shy Orville, who spoke only when he had to and could sit for hours in a group without uttering a word. After Wilbur's death she was more than ever a buffer-contact for Orville.

Though neither brother had attended college, both looked on Oberlin as a kind of foster alma mater. The far-visioned college in 1910 was the first of many to grant them honorary degrees. Katharine was elected trustee of the college and when she attended board meetings Orville invariably was with her. After her marriage she traveled faithfully from Kansas City for trustees' gatherings—without Orville, and without going on to Dayton to see him.

Her life with Henry Haskell was a happy, busy one, though brief. Born not far from Oberlin, in Huntington, Ohio, he was raised by American missionary parents in Bulgaria. Influenced by this background, he traveled widely and was known as an authority on foreign affairs. Joining the *Star* shortly after graduation, he remained on the staff more than fifty years, and on his fiftieth anniversary with the newspaper received messages from all over the world. He succeeded his wife as a trustee of Oberlin College, where a fellow board member described him as "brilliant, a master of his craft who has not lost his youthful ideals . . . the conversation of few reflects such wide reading or such charm . . ."

When Katharine was stricken with pneumonia in March, 1929,

and it became apparent she could not recover, her husband asked her if she wanted to see Orville. She replied: "He may come if he wishes."

He reached her just in time.

"Here is Orv, Katharine," Haskell said. "Do you recognize him?"

"Yes, of course," she answered.

Katharine was buried beside Wilbur in Dayton's Woodland Cemetery. During the funeral services planes from Wright-Patterson Field dropped flowers on her grave.

Orville lived nineteen years longer, alone in the Oakwood House. More reticent and withdrawn than ever, he was seen so seldom he became almost a legend. In his will Oberlin received a legacy of over $360,000.

Now and then a champion of Katharine comes forward insisting that she has not had her due. On the twenty-fifth anniversary of Kitty Hawk, while she still was alive, the Cleveland *Plain Dealer* editorialized that "there would have been no Kitty Hawk without Kitty Wright" and "the brothers have testified to the vast assistance rendered by their sister . . ." A Congressional Medal for her was proposed, but nothing came of the suggestion. However, she was decorated by the French government and made an Officer of Public Instruction in 1923 at the same time that Orville received the Legion of Honor medal.

Katharine's husband erected a fountain in her memory in the gardens of Oberlin's Fine Arts Building. It is a replica of sculpture by the Renaissance artist Verrocchio, seen in the courtyard of Florence's Palazzo della Signoria. The joyous little boy with the dolphin and the sparkling water is peculiarly appropriate as a memorial to the vivacious Katharine.

Not far away on the campus her brothers' names also are cut in stone, in the physics laboratory named for them.

Thus are the three Wrights remembered at Oberlin College, where romance bloomed for one—and brought heartache to another.

Wayne B. Wheeler

"THERE GOES WHEELER ON HIS WHEEL."

The serious young man pedalling furiously, coattails flying, was a familiar sight around Cleveland, Ohio, in 1894. He was Wayne B. Wheeler, freshly graduated from Oberlin College, embarking on his life vocation.

He was launching a career that would make him Dry Boss of America and, for a time, the most influential single individual in the country.

Now, however, his name meant nothing as he announced himself to the minister of every church he passed and rang doorbells up and down residence streets. He was soliciting memberships, collecting pledges and occasionally cash, for the Ohio Anti-Saloon League. Few had heard of the League, for it was no better known than Wheeler.

The previous year, gentle Howard Hyde Russell, Congregational clergyman in Berea, Ohio, had founded the League in ceremonies at Oberlin's Old First Church on the campus.

Wheeler, with a few other students, sat in the front row of the balcony, which extended far out over the lower floor. Wheeler, leaning on the railing and almost touching Dr. Russell, listened spellbound!

At the conclusion of the program he pledged to give twenty-five cents a month to the fledgling association, a generous sum for him at the time. The rest of his life, though he raised six-figure amounts for the League, he never failed in his monthly contribution, increasing it as personal income permitted.

Dr. Russell soon needed an assistant and asked faculty members of Oberlin College, his alma mater, to suggest someone from the graduating class. Such a candidate, he specified, must be a hard worker, have frugal money sense and be an able public speaker. Without exception, professors recommended Wayne Bidwell Wheeler. Enthusiastically they detailed his record for Russell.

Wayne was born in Brookfield, Ohio, near the Pennsylvania border. His father was a farmer. He and his wife could not understand why their son wanted further training than was available in local schools. Wayne, undeterred, taught country school a term or two, then enrolled in Oberlin Academy and went on for four years more at the college.

He supported himself over the entire period. During school months he took odd jobs on campus. In vacations he sold Bibles and other books throughout northern Ohio, with teams of college boys as salesmen under his direction. Finally, ready for commencement, with all his expenses met, he had a small bank account besides. He was the outstanding orator and debater in his class, and, his teachers emphasized, would have had top rating had he been free from the necessity to earn his way.

Dr. Russell, convinced, hurried off to look up the boy. He found him in the basement of a dormitory. His appearance was anything but impressive. Short and slight of build, in tattered and not too clean overalls, with a smudge on his face, he was at work as the hall's janitor.

He felt honored by this visit from the Berea preacher whom he remembered so vividly. Standing, broom in hand, he gave him his deep attention. Russell presented his proposition as a Christian's opportunity to serve God and fellow man.

Wheeler had about made up his mind to accept a business proposition. But he was moved by Russell's eloquence and appeal, as he had been in the balcony of "Old First." He agreed to the offer —for one year. It would be his contribution to a cause he believed in.

Little did the serious young man think the one year would spread over a lifetime. Hardheaded and practical as he was, he never lost his link with the spiritual side of life as he gave himself to advancing the interests of the Anti-Saloon League.

The League's incorporators, few in number and far from wealthy, were devout church folk and other idealists. They had no united scheme to win converts to the gospel of abstinence. Finances, as nebulous as their plans, warranted only a small allowance for the new aid. There was barely enough in the treasury to pay for Wheeler's wheel, which would take him around the first area he was to tackle. This was to remain his sole means of transportation for many years.

The League, Ohio in origin and Ohio in make-up, had no aim of expansion beyond the state.

Wheeler's genius, dubbed "Wheelerism" in admiration by friend and foe alike, pushed the Anti-Saloon League to national status, a power in every state of the Union.

Twenty-five years after assuming his post, Wheeler experienced success as seldom befalls mortals. His crusade triumphed completely.

Prohibition was inaugurated in the entire country by ratification in 1919 of the Eighteenth Amendment to the Constitution and passage of the Volstead Law (over President Woodrow Wilson's veto) to implement its enforcement. The "Dry Age" lasted fourteen years.

Persistent temperance indoctrination for many years laid the foundation. Home-front patriotism during World War I and vigorous promotion of postwar recovery helped make the measures acceptable. The catalytic agent that brought the strategy to reality was the Anti-Saloon League. It was directed by many capable men. But the world gave the credit to Wheeler. His was the main hand in drafting the amendment.

The Volstead Act took its name from Andrew J. Volstead, Minnesota congressman who introduced it in the House. Wheeler's enemies derisively christened it the "Wheeler Act." It was not entirely a misnomer, for he generally was conceded the true author.

Prohibition and Wheelerism became synonymous. Wheeler WAS the League in the eyes of the nation. If he did little to offset such assertions, it was not from conceit, but rather because facts confirmed such estimates. He knew what he had accomplished in the past. He had faith in his own leadership currently and for the future.

It was no easy responsibility. Wheeler drove himself tirelessly and expected all on his staff and in the fellowship of a widespread movement to do likewise.

Though often accused of receiving a high salary, his League wage always was on a modest scale. He was content with it. Had he directed his energies and talents to business or public life, he would have gone far. He was a master of law and politics and deftly manipulated techniques of both to further his goal.

Early in his connection with the League he saw its need for legal counsel. Straightway he began to study law and was graduated from Western Reserve University's Law School in Cleveland. At the same time he was discharging all his obligations as superintendent of the northeastern Ohio district, making speeches, managing money-gathering programs, and practically every Sunday addressing a church group.

Soon he was appointed League attorney for all Ohio. By his own count he handled two thousand cases involving local liquor irregularities and gave assistance to liquor control boards. He was beaten in less than ten court appearances.

One of his first adventures at the polls meant the downfall of Robert E. McKisson, Cleveland's colorful mayor from 1895–98. Following the mayor's welcoming talk before a national retail liquor dealers' convention, Wheeler set out consistently to block him. He endorsed his rival, John H. Farley, and at the next election Farley was chosen over McKisson, who was trying for a second term.

When he was thirty, Wheeler fell in love. Up to then he had had no time for romance. Girls did not interest the solemn young man with a seemingly one-track mind and a single purpose in life. However, all this was changed in one evening when he met a beautiful young woman, Ella Belle Candy.

According to one version, he saw her first at a temperance convention in Columbus. In the crowded auditorium there suddenly was only one person, as far as Wheeler was concerned—Miss Candy, though he did not know her name. Nonetheless, before he had wangled an introduction to her, he knew he was looking at his future wife. Another story is that he was introduced to her through a mutual friend of Oberlin College days. In any case, it was love at first sight on his part.

Miss Candy was not so sure. Daughter of Robert Candy, owner of the Busy Bee restaurant chain and, appropriately enough, a candy manufacturer, she was a popular girl and at the moment had another insistent swain. Wheeler, self-confident in love as in career, persevered and was accepted, as he had known he would be. His bride was a gifted singer who had studied at Oberlin, but after Wheeler's day.

Later, Mrs. Wheeler became prominent as a soloist in Columbus and Washington churches. Her father was a substantial backer of the Anti-Saloon League and looked with favor on the match.

Some authorities state that Wheeler neglected family and home for exclusive concentration on League affairs. This has been countered by surviving relatives who describe him as outgoing, jolly, and ready for fun.

His work, on the other hand, which he considered of vital importance, did have to come first. When not absent at meetings or conferences he brought home bulging brief cases and poured over the contents far into the night. He regretted such intrusion into his domestic life, but felt it unavoidable.

Writing while on a train in 1926, he commented to a son that he had left home regretfully as this was "a very special day—your mother's and my 25th wedding anniversary. But," he added, "warfare ignores such incidents." His immediate circle accepted this preoccupation, seeing him as a dedicated person who could not side-step his duty, as he saw it.

Wayne Wheeler could look back over the interval with pride in his accumulated attainments. In 1903, two years after marriage, he was made League superintendent for Ohio, with headquarters set up in Columbus.

His grasp of state politics and his influence were demonstrated when he engineered the defeat, in 1905, of Myron T. Herrick, of Cleveland, up for re-election as Ohio governor. During his first term Governor Herrick forced certain changes he considered necessary and fair in a local option bill. Its purpose, to keep saloons out of residence districts, thereby was weakened, according to temperance advocates.

Wheeler induced John M. Pattison, Cincinnati Democrat and avowed teetotaler, to run against Herrick. It was an uphill campaign and afterward Wheeler liked to talk about it. His favorite stories concerned stanch Republican drys who objected to supporting Democratic Pattison, insisting they always voted the straight "Lincoln party ticket" in honor of that great President. "I used to tell them Lincoln wasn't running this year," Wheeler would finish the tale, with a flourish and a flash of his famous grin.

Pattison came out ahead, he and his lieutenant governor being the only Democratic victors in an otherwise Republican landslide. Some hint of Wheeler's effort in the campaign was apparent in his report of 3,000 meetings scheduled and distribution of 75,000,000 pages of printed material.

He wrote many municipal anti-liquor ordinances and so efficiently backed local option laws that fifty-eight of Ohio's eighty-eight counties lined up on the dry side. He was pressed into service for advice and speechmaking in other states. His reputation mounted with brilliant pleadings before the U.S. Supreme Court.

As a natural result, the League, now country-wide in scope, moved him to Washington, D.C., as general counsel in charge of national legislation. Title was unimportant. Wayne Wheeler dominated the organization . . . as the liquor interests were aware.

His office faced the Capitol. He could get there in a hurry if word reached him that some temperance measure was faring badly. Through a card index he tabulated senators and representatives. If one wavered in his zeal, Wheeler's telegrams to dry constituents brought pressure from home that usually set the lawmaker on the path again. By such techniques he calculated he controlled 206 "bone dry" lawmakers in one session. This sort of thing gave him the name of "the bully lobbyist."

He was one of the first in the League to focus on the daring concept of nation-wide abstinence. When he arrived in Washington in 1915 this had jelled into definite policy. He and the League were looking ahead in their own words to "prohibiting forever intoxicating beverages in the United States."

Wheeler lost no time in calling on President Wilson to discuss the subject. Ever-confident, the League's emissary carried his own preliminary outline of covering legislation. The President appears to have been noncommittal.

With the declaration of war, Wheeler was quick to press for limitation of alcohol manufacture as a food conservation step. Wilson's first Secretary of State William Jennings Bryan was a loyal Wheeler ally. Secretary of the Navy Josephus Daniels debarred liquor from navy ships and shipyards, an action hailed by the drys as a victory.

Twin mechanisms, the Eighteenth Amendment and the Volstead Act revolutionized the habit of Americans. Temperance was now the law of the land. One might conclude that Wheeler could rest on this dizzy pinnacle of achievement, his lifetime mission fulfilled. That is exactly the way his associates reacted.

John Barleycorn was conquered!

The League began to break up. Key personnel, the majority of them clergymen, were hunting pulpits or other openings. Membership diminished and contributions withered.

The prophetic Wheeler, on the other hand, realizing that even more challenging tasks would confront them, tried to rally his colleagues. A stronger offensive, he insisted, was essential, if prohibition was to be safeguarded and maintained. Legislators had to be kept from backsliding. Liquor's hierarchy was not out, merely downed. Like the astute generalissimo he was, he recognized that favorable outcome in one battle did not guarantee the war was won.

In the 1920 elections he sought to have dry enforcement planks inserted in platforms of both parties. To this end he enlisted the aid of Bryan, who was attending both Republican and Democratic conventions as observer and reporter. The two nominees selected were Warren G. Harding by the Republicans and James M. Cox, his Democratic opponent, both Ohioans. Wheeler was well acquainted with them. Cox he had fought before, labeling him a wet during his term as Ohio governor, and he remained on the Wheeler black list.

While in the Senate, Harding had stood with the drys, voting to submit the prohibition amendment, and had been for passage of the Volstead Act and for similar bills. Wheeler was close to Harding, who was considered "a temperate man," but not by any yardstick a teetotaler.

It was said that during the campaign Wheeler persuaded Harding to embrace personal abstinence under threat of withdrawing League endorsement. Wheeler had Harding's ear in numerous instances, including appointment of Roy C. Haynes, Hillsboro, Ohio, newspaper editor and dry crusader, as the first Prohibition Commissioner.

When it appeared that Andrew J. Volstead's re-election to the House was in jeopardy, Wheeler canvassed the dry electorate in his Minnesota district and saved the seat of this valuable friend of temperance.

Planning well ahead for the next national hustings, the League head practically single-handedly prevented consideration of Governor Alfred E. Smith for the 1924 presidential ticket. The New York governor had urged a referendum which would have killed the state's ratification of the Eighteenth Amendment, and in other actions showed himself "unsatisfactory" to the drys.

It was an interlude of king-making for Wayne Wheeler. Candidates courted his approval and feared his frown. His nod turned judgeships, political appointments, and patronage to those he felt would lend a hand to insure that America stayed dry. From one end of the nation to the other he and his underlings kept themselves alert and vigilant for laxness and violations in liquor control enforcement. And in the early difficult days of the new enactment plenty of loopholes had to be plugged.

There were areas of conflict within his own ranks. Some confederates objected to his habit of assuming the mouthpiece role, of putting himself out in front as the indisputable oracle for the entire League. Jealousy prompted a few malcontents, while others sincerely differed with his operational blueprint. Invariably, however, his skill and the results he obtained compelled respect and deference. Where Wheeler sat always was head of the table. This might be an annoyance, but no one cared to attempt unseating him.

Legalized prohibition required him to maneuver on two fronts: against liquor interests seeking a comeback, and bootlegging lawlessness. Inroads by brewers and distillers he had anticipated. But the crime rise bred by illicit production of alcohol he had not expected.

Previously, condemnation had seldom bothered Wheeler. It was usually from traditional wets or well-heeled liquor companies. Such derogatory innuendoes he often reprinted and circulated as evidence of his effectiveness. On more than one occasion an attack was launched against him from the floor of Congress while he sat in the gallery relaxed and smiling characteristically.

A new kind of invective came to be leveled against him and he was deeply upset a few months before his death by a particularly vicious series of newspaper articles. Editorials and cartoons presented him as a wholesale poisoner, accountable for widespread blindness, fatalities, and other ills arising from consumption of bathtub gin and similar illegal concoctions.

Wheeler interpreted aright the ominous portents. The foundations of his lifework were beginning to crumble. But he did not surrender.

In 1926, during investigation of Senate campaign expenditures, James Reed, a "wet" senator from Missouri, long a bitter and vocal anti-prohibitionist, summoned Wheeler. Publicly announcing he would "grill" the witness, Reed exhausted every approach in a grueling cross-examination. In vain he sought to show the drys guilty of improper use of funds in influencing legislation.

Wheeler was very ill and spent the hours between appearances in bed. While he was testifying, his wife sat as near him as possible, with restoratives in hand. He would have been within his rights had he refused to answer. But the dry leader, instead, replied to all questions courteously and fully. Even adversaries, who had waited for the kill, commended Wheeler. Reed lost face, having failed to uncover any wrongdoing on the part of the League or Wheeler.

Nonetheless, the League's prestige was receding. Opposition to prohibition grew more vindictive. Antagonism arose from all sides, and not alone from the wets. Original sponsors were disillusioned by accompanying corruption and other undercover offences. In the face of these discouraging trends, Wheeler's health worsened steadily.

Hoping a change would benefit him, his family decided to spend the summer of 1927 at their cottage in Michigan. One evening in August when Mrs. Wheeler was preparing dinner, a gasoline stove exploded. Flaming oil cascaded over her, igniting her thin summer clothes. She ran screaming to the porch where her husband and her father were sitting. Mr. Candy leaped to his feet and instantly fell to the floor, dead from a heart attack. Wheeler grabbed a rug, upsetting tables and chairs, and smothered the flames. The burns had made too much headway.

She succumbed the next day.

Wasted and weakened by shock from the two tragic deaths and his own illness, Wheeler "looked like a skeleton with yellowed skin taut over high cheek bones, eyes dull and sunken," as a contemporary described him. Yet he fought on.

A short time later, having arranged the double funeral of his wife and her father in Columbus, he traveled to Lake Winona, Indiana, for the executive board meeting at the League's international convention.

He mounted the podium as of old, but he swayed as he went. Scarcely able to stand, he could give only a brief summary of the extensive address he had prepared. His voice was faint and quavering. The audience sat tense and hushed, fearing his collapse momentarily.

No one in attendance at that meeting was surprised to learn of his death September 5, three weeks after the tragedy in Michigan. He was fifty-eight, a martyr to overwork and a vanishing objective.

Dr. Russell, who had inspired him to shoulder arms in the first place, was beside him at the end. In Central Methodist Church, Columbus, where the double funeral had taken place so short a time before, Dr. Russell conducted the memorial for Wayne Wheeler. He thanked God for Wheelerism, His gift to humankind.

Wheeler's critics joined his champions in eulogizing the Dry Boss for his sincerity, his integrity, and his ability. Newspapers throughout the land broke out in front-page headlines about him, among them those formerly given to denunciation of his tactics.

"No other private citizen of the United States has left such an impress on national history," extolled the *Washington Post.* The *Cincinnati Enquirer,* heretofore a vigorous antagonist, called him "the strongest political force of his day. The wets hated him and maligned him but found him always invincible."

Not even Colonel Charles A. Lindbergh received more columns of attention earlier that year, in May (1927), when he soloed across the Atlantic. Wheeler had noted the event with pointed comments about the young flier, an abstainer, welcomed in Paris by the "wet" U.S. Ambassador Herrick, with whom the League leader had crossed swords so long ago.

Wheelerism died with Wheeler. Six years after him, prohibition, undermined beyond rescue, faded into the mists with repeal in Franklin D. Roosevelt's administration. The reform, the way of life for which Wayne B. Wheeler sacrificed himself, disappeared. But he was spared the knowledge.

Though very different from what he envisioned, Wheeler left a legacy to his country. Saloons, as they once were, doing business at all hours, unchecked, are no more. America rejected his idea of total abstinence, but sees to it liquor is dispensed under stringent control.

The League, therefore, has justified the anti-saloon part of its name. Today the League functions quietly in unpretentious quarters in Westerville, Ohio. It has veered completely away from Wheeler's aggressive militancy. Largely a venture in publishing, it circulates material in schools and colleges to acquaint youth with the dangers in the use of alcohol.

As contrasted with its reverberating thunder under Wheelerism, the Anti-Saloon League is "a still, small voice."

Wayne Bidwell Wheeler has had no successor.

Mark Twain

THIS IS THE STORY of the world's first transatlantic luxury cruise. A "select company" of sixty signed up for "a pleasure excursion to the Holy Land via Europe" aboard the 1800-ton side-wheeler *Quaker City*. Among them were half a dozen wealthy and pious Clevelanders.

Another group consisted of members of Reverend Henry Ward Beecher's Plymouth Church, in Brooklyn, where the expedition was organized.

Also on the roster was Samuel L. Clemens.

The name meant nothing to his shipmates, nor did his nom de plume, Mark Twain. He was not yet a celebrity.

It was Saturday, June 8, 1867, when the *Quaker City* embarked from New York.

Using steam and auxiliary sails, the ship was "provided with every comfort, including a library, a new Chickering piano and an organ," according to the elaborate prospectus.

The itinerary was high adventure and would be ambitious even for modern travelers. With the vessel as home base, voyagers inspected Europe's name places from Paris to Pompeii, climbed the Pyramids, touched at Greece. They stocking-footed it into Constantinople's mosques, went ashore in the Crimea, camped in Jerusalem, and rode muleback to Nazareth. A package deal for nearly six months. Cost: $1,250.

Little did the earnest travelers suspect they were to become "Innocents Abroad," caught forever like bees in amber, as characters in Mark Twain's book of that title about the trip.

In *Innocents Abroad,* published two years after the famous trip, he poked fun at the sight-seeing, uttered whimsical sallies about venerated Biblical landmarks, chuckled over pompous fellow tourists as "venerated fossils skipping forth on a six-month picnic," and at the same time managed some serious guidebook descriptions of places visited.

Forerunner of modern travel literature, it was an immediate best-seller and is singularly readable today. *Innocents Abroad* launched its author securely on the path that was to lead to high achievement, topped by *The Adventures of Huckleberry Finn,* still unchallenged as the great American novel.

All that was far in the future for the "carroty-topped," thirty-two-year-old Clemens, "scarcely genteel in appearance," lolling alone on the *Quaker City* deck. He had come aboard unacquainted with anyone.

However, he soon was welcomed as a congenial fourth by three of the Clevelanders: a young banker and scion of a first family, Solon Severance, about Clemens's age; Severance's aristocratic, devout wife, Emily, and Mrs. A. W. Fairbanks, wife of the editor and part owner of the *Cleveland Herald.*

During those fabulous months at sea, Clemens and the Cleveland trio forged lifetime friendships that brought him and his family often to the Ohio city. Following the cruise, he came to feel so at home there that he would have settled in Cleveland had his efforts not fallen through in a business deal with Fairbanks.

When the *Quaker City* left its New York City dock at the foot of Wall Street, Clemens was little known beyond the West Coast, where he had been contributing to newspapers and had just published his first book, *The Celebrated Jumping Frog of Calaveras County.* He was staked to the cruise—the fare being a considerable sum in those days—by *The Daily Californian.* He sent the newspaper fifty articles Sunday after Sunday and he wrote a few for New York newspapers. This output formed the basis for his *Innocents,* his second book.

The Severances were among the few young people on the ship, and Clemens was attracted to them immediately. They had made a traveling companion of Mrs. Fairbanks. This forceful woman and the shaggy-haired, seemingly indolent Clemens were drawn together by a common objective. Each was a newspaper correspondent.

Mary Mason Fairbanks was an experienced journalist, author of a popular column in her husband's newspaper under her by-line "Myra," transposed letters of her first name. The *Quaker City* venture was a sensation and had aroused great interest. She came along to write dispatches for the *Herald.*

Cultured Mrs. Fairbanks, who had more advantages than most women of her day, had attended Emma Willard School in New York State, and was better educated and more self-confident than Clemens. Frequently gripped by doubt of his own ability, he fell into the habit of showing his manuscripts to her. Soon he was seeking her appraisal regularly, and calling her Mother, a term of endearment and jest, for she was only seven years his senior.

Emily Severance, with no professional training or air, also was writing about this well-chronicled voyage. She recorded her observations in a diary which she posted piecemeal at every port to her Ohio home folk. The Severances were an illustrious clan, still prominent in Cleveland. Solon's nephew, John L. Severance, years later, perpetuated the family name in Severance Hall, which he built as home for the renowned Cleveland Symphony Orchestra.

Emily, whose twenty-seventh birthday occurred en route, had been persuaded to leave her three babies, two of them twins, in care of nursemaids and her matriarchal mother-in-law, to accompany Solon, who was ailing. The sea air, it was hoped, would benefit him.

Naively impressed with everything, Emily Severance missed nothing. Her almost daily messages that helped assuage her constant homesickness were published as *Journal Letters* by her daughter, Julia Severance Millikin, one of the babies she longed for every day she was away.

This volume, the second that grew out of this nineteenth-century *Pilgrim's Progress,* is a serious commentary, in sharp contrast to Mark Twain's. But, like his, it holds an appeal for today's tourist.

Journal Letters was issued in a limited edition in 1938, long after the deaths of both Mrs. Severance and Mark Twain. It was intended only for her descendants. The volume has been little noticed, though in it, Emily, with brisk pen and sharp eye, gives vivid glimpses of America's foremost man of letters on the eve of greatness.

Mrs. Severance and Mrs. Fairbanks found their Missouri comrade "irresistible," the "ruling spirit of the ship and a capital person for ocean life . . ."

"There is something about him, I know not what," Mary Fairbanks wrote, "that interests and attracts."

They both considered him a diamond in the rough. They had

no hesitancy in supplying the polish, and tackled his prose, his careless dress, his Christian shortcomings.

He took all the prodding good-naturedly, coming back for more again and again. He freely admitted that these two Cleveland women had profoundly affected his career, influencing his literary style, his manners, and his marriage! But they did not succeed in their religious crusade in his behalf.

When *Innocents Abroad* came out, Mrs. Severance wrote to him about it in October, 1869, and he replied:

> I thank you most kindly for your good words . . . I am glad you like the book, and am not in the least surprised that you find things in it that should have been left out . . . But for you and Mrs. Fairbanks it would have been a very sorry affair. I shall always remember both of you gratefully for the training you gave me—you in your mild persuasive way, and she in her efficient, tyrannical and overbearing fashion.

This last, of course, was more of his drollery and was thoroughly understood by Emily, who knew of his devotion to Mrs. Fairbanks.

Clemens kept in touch with the Severances and Fairbanks all his life. A volume of his letters to Mrs. Fairbanks has been edited by the Mark Twain authority, the late Dixon Wecter, who states that Mary Fairbanks was second only to Mrs. Clemens in transforming him from a "wild west humorist" to a true literary craftsman.

Mary Fairbanks at once sensed his genius—perhaps was the first to evaluate fully his talent. Her belief in him seems to have made her all the more alert against syntax lapses and the profanity and irreverance he mixed with mirth. She was vigilant especially to weed out crude and raw passages that would offend fellow passengers.

Meekly and gratefully he heeded her and dutifully deleted. Entire manuscripts were abandoned, if she so directed.

"Well, Mother Fairbanks has just destroyed four hours' work for me," he once remarked ruefully after a deckside conference with his stern but adoring mentor.

Solon came on deck one morning, Emily wrote, to find him "tearing to shreds batches of closely written sheets of paper and throwing them overboard, Mr. Clemens mumbling the while about 'Mother Fairbanks.' "

The two women, ever optimistic of a spiritual awakening in him, saw to it that he attended the ship's frequent prayer meetings and church services. Along with attempted indoctrination he also was being exposed to Victorian propriety and drawing-room etiquette. Meanwhile, as he himself said, "Mother" Fairbanks sewed on missing buttons, patched and mended and saw to it rumpled suits were pressed.

When Clemens brought his pieces to Mrs. Fairbanks for criticism, he invariably dropped pencils into Emily Severance's lap for sharpening. "No one else could point them with such precision," he asserted. As she returned them one day, she said, "Now these are ready for you to make fun of us! I wish you would use them instead to write something sober to be put into the *Atlantic Monthly*, for instance."

Emily whittled more than pencils. The pseudonym which Clemens had adopted and which had not yet attained its luster, she looked upon skeptically. These words, "Mark Twain," meaning two fathoms deep, referred to soundings on the Mississippi River, where Clemens had been a steamboat pilot. That rough life was beyond the experience of the sheltered Emily. She countered his river-front jargon, his folksy, sometimes off-color anecdotes and, like Mrs. Fairbanks, felt free to pass judgment on anything he wrote.

The Holy Land schedule was the underlying objective of the excursion, which in reality was a Protestant pilgrimage. It had attracted serious-minded oldsters, practically every one an ardent church member—save Clemens. "The solemn patriarchs made this, not the advertised pleasure cruise," Mark Twain declared, "but a funeral without a corpse."

A strict Presbyterian, like most of the Cleveland contingent, Emily found the "first Sabbath on board" greatly to her liking, "with an excellent sermon and organ hymns" and "hopes it is the commencement of a series of such meetings." It was. Mark Twain could not resist the encircling piety.

"There was church every Sunday at eight bells, prayer meetings every night. . . . We never played the piano except for devotions," he explains in *Innocents Abroad.*

> They pray every night for fair winds when they know as well as I do that a fair wind for us (going east) is a head wind for those going west. A problem for the Almighty's blowing. . . . The pilgrims danced quadrilles once, of three ladies and five gentlemen (the latter with handkerchiefs around their arms to signify their sex), but this melancholy orgy was voted sinful and dancing was discontinued.

Clemens's inner well-being continued to concern Emily. "It seemed an accident," she reported in her diary, "but it was planned, that one of the clergymen and Mr. Clemens were drawn into religious conversation. Afterward the minister confided in me how much he hoped that from this voyage many souls might be born again." One uppermost in her mind was "Mr." Clemens, as she always referred to him.

The "Sabbath" was rigorously observed on land and at sea. Mark Twain, ranting against "self righteousness," fumed that en route to Damascus what was a "three days' journey with the sorry relics we bestrode" had to be squeezed into less than two, despite the "tired, ill-treated horses," because three pilgrims would not travel on the Sabbath day. Earlier, in Italy, Mrs. Severance gave up going to Garibaldi's house because the outing came on that day. She divulged to her Bible-reading father, Dr. Peter D. Allen, then living in Oberlin, Ohio, that she would have by-passed the luncheon "given by the Emperor and Empress of Russia, had it not been set ahead from the Sabbath to Monday." The affair took place at Yalta in a palace belonging to Grand Duke Michael, the Czar's eldest son.

"The Empress," Emily described as "a tall slender lady who wore a suit of white foulard with a broad blue silk sash . . . a small round hat and carried a seaside umbrella. . . . It was a real event. Most of us had not worn our black silks since leaving New York and we embraced the opportunity." An address, "prepared by a committee of the passengers, of which Mr. Clemens was made chairman, was read to the Emperor . . . Mrs. Fairbanks has made a copy of it so that you will see it in the *Herald*."

One of their first landings had been made at Marseille, from which Paris was reached by train. Emily found it "gay and charming." On "Sabbath morning we walked a long way through the Champs Élysées to the American church, returning in the afternoon for Communion."

Clemens occupied himself otherwise in the French capital. He took in a bit of night life, watching a cancan dance. "I placed my hands before my face for very shame. But I looked through my fingers."

In Florence, Emily and Mrs. Fairbanks reveled in the city's art treasures. Mark Twain, struck by contrasting poverty of the people and the richness of cathedrals, exclaimed to the "filthy beggars" who swarmed around him when he left the grand Duomo: "Why don't you rob your church?"

Wearied by Renaissance religious pictures, he wished one of the old masters, "like Titian, had passed up a martyr or two" and gone instead to England to capture a portrait of Shakespeare, or maybe a picture of "Columbus returning in chains after the discovery of the world."

Rome was the "filthiest place imaginable," to Emily. Her militant Protestantism decided "the Papal church is dying," and "the Pope soon will abdicate. Before long there will be no more Popes." Wandering about the Colosseum where the "barbarians" set wild beasts upon the early Christians, Clemens commented that when the Christians came into power they in turn taught the barbarians the error of their unbelief by tortures of "the pleasant Inquisition."

Constantinople, from the "deck beautiful beyond any place" Emily had seen, on closer inspection proved "filthier than the Italian cities." She confessed she was disappointed in St. Sophia. Mark Twain was too, but expressed it differently: "It is the rustiest old barn in heathendom."

The Holy Land became "a Presbyterian Palestine" to the *Quaker City* pilgrims, acording to Mark Twain. The strenuous two weeks for Emily were "her chance for more light from His Blessed Book." Heat was intense, dust worse. All became ill, though "food, often eaten under olive trees, was excellent, prepared by our dragomen (guides)." At Beirut she inspected missions, and at the Bay of Haifa she shared a tent with Mrs. Fairbanks. Up at sunrise they climbed Mt. Carmel, a six-hour horseback ride, with lunch of mutton and pomegranates on pewter plates and "rest in our shawls in a fig grove."

Seeing two men kiss each other, Mark Twain concluded it an all right custom for "a man would not be likely to kiss one of the women of this country."

Emily was greatly moved when finally "I stood at our tent and looked out at Nazareth." Clemens visited the grotto containing the Virgin's Kitchen and Living Room, where she and "Joseph watched the infant Saviour play with Hebrew toys" and wondered why all the great Holy Land "events occurred in grottoes." He wrote that after "they imposed another pirate on us"—here . . . an Arab guard —"we took our last look at the city, clinging like a whitewashed wasp's nest to the hillside."

On the rough road to Jerusalem they rode "side saddle on sure footed horses," Emily's "a fat gray pacer." They started off one day at 2 A.M. and "always had a blessing with breakfast, which was in the open by candle light." . . . She would never be sorry she had come to Palestine, but she never wanted to return.

In Jerusalem, Mark Twain was overjoyed to find the genuine center of the earth marked by a column "which has moved three different times of its own accord." The proof that this is the center of the earth is the fact that from "under this column was taken the dust from which Adam was made." He concludes this must be true for "in six thousand years no man has ever been able to prove that the dirt was not procured here whereof he was made."

As the journey progressed, Clemens saw a great deal of a delightful eighteen-year-old passenger, whom he designates as Cub in his *Innocents.* The youth was Charles Langdon, son of a well-to-do coal dealer of Elmira, New York.

One day, while the *Quaker City* was anchored in the Bay of Smyrna, Charlie took Clemens to his cabin and showed him an ivory miniature of his older sister, Olivia. Back in the States, Clemens lost no time in trying to make her acquaintance, for he had fallen in love with her likeness.

In New York City he hunted up Charlie at the St. Nicholas Hotel and was promptly invited for dinner with him and his father. "Livy" was there, too. Clemens found her even more alluring in the flesh than in ivory. "She was slender, beautiful and girlish," he wrote in his *Autobiography*. There were more meetings. But he lacked the courage to propose.

Clemens came to Cleveland (September, 1868) renewing shipboard contacts and stayed at the Fairbanks's handsome home on lower St. Clair Street. Into the sympathetic ear of "Mother" Fairbanks he poured the tale of his infatuation with Livy, and his overwhelming sense of unworthiness.

Mrs. Fairbanks enthusiastically endorsed the romance, insisting Miss Langdon would be lucky to have him for a husband. "'Mother' urged me to pop the question," he recounted.

He followed her counsel and a week later wrote his Cleveland "Mother": "sometime in the future she [Livy] is going to be my wife . . . I think we shall live in Cleveland, next door to you . . . [if] you can persuade Mr. Fairbanks to sell me a living interest in the *Herald*. . . ."

When in Cleveland, Mark Twain, always lured by printer's ink, spent a good deal of time in the offices of the *Herald,* though he thought the editor "dull and dour" compared to his wife, who was eleven years younger. Fairbanks, on the other hand, liked Clemens and offered him part interest in the paper and a yearly salary as a member of the staff.

Clemens, however, considered the proposition unsatisfactory and went instead to the *Buffalo Express*—and into financial difficulties.

He sent word of his marriage plans to his Cleveland friends: "The Severance and Fairbanks households must be at our wedding [later set for February 2, 1870], without fail. So, you must stand by ready to drop everything at the tap of a gong, and start!"

The union proved to be one of the literary world's love affairs, akin to that of Robert and Elizabeth Browning. "Mother" Fairbanks had been correct in her judgment about this, too.

One of Mark Twain's first lectures took place in November, 1868, in Cleveland, on the invitation of Mrs. Severance. It was a benefit for the Cleveland Orphan Asylum, one of her charities. The talk, "The American Vandal Abroad," all about the *Quaker City* trip, netted the speaker $100 and the orphans, $594.

For decades, well-attended dramatizations of the Mark Twain stories were staged in Cleveland, including a memorable run of *The Prince and The Pauper,* directed by David Belasco, and presented by Daniel Frohman.

Emily did not "convert" Mark Twain. But, as her daughter wrote in the epilogue to the *Journal,* "she helped to gentle him."

The last afternoon on shipboard Clemens dashed off a long poem, his "Good-Bye" to Emily. It was printed for the first time in the *Journal,* a few lines of it following:

Their voyage done, the fleet that plowed
Together o'er the main
Spread their broad sails and sped away,
No more to meet again!

Some shall be famed in many lands
As good ships fast and fair,
And some shall strangely disappear,
Men know not when or where.

Philip Sheridan

GENERAL PHILIP SHERIDAN is Somerset's hero, its claim to fame. He greets you from the heart of the Ohio village where he grew up. In the center of the public square, forcing all heavy, interstate traffic to swing around it, is a mammoth equestrian statue of the cavalry genius of the Civil War.

Little Phil—his troops' sobriquet of endearment and respect—sits astride a prancing horse, in full general's regalia, at his side his famous sword. In one hand he reins his steed, with the other he waves his hat in the air.

The statue symbolizes one of the celebrated incidents of the war—the victory he snatched from Confederates at Cedar Creek in the Blue Ridge of Virginia. The Cincinnati poet and painter, Thomas Buchanan Read, immortalized the exploit in "Sheridan's Ride," which begins:

> Up from the South, at break of day,
> Bringing to Winchester fresh dismay. . . .
> And Sheridan twenty miles away.

Poem and bronze are memorials, too, to his horse, Rienzi, a powerful big animal who, Sheridan declared, carried him through eighty-five battles. As to the day that made Rienzi famous, the general himself is authority for the statement that he galloped all the way—all the way from Winchester into the melee of the living and dying, the dust and smoke and din that greeted horse and rider in the Shenandoah Valley:

> With foam and dust the black charger was gray;
> By the flash of his eye, and the red nostril's play,
> He seemed to the whole great army to say:
> "I have brought you Sheridan all the way
> From Winchester town to save the day!"

Motorists, more hurried than history-minded, curse the Sheridan monument, there where four highways intersect. This main throughway, U.S. Route 22, is the old Zane's Trace which was begun in Washington's time to channel a road from Wheeling, across the State of Ohio, down and into Kentucky. It is a busy highway today and always has been.

From the beginning this thoroughfare was choked with westbound settlers. In endless procession they moved over it on horseback and in long Conestoga wagons. These were colorful conveyances pulled sometimes by oxen or by six and eight horses festooned like circus animals with jingling bells and glowing streamers.

Though other communities are wont to demolish and discard landmarks in meek deference to the speed age, Somerset turns deaf ears on such clamors about Little Phil and his horse. It appears they will not have to budge an inch. Somerset keeps a big American flag flying over the general's head and flowers blooming at Rienzi's feet. Embossed at the base is the signature of the sculptor, Carl Heber, of New York City.

Sheridan arrived in Somerset as a year-old baby. His parents were Irish immigrants and first located in Albany, New York, where his father, John Sheridan, worked as an ordinary laborer on the Erie Canal. It is generally accepted that Phil was born there in 1831. After the war, when so many of his fellow generals and other prominent veterans were put forward as possible presidential timber, General Sheridan was bypassed.

A story circulated that his birth occurred in Ireland on the eve of his parents' departure. If true, this would have disqualified him for the presidency. Further, the fact that he was a Roman Catholic was prejudicial to his nomination in those days.

At any rate, he was one of the few top-ranking Civil War officers who did not use his military record as a springboard for high political office.

He left Somerset for faraway West Point in 1848. The few years of boyhood in the village were enough for Somerset citizens to hold him in affection and admiring memory forever. He himself was devoted to the hometown and to his relatives there. Despite demanding responsibilities and crowding honors he was loyal to the earlier, simpler scene and managed to return to Somerset regularly as long as he lived—which was not long, as he died in 1888.

People in the business places on Somerset's square surrounding his statue are always ready and able to talk about Sheridan. He clerked in more than one of these stores to add to his father's always slim income. A building here, preserved as Phil knew it, is the Virginia-style courthouse, of which Somerset is rightly proud. A graceful tower rises from the pitched roof. Over the middle doorway, topped with arch and keystone, is lettered this amusingly garbled couplet:

> Let justice be done
> If the heavens fall.

Villagers like to tell the story that when Somerset was the seat of Perry County—before New Lexington took it away—a pioneer lawyer had become disgruntled at a verdict that went against him in the newly opened courthouse, which was not quite completed. Bitterly the lawyer declaimed the old, correct motto, substituting "if" for "though" as the more appropriate for such justice. Stonemasons, putting on final touches, overheard him, and, not grasping the irony, chiseled in his exact words. Traditionally inclined Somerset keeps them.

The Sheridans occupied a neat cottage, on what is now Sheridan Avenue, as their original home. It was dubbed "Happy Alley" by Phil's Irish mother, who never lost her County Cavan heritage of wit and gaiety. She had a strong influence on Phil. The two were close throughout their lives.

Another son, "Mike," later Colonel Michael, aide-de-camp on his brother's staff, was better known and more of a mixer as the two were growing up. The future general was never overly talkative or gregarious.

The father, industrious but not prosperous, worked on the pike then being "macadamized," a crushed stone surface newly invented by a Scotsman, John McAdam.

Phil's Irish temper flared easily and he fought "at the drop of a hat." In youthful squabbles, as in war, it was said he always came out a winner. Schoolmates were soundly thrashed for calling him "monkey boy" or otherwise twitting him for his appearance. Indeed, he was odd-looking. The large head and full chest seemed top-heavy on his short legs. Phenomenally long arms—one day to be put to good account with sword and saber—dangled to his knees.

By the time he was ten, Phil Sheridan had whipped every boy in town who was his own age, as well as many older and bigger youngsters. One fracas with a schoolteacher he disposed of by a disappearing act. With the schoolman in close pursuit, brandishing a businesslike hickory switch, Phil took to his heels down Main Street. Into the shop of a friendly tinsmith the boy raced. Sensing a crisis, the craftsman quickly lifted a huge copper kettle he was riveting and turned it over the lad. When the breathless pedagogue rushed into the shop his pupil was nowhere to be seen.

School held only casual interest for Phil, until he developed a passionate desire to attend West Point. Then, tutored by a well-versed townsman, he crammed himself all one summer with mathematics and other subjects heretofore neglected. More obstacles than the academic loomed against his admission to the Point. Foremost was his short stature, which all but barred him.

He knew no influential statesman to whom he could appeal as sponsor of his candidacy. Instead, he resorted to the simple device of writing directly to his congressman. His straightforward letter so impressed the lawmaker that he named him for appointment.

Moreover, Phil had to hurdle his father's objection and disapproval of West Point. The school on the Hudson was receiving some criticism, particularly in the frontier, as undemocratic and snobbish. John Sheridan viewed it as an institution for well-educated sons of rich Americans, and no place for a poor Irishman's boy from a backwoods school in Ohio. Worst of all, it was strongly Episcopalian. Phil might stray from his faith attending that secular academy.

John Sheridan laid his worries before the white-robed Dominicans in the spacious grounds of the Catholic center on the edge of town. The Sheridans were communicants of St. Joseph's, beside a priory here in the rolling hills. Father Nicholas Young, nephew of the sainted Father Edward Fenwick, who founded St. Joseph's, gave careful attention to the problem. He called in another priest, Father Joshua Young.

Throughout all his young life Phil's spiritual needs had been in the hands of these Dominicans. The two clergymen, after duly conferring, agreed with the senior Sheridan. Seventeen-year-old Phil should not be permitted to enroll at West Point.

"What shall I do with the boy?" the distraught father asked.

An old saying around Somerset is that one of the priests solemnly answered, "Rather than let him go to that academy, I'd prefer to see you take him out in your back yard behind the chicken coop and slit his throat!"

Apparently Phil's parent considered this a bit too drastic an alternative, for Phil had his way. While he passed the entrance examinations, nonetheless his father's foreboding about difficulties ahead were borne out. The strange-looking fellow from Perry County had a rough time against better-prepared lads and the elegant ways of wealthy young men, among them Southern planters' sons who would be more than campus antagonists someday.

Sheridan, better in cadet drill than in the classroom, soon was excelling in cavalry maneuvers, master of horse and sword. In the saddle he appeared a tall man, at ease, confident. Unmounted, his uniform accentuated his body's ill proportions, the military cap resting awkwardly on his massive head. Plebes taunted him.

Ridicule was not a new experience. He used his fists as effectively as in Somerset. One such quarrel threatened to terminate his soldiering. He was late for drill and was reprimanded, unjustly he thought, by a captain, a petty martinet who was officer of the day. Meeting the officer off duty, Phil gave him what he considered a well-deserved trouncing. The captain had him disciplined by a year's suspension from the academy.

Top man in his class when he finally graduated (1853) was James B. McPherson, of Clyde, Ohio. As a general in charge of the Army of Tennessee, he was killed, age thirty-six, before Atlanta. Opposing Confederates were led by another member of his class, General John Bell Hood. Still another classmate, Union General John M. Schofield, was supporting Sherman at the time.

Sherman, eleven years older than Sheridan, was born and reared in Lancaster, eighteen miles east of Somerset on the pike. It was not until the war brought them together that they came to know each other, though Sherman had a boyhood memory of Phil as a youngster at St. Joseph's

"Cump" Sherman, at the death of his father, Charles, an Ohio circuit judge, was adopted by the Shermans' neighbors, Senator Thomas Ewing and his wife, who lived near them in Lancaster. Daughter of the well-to-do Irish pioneer Hugh Boyle, Mrs. Ewing was an ardent Catholic, though the senator and the Shermans were not. Judge Sherman's widow, a Presbyterian, offered no objection when Mrs. Ewing wanted one of the Dominicans from St. Joseph's to baptize "Cump."

At the ceremony the priest added the name of Saint William to young Sherman's "heathen" Tecumseh. Judge Sherman had named his son for the magnanimous Indian chief. The boy who heretofore signed himself "Tecumseh Sherman," now used the signature "William Tecumseh," or "W. T." But he was always Cump to his intimates.

Though Mrs. Ewing did not press her religious tenets upon him, Cump frequently was included when she piled her brood into her carriage and, with a coachman in charge, took them all to St. Joseph's for mass and communion. For the long drive, they had to leave before daylight, and often she and her sleepy charges were not back in Lancaster until after dark.

It was on such pilgrimages that Cump saw the black-haired Phil—and ignored him as too young for his attention.

Many years and many battles were ahead before General Sherman would confide to his wife, Ellen, Mrs. Ewing's daughter: "Grant, Sheridan and I are the popular favorites. . . ." He was writing factually and not at all in conceit. The three rose to a pinnacle in public regard. They were the "Big Three of the Union." And all were Ohioans.

Neither priest nor parent needed to have had misgivings about West Point weakening Phil's religious convictions. He never wavered in zeal for his church. He had been well grounded in in Somerset. Fink and Dittoe, proprietors of the dry goods store where he measured out calico and counted buttons for customers, were members of families responsible for establishing Catholicism in the community.

In 1805 Jacob Dittoe and his brother-in-law John Fink drove their ox teams into the hilly land a few miles from the settlement. It was called Middletown, since it was midway between Lancaster and Zanesville. They renamed it Somerset for their native town in Pennsylvania. They were Catholics, but they found no others of like creed, no church, no priest.

Longing for the worship they loved, they petitioned Bishop John Carroll, of Maryland, whom they had known "back home," to send them a priest. In his urgent piety Dittoe offered land for a church and home for clerics—"320 acres covered with oak, hickory and walnut. We will exert ourselves in making improvements," Dittoe wrote the bishop, and promised "to have a good house ready for the pastor."

Father Edward Dominic Fenwick, scion of a distinguished Maryland family, was dispatched. He was already an overburdened missionary in Kentucky. The assignment was an arduous one.

Few Catholics had emigrated to Ohio, and those here were

widely scattered, with no organization to meet spiritual needs. Young Fenwick packed his saddlebags with altar stone, vestments, and all requisites for the mass and sacraments. When he came upon Catholics he set up his altar and conducted services in settlers' homes.

It was an uncharted country that he traveled, sometimes not encountering a habitation for days. Often overtaken at nightfall without the prospect of shelter, as he noted in his diary, "I would hitch my horse to a tree, make a pillow of my saddle, recommend myself to God and go to sleep with bears all about."

He would be remembered in after years with love and reverence as "The Apostle of Ohio." In 1821 he was named a bishop, Cincinnati his episcopal see. He was the first Catholic bishop in the state.

All that was far in the future as he guided his horse through dense woods on a chilly October day in 1808. He had been on the way several hours and now was not sure of his whereabouts. He slackened the reins and gave his horse its head. It turned into a path faintly worn through an oak grove, the trees resplendent in deep mahogany reds. Everywhere colors of fall lighted the landscape—scarlet dogwood against gold of beech, woodbine's flaming vines, and the play of sunshine and shadow.

Weary as he was, and confused about his route, the young friar crossed himself and thanked his God for the beauty of His handiwork in this lonely countryside. Suddenly the horse cocked its ears, alert to an untoward something. Fenwick pulled him to a stop—and listened, too. A far-off sound echoed, an ax being driven again and again into a log or a stout tree.

Urging the horse as fast as he dared negotiate the unfamiliar terrain, Fenwick headed for the wood chopper. As he drew closer he sniffed the good fragrance of a wood fire and saw wisps of smoke tangling in the trees—welcome promise of a homestead!

A clearing opened, centered with a substantial log dwelling. It was the home of Jacob Dittoe. He was the woodsman. He fell on his knees before the horseman. His wife and children gathered in the dooryard. One man was sent off to summon the Finks, and another the rest of the Dittoe family. Soon a flock of twenty or so were surrounding Father Fenwick.

Deprived for years of the consolations of their religion, their joy was inexpressible. The missionary was received as a messenger sent from heaven for their salvation. He was no less moved.

The Mass he said in that humble cabin he considered the start of

Catholicism in Ohio, and he placed the year, 1808, as the founding date of St. Joseph's—first Catholic church in the state. However, it was ten years before a church building was consecrated. Meanwhile, Father Fenwick, and friars delegated to assist him, conducted services in homes as they moved through the state.

St. Joseph's first building was a small log affair on the tract Dittoe had donated. Bare ground formed the floor and windows were mere openings in the walls, lacking even bear-grease-treated paper for covering. It was without heat. A "warming house" beside it had a broad hearth where, in cold weather, worshipers could warm themselves before Mass and afterward fortify themselves for the cold ride home. When begun, only ten Catholic families were on the rolls, but the number mounted with a tide of new immigration and soon the little chapel was overcrowded.

The year the Sheridans settled in Somerset, Bishop Fenwick, victim of the cholera epidemic, died in Wooster while on an apostolic tour visiting the many congregations he had organized in Ohio.

First witness of his labors, St. Joseph's, the third edifice after fires and rebuildings, rises amidst the broad acres of the original gift tract, the towering priory beside it. In the cemetery, shadowed by the church they founded, Jacob and Catherine Dittoe lie in land they gave.

The John Sheridans, before the outbreak of the Civil War, moved nearer their church. Between duties on the West Coast, Lieutenant Sheridan built a home for his parents on the New Lexington Road on the outskirts of Somerset. The attractive "Steamboat Gothic" house with its perpendicular clapboards and molding trim, is on a woodsy knoll, the valley dropping away to the rear.

Little Phil may have chosen this site because of the great oak under which political rallies were held in his youth. He was often among the milling crowds that stood beneath the great branches, enthralled in those days of flowery oratory by such luminaries as William Henry Harrison, stumping for the presidency; Ewing from Lancaster and Tom Corwin from Lebanon wooing votes for the United States Senate.

Many still come to this site. The house is pointed out as Sheridan's birthplace by glib tourists untroubled by accuracy and oblivious to the boulder by the roadside where a plaque details the entire history.

Phil's brother John lived here for a period with the latter's daughter, Nellie, who served a long term as Somerset's postmistress.

She was Mrs. T. C. Wilson, but her husband died on their wedding night and she remained "Miss Nellie" to Somerset.

While his parents were alive, Sheridan was often here. He was attached to the house and thought of it as the family homestead. His mother outlived his father, dying in her late eighties only shortly before her illustrious son's death. She prized highly a priceless collection of campaign relics Phil sent her from time to time, such as the inkstand on Robert E. Lee's desk when he signed the surrender terms, and the saddle—a regulation McClelland—with military trappings, Sheridan used on the ride from Winchester.

Sheridan's reputation soared with his brilliant battlefield tactics until, by his blocking of Lee that led to Appomattox, he was regarded with veneration in the North. And nowhere more than in little Somerset.

The South decried him for his scorched earth policy in the Shenandoah after Winchester, which he maintained was a military necessity, and for his stormy administrations in Southern military districts during Reconstruction.

But when Grant was elected President and Sherman was made commanding general of the United States Army, there was high recognition for him. He was made a lieutenant general, and later, succeeding Sherman, finally was raised to a full general. In the meantime, appointed military observer during the Franco-Prussian War, he was the guest of Bismarck and the King of Prussia.

Small wonder Somerset cherished such a man. On his visits, a guard of honor escorted him from the railroad station and invariably a fete-day atmosphere prevailed.

Little impressed by show or pomp, Sheridan wore civilian attire whenever he could discard his uniform with its glamorous medals. He put on weight as he grew older and his clothes usually were too tight. Out of uniform, he was careless of his dress. His mustache was scraggly. His hair, perpetually in need of a trim, stuck out from under a tall silk hat too small for his head. Coats were minus buttons, shoes unpolished. He disliked gloves. The short, stocky man looked as if made up for a comedy part, until one glimpsed his red, weathered face. Immediately any thought of his unusual figure was forgotten. Force and personal magnetism were apparent, the extraordinary qualities that caused Grant to declare: "I rank Sheridan with Napoleon and Frederick and the great commanders of history."

Assistant Secretary of War Charles A. Dana walked through the ranks with Sheridan just after he had been made a major general, following his "ride" from Winchester. Dana reported in the *New York Sun* that Sheridan's men showed deeper affection for him than he had seen displayed toward any other officer. Yet, Sheridan was considered a stern, uncompromising disciplinarian and exacting commander. The explanation for his troops' feeling for him, Dana concluded, lay in a statement of Sheridan: "I never command my men with paper orders from the safe rear, but from up front with them where the fight is hottest."

Though he was to be hailed for the greater, final victory of the war against Lee at Five Forks, the public first made him its idol after his dash from Winchester to rally the Union troops. Read's poem, inspired by the achievement, appeared two months later. It was composed during one afternoon and read the same evening in Cincinnati by James Edward Murdock, then one of America's favorite actors, at a benefit performance for wounded Union veterans. Cheers and standing ovations interrupted the delivery. It was an immediate hit, recited by everyone, and added to the general's fame.

Gruff, modest Little Phil made one comment on Read's verses: "I was only sixteen miles away!"

Warren G. Harding

WARREN, YOU WERE EVERY INCH A PRESIDENT."

Mrs. Warren G. Harding choked out the words as she stood beside her husband's casket. She was fighting for composure aboard the funeral train bringing his body home through the August heat of 1923 following his death on the West Coast.

Home was Marion, Ohio. And Marion, as this is written, holds the same sentiment about Harding that was uttered so long ago by "the Duchess," his name for his wife.

Whatever appraisal the rest of the country makes of the twenty-ninth President, his memory in Marion is revered. His public record lies under shocking charges against some of his appointees; mystery and scurrilous innuendoes befog his private life.

In Marion, however, the clouds part. Warren Gamaliel Harding stands forth in pure, white light. He is Marion's hero.

Here he grew up; built his home; owned and edited a successful newspaper; went to Columbus as state senator, then lieutenant governor; to Washington as U.S. Senator—finally, President. His front porch at home was the launching pad for his "back to normalcy" campaign that orbited him into the White House.

Returning frequently from the national capital's regions of outer space for brief respites in Ohio, he stopped to chat with everybody up and down the main street, as affable and unpretentious as if he were not the First Citizen of the land.

He *looked* like a President, more like one than any chief executive before or since. Tall, full-chested, he had the stance and magnificent head of a sculptured Greek god. Yet he remained a Common Man. He was Marion's own and Marion loved him. From such ingredients was born the local Harding cult—as has happened elsewhere when some magic personality catches the imagination of his fellows.

In this bustling mid-Ohio city, now grown bigger, there are still many who knew him. Tears flush eyes as they talk of him, recall little attentions at his hand, acts of unaffected friendliness, speak of his greatness.

They counter criticism of Harding's administration with enumeration of its accomplishments. His Limitation of Arms Conference in 1921 halted a furious naval race and brought America, France, Great Britain, Italy, and Japan into a peace pact. Repeatedly preaching economy in government, he backed legislation providing the national budget system. The result was a reduction in taxes of approximately a billion dollars annually and a reduction of public debt by almost a hundred million dollars monthly. Incredible, isn't it, against today's astronomically contrary trends? Harding champions ask rhetorically.

Despite corruption charges that engulfed some of his cabinet members and department heads, Marion reminds the world of the able, respected men Harding picked—like Charles Evans Hughes, as Secretary of State; Herbert Hoover, Secretary of Commerce; Andrew Mellon, Secretary of the Treasury; Will Hays and Harry S. New, successively Postmasters General; and Henry C. Wallace, Secretary of Agriculture.

Ominous rumblings of something amiss in Washington were coming to Harding as he left for his tour to Alaska.

Scandals erupted full force after his death: to submerge Secretary of Interior Albert B. Fall in oil illicitly drained from Teapot Dome and Elk Hills fields; to send to prison his head of the Veterans Bureau, Colonel Charles R. Forbes, and Alien Property Custodian Colonel Thomas W. Miller. Attorney-General Harry M. Daugherty, who was Harding's crony, was indicted but escaped conviction. Two lesser lights were suicides . . .

In the face of the holocaust Marion answered: "No graft ever touched Harding. He was betrayed by those he trusted."

Such a credo was substantiated six months after Harding's death by the quashing of implications that there had been something shady on his part in his sale of the *Marion Star*. The transaction was effected on the eve of departure for his western tour. He received over half a million dollars, which seemed excessive for a newspaper of the *Star's* potential. Whispers spread that the money was a "cover-up" for some political obligation. This was given voice in a speech by a retired New York banker, Frank A. Vanderlip. Promptly grilled by a congressional committee on the scent of irregularities in the Harding official family, Vanderlip admitted he had no grounds for his charge and withdrew it. The *Star's* new owners explained they had contracted with Harding to write editorials following his term in office. On the basis that such contributions from a President of the United States would be profitable to the paper and in syndicated rights, they had arrived at the purchase price. Once more Harding's reputation emerged unscathed. His memory was attacked in subtler fashion.

Stricken in San Francisco, Harding was reported in news dispatches as recovering when he suddenly died. As time passed, rumor and outright allegations were advanced by reputable and not-so-reputable writers that there had been something unnatural about his death . . . he had taken poison . . . or his wife had given it to him. Motivation in either case was to spare him what already was apparent were to be earth-shaking disclosures.

The sinister talk about Mrs. Harding was tied to her refusal to permit an autopsy, and more, to her destruction of papers belonging to her dead husband. The conclusion: she was deliberately concealing something.

Any uncertainty concerning Harding's death was settled, it would appear, not long afterward in a magazine article by one of the attending physicians, Dr. Ray Lyman Wilbur, president of Leland Stanford University, who stated that the President "was struck down by apoplexy and lost his gallant battle against pneumonia just when victory seemed to be his." During the Chief Executive's illness in San Francisco, Dr. Wilbur had been called as consultant by Dr. Charles E. Sawyer, the Hardings' personal physician and friend, accompanying them on the western odyssey.

Despite Mrs. Harding's ill-considered disposal of some of her husband's papers, a large cache survived. These the Harding Memorial Association held in locked files in Marion until the fall of 1963, when the collection, estimated at over 300,000 items, was given to the Ohio Historical Society. Once these documents are made available for study, it is possible certain puzzling obscurities regarding Harding may be resolved. By withholding the accumulation for so many years, the Memorial Association, though unintentionally, added to mysteries hovering over Harding.

On the eve of the centennial of his birth (1965), with interest reviving in him and his era, Marion confidently expects the documents' contents will bolster its regard for Harding and further justify its sturdy defense of its most famous citizen.

In 1927, when he was four years dead, a bombshell dropped. In a book, *The President's Daughter,* issued by an unidentified publisher, the author, one Nan Britton, claimed that she was the mother of a child fathered by Harding. Coming on the heels of startling exposures of shenanigans during Harding's years in Washington, the book soon reached top figure circulation. Booksellers and reviewers handled it gingerly. Those libraries that stocked it consigned it to the restricted shelf. It was *sub rosa* reading for the nation.

Compared with the detailed clinical delineation of sex by today's authors, Nan Britton is restrained indeed. For her sensational splash she relied on a name—that of the President of the United States.

Hers is the story of an adolescent infatuation, which began, she says, when she was fourteen and Harding was in his mid-forties. He was unaware of her existence and she had to be content with seeing him from afar—watching for him coming and going up and down the street, making a collection of his photographs . . .

By her own admission she made the initial overture to Harding. Her father, a local doctor, died. She needed work and asked Harding to help her obtain a position. In New York City he found her a post in the office of a friend. She contends they met frequently in that city, in Washington, and in Chicago during the Republican convention that nominated him. On her say-so they traveled together. He never saw "their" child, she states, but added that he gave her money on many occasions for her own and the girl's support.

She tells about approaching Harding's family after his death, seeking a share of his estate for her daughter. She lacked proof of Harding's paternity. She could show no letters from him as she had destroyed all communications from him at his insistence. His relatives rejected her claim. She brought suit—and lost. And so, she told all in her book.

Marion found the Britton diatribe the cruelest of all onslaughts against Harding's memory. The woman had waited until he was dead to broadcast her assertion. He could not defend himself. Unshaken in loyalty to him, Marion recalled the blurb under Nan Britton's name in the Marion High School yearbook, *The Quiver,* when she was graduated in 1914. It read: "We all know 'Nawn,' talking she knew not why, and she cared not what."

Despite—perchance because of—these slings and arrows darting so mercilessly and unceasingly at Warren Harding, Marion went about creating many tangible symbols to honor him. Most striking is the memorial to him, an outstanding mausoleum, erected through voluntary gifts from local citizens as well as from admirers throughout the country, including school children.

The President, with his wife beside him, lies in a circular temple of glistening white Georgian marble. Laced with shrubbery and trailing vines, it stands dramatically on a rise of greensward dominating a ten-acre tree-lined plot. An Ionic colonnade surrounds the cloister where the tombs repose, decorated with bronze wreaths, his of palms and hers of roses.

The memorial was dedicated in 1931 by the then President of the United States, Herbert Hoover. After allowing himself some eulogy of the dead man before him, rather tactlessly, considering the occasion, he spoke of him as "a man whose soul was being seared by a great disillusionment . . . [Harding] had a dim realization he had been betrayed . . . by men he believed were his devoted friends." Hoover continued, "It was later proved in the courts of the land that these men had betrayed not alone the friendship and trust of their . . . friend, but had betrayed their country. That was the tragedy of the life of Warren Harding." Among the other speakers were former President Calvin Coolidge and Charles Evans Hughes, then Chief Justice of the United States Supreme Court.

Harding's home on Mount Vernon Avenue is another Marion shrine. Under terms of Mrs. Harding's will, the house, with its furnishings, personal and official memorabilia, is maintained as a public museum by the Harding Memorial Association. Warren Harding and Florence De Wolfe built it in 1891 and were married in it. For the ceremony they stood at the newel post.

The bride, eight years Warren's senior, had been divorced from Henry De Wolfe and was the mother of a boy, Marshall Eugene, about ten. Her stern and wealthy father, Amos Kling, had bitterly opposed her first husband. He saw no more promise in Harding, then struggling to get the *Star* on its feet. Kling's daughter, as proud and self-willed as her father, determined to have her wedding in her own home. Her father did not attend. However, he was reconciled to them when Warren became Senator Harding.

A campaign poster among the many exhibits sums up in humorous vein Marion's feelings about Harding: "Listen Pilgrims! Marion is for Warren Gamaliel Harding for the presidency of the United States from the homeliest of homeless dogs on the streets to the most influential and staunchest of her citizens, Democrats not excluded."

A different kind of monument to the Hardings is the *Star*, on North State Street. It still is "Harding's paper," though not even its building is the one he knew. Following their marriage, Mrs. Harding for years worked side by side with him in the old, crowded plant. She handled circulation. The newsboys learned there was no nonsense about her. She wasn't above meeting out a sound spanking for misbehavior. (The technique was more generally practiced in that era.)

When Harding was in the White House, these carriers, grown now, called on her in a group. She jokingly asked those to stand whom she had paddled. All rose to their feet. One, James C. Woods, later the *Star's* business manager, got his trouncing for rigging up a wire to catch static electricity from the cumbersome leather belt of the press. He touched Mrs. Harding with it. The spark made her jump . . . and angry. She snatched the cord from Woods and used it on him. From then on Jim, like the other boys, and Mrs. Harding were firm friends.

The city's three-million-dollar high school is Harding High. An older building first used as a high school was so named by student demand the day Harding was elected President. When this was made a junior high, boys and girls carried the Harding name with them to the new building. It was in the first Harding High School that history teachers labeled a textbook reference to Harding as inaccurate and unjust and held out against buying the book until publishers revised the passage.

The town's important hotel is Harding Hotel, a civic and social center. A life-size portrait of a very distinguished Warren Harding hangs in the lobby. Not far away in downtown Marion another tribute to him is a memorial plaque on his pew in Trinity Baptist Church, where he was a member.

The large auditorium in the clubhouse of the 400-member Marion County Federated Women's Clubs is dedicated to the memory of the President's sister, the late Abigail ("Daisy") Harding Lewis, one-time Marion High School teacher, locally as beloved as her brother. Her husband, Ralph T. Lewis, a member of the Harding Memorial Association and a prominent local businessman, for many years operated a grocery store. One of his best customers was Warren Harding, who regularly brought in the weekly food list, and at the conclusion of his transaction invariably bought twenty-five cents' worth of Beeman's pepsin chewing gum for the Duchess.

The reminiscences of Harding's brother-in-law follow the usual Marion pattern: "No one who knew Warren could help but love him . . . Harding never forgot his family. He wrote long letters to Daisy, sent her flowers and every Sunday morning a bouquet from him was delivered to their mother."

Closely linked with the Hardings is White Oaks Sanitarium, a cluster of mellow buildings sprawled under fine old trees in a hundred-acre tract on the edge of town. It was established by Dr. Charles Sawyer and inherited by his son, Dr. Carl W. Sawyer, when he was the "young Dr. Sawyer."

Dr. Carl, now bent and burdened with years, has held the position as president of the Harding Memorial Association since 1934. He has been custodian of the Harding papers, one of the few who has had access to them. From boyhood he knew the Hardings. Few knew them better.

His parents and the Hardings were close friends, constantly in and out of each other's houses. When Dr. Carl and his wife were married in Madison, New Jersey, the Hardings attended the wedding. Harding, then Ohio's lieutenant governor, gave the bride away.

After Harding was elected President he persuaded the senior Dr. Sawyer to go to Washington, primarily that he might continue his care of Mrs. Harding, who had chronic spells of sickness from a kidney ailment. She was a frequent patient in the Sawyer sanitarium and died there a year after her husband passed away.

Enigmatic and wise as some ageless seer, Dr. Carl kept his counsel as to "the truth about Harding." Dr. Carl has been heard to say, however, that nothing could alter one whit his lifelong opinion of Warren Harding and "No one could think more highly of a man than I do of him."

Dr. Carl Sawyer, as he often did, accompanied his father one January evening in 1911 to an informal gathering at the Harding home. The previous November Harding had lost the Ohio governorship to Judson Harmon. After two terms in the Ohio senate and one as lieutenant governor, it was his first political defeat and it depressed him. To cheer him, one of the party said, "Warren, we will make you President of the United States." Harding laughingly pooh-poohed the suggestion. Later, as the party rose to go, Harding stood with his hand on the newel post in the hall and everyone was struck with his handsome statesmanlike bearing.

"He's every inch a President," someone murmured, with which in one accord all exclaimed, "We'll make you President yet!"

With the good nights exchanged, little Dr. Sawyer added, "See that you do, my friends."

The group, aptly labeled by Dr. Carl as the "unseen strategy board," stood by him from that day until the end. Under their quiet guidance, Harding's political star rose again. In 1914 he was elected United States Senator.

Harry M. Daugherty, of Washington Court House, Ohio, who had been watching Harding's rise in state politics, also thought he looked like a President. Over such qualified contenders as former Illinois governor Frank O. Lowden and General Leonard Wood, whose record included service as Governor-General of Cuba, Daugherty's tactics won Harding the presidential nomination in 1920.

"I found him sunning himself like a turtle on a log and I pushed him in the water," is a saying traditionally attributed to Daugherty about the maneuver.

Since Harding largely ran his campaign from his home, with his porch as rostrum, voters traveled to him rather than he to them. Marion became the center of the nation. Harding strolled across his lawn to the home of his next-door neighbor, George B. Christian, Jr., and asked him to be his private secretary in the White House. The fact that Christian was a Democrat made no difference. He was Harding's friend.

Christian served him faithfully to the literal last and might be said to have uttered Harding's final words. Acting as substitute for his ailing chief, he was reading a prepared presidential speech before a scheduled Los Angeles audience at the very moment Harding died in San Francisco.

Harding was born November 2, 1865, the son of a struggling country doctor, a former veterinarian, and a knowledgeable mother. Money was scarce. The father, like his famous son in later years, found it hard to press those who owed him money. Harding worked his way through Ohio Central College, a glorified high school at Iberia, Ohio, now extinct.

Briefly he taught school, but found "it was not for me." He learned the printer's trade and, with a printer's rule in his threadbare suit, he rode into Marion on a mule, excited at the wonders of the city of 4,000 (population now 60,000).

He wangled a job on the *Star*. Two years later he persuaded C. H. Schaffner, a county bank official, to lend him $300 to buy a half interest in the paper. Schaffner, named years afterward by Harding as his executor, liked to say it was the best investment he ever made.

The young Harding wrote editorials boldly Republican in a strongly Democratic community, acquired readers, managed the advertising, and in two years was sole owner.

People liked him on sight, more so as they came to know him. He had the knack of showing genuine interest in everyone he met. He remembered their first names, inquired about the newest baby, about crops and ailing aunts. He had time for children and animals.

Anecdotes about him, verging into legend, abound in his home precincts. One concerns a bedraggled kitten that tagged after him, mewing and protesting as he walked downtown. He picked it up. He stopped a small boy he knew—he knew everybody—thrust the kitten into his hands, gave him a dime, and bade him keep it or find a home for it.

Another time, striding on his way to the *Star*, he noticed a farmer driving into market with a crate of pigeons as part of the load on his wagon. The birds were packed to suffocation. Harding stopped the farmer, bought the entire lot and, when the man was out of sight, released the birds.

Harding was twenty-six when he married Florence De Wolfe. It has been said the courting was more on her part than on his; that she was domineering and overambitious, aligning herself with Daugherty to push her husband into the presidency when he would have preferred to remain in the Senate.

Marion will have none of such talk. If she was aggressive, her practical sense helped advance her husband's business. If some considered her a bit more formal than he, others recall her as a pleasant hostess. All in all she is respected, and credited with undeviating devotion to her husband's well-being.

Whether Harding was a reluctant presidential candidate or not, once in office he yearned to go down in history as the best loved of all who had preceded him. When death cut short his term a bit more than midway, it appeared his wish might be realized. He had been elected by a record plurality of over seven million. At his passing a spontaneous outpouring of grief and affection on the part of the electorate swept through the entire country.

As the train bearing his body headed east, crowds, solemn and patient, lined the right of way and waited at every stop, their vigils frequently beginning at dawn. After ceremonies in Washington honoring the dead President, he was brought to Marion for burial. The day of the funeral uncounted thousands, many from outlying districts, massed in quiet tribute along every curb and tree lawn. Cordons of Ohio National Guardsmen kept order on streets leading to the plain home of the President's father, Dr. George T. Harding. Here final services were held in the modest sitting room.

While the cortege of family and notables moved slowly toward the cemetery, onlooking citizens unashamedly wept. They mourned a man who had reached the heights, but was never too important to be one of them.

That was 1923. Marion continued to mourn him, to refute all the negatives as they were stacked against him, to see him "every inch a President."

Whatever revelations may be forthcoming from the long-secret papers, no evaluation of Warren G. Harding can be complete without recognizing this Marion image of him, sustained unfalteringly through the decades.

James A. Garfield

Astride the lead horse towing the canal packet *Evening Star* was a powerfully built youth with blond hair sun-bleached to almost white. His legs were too long for his patched pants and his wrists reached beyond the sleeves of his homemade jacket.

James Abram Garfield spent the summer of 1848 as driver and bowsman on the inland waterway that connected Lake Erie with the Ohio River. A matter of jogging along at a leisurely three miles an hour, the trip was high adventure to the boy. His pay, fourteen dollars a month, plus keep, he considered substantial earnings.

To land the job, he had walked seventeen miles to Cleveland from his home in Orange Township. His father, Abram Garfield, had bought about a hundred acres here, paying $2.50 each. He had put up a snug log cabin. In it Jim was born in 1831. Before he was two years old his father died from exhaustion or pneumonia, or maybe both, after fighting a fire that crept through the woods dangerously close to the cabin.

Jim was brought up on talk of the canal. Before his birth, his father had contracted to dig three sections for it in central Ohio beside the Tuscarawas River. He underestimated problems of earth and rock removal and lost money. But the family interest continued in the canals that crisscrossed Ohio, opening the state to commerce and prosperity.

The boy's canal experiences are described in the voluminous diary he wrote throughout his life. Entries contained such facts as: the *Evening Star* carried "52 tons of copper ore," which was loaded at Cleveland and destined for Pittsburgh. The route wound through rich bottom lands of the Cuyahoga River valley to Akron, a booming exchange point, thence over a crosscut, and on past Ravenna,

Warren, and Youngstown, where water fronts were lined with new mills and warehouses.

An extension from the New York State Erie Canal took the *Evening Star* to Beaver, Pennsylvania, and on to the Ohio River, where a steamboat tug maneuvered the packet to Pittsburgh. A round trip from Cleveland, with stops for delivering and picking up salt, stone, coal, and whatnot, sometimes lengthened the journey to a full month.

Garfield was introduced to a new and expanding world. On the busy wharves of the canal, boisterous men heaved cargoes from far-off places. Tough boatsmen swore and fought and sang lusty chanties, dozens of them:

> Low bridge, everybody down.
> Low bridge, we're comin' to a town.
> So haul in the tow line
> And pull up the slack!
> Take a reef in your shirt tail
> And straighten your back. . . .

It was an exhilarating change from chopping wood, cradling wheat, and black salting (bleaching out wood ashes for potash), all within the circumscribed area of neighbors' farms.

The hitch on the canal and his humble place of birth were to be political assets. When he went to the White House in 1881, he was the last of the log-cabin presidents. The austerity of it all appealed to the American pioneer spirit still alive in the land.

Small wonder that this dramatic life inspired his contemporary, Horatio Alger, Jr., to write what proved to be a best-seller, *From Canal Boy to President.* Harvard-educated Alger, who had quit his fashionable Unitarian pulpit to work with underprivileged boys, authored a rags-to-riches series that ran to 20,000,000 copies. In his Garfield tale not a detail had to be invented. Every unfolding chapter illustrated the Alger theme: a lad could make poverty and temptation steppingstones to dazzling achievement.

Whatever befell Garfield seemed to push him toward success, even his encounters with brawling ruffians on the canals and his near-to-drowning duckings.

Packets jockeyed for position in the canal locks. When, as a "green" hand, he hesitated to "steal" a place from a boat that had the right of way, a sailor called him a coward. Garfield swung husky fists so effectively he almost killed the fellow. He gained new confidence in himself and respect from the crew, including the skipper, his cousin, tough Captain Amos Letcher.

Again and again when Garfield steered the *Star* into a lock, a bowline would tangle, become taut, and plunge boy and horse into the water. This happened fourteen times by his own count. He could not swim.

During one such episode he was caught in the dragline and it seemed for a terrifying half-hour he would never make it to the deck. It was midnight and none of his sleeping mates heard his cries for help. His strength saved him.

Once aboard, he sat in dripping clothes completely shaken by his narrow escape from death. His thoughts turned to God—so the incident appeared in his adult reminiscences.

There was no doubt as to one effect of these immersions in stagnant water: he contracted a serious case of malaria fever. He was so long recovering he could not resume the canal post.

The seeming misfortune was turned to advantage. Always alert to further the promise she saw in Jim, her youngest son, his mother decided that if he could not do heavy work, it was a good time to add to his sketchy schooling. The strong-minded woman, who never would admit she was poor, somehow gathered together fifteen silver dollars and sent Jim off to the Geauga "Seminary" at Chester. It was an easy twelve-mile walk for him as he swung along the road, his trustworthy ax and a small bundle of clothes in hand.

"Nothing hinders us from learning if we wish to," he said of his first tastes of algebra, philosophy, grammar and a "singing evening." Precursor of the public high school, the academy admitted both boys and girls.

One of its pupils was Lucretia Rudolph, from Hiram, Ohio. Garfield gave her only a few passing glances. Yet, the quiet sunbonneted girl would one day go to the White House as his wife.

The malaria soon was behind him. With his mother's nest egg for tuition, he had no difficulty earning enough for living expenses of $1.06½ per week, which included "board, room, bed, washing done—everything," he wrote, "except wood and candles."

Frequently he cooked his own meals: mush and molasses, salt pork and boiled potatoes—sturdy fare uninhibited by any concern about vitamins or balanced diets.

There was plenty of wood for his stove and stoves of professors who paid him for keeping their wood boxes filled. In addition, he felt fortunate in being hired "to put on siding at seventy-five cents a hundred feet." But he would "not be able to send Mother anything," he told his brother.

His mother, whom Garfield mentions so often and so devotedly in letters and autobiographical jottings, met her widowhood resourcefully, refusing the aid of numerous relatives in the area. She herself would care for her "four saplings," as Abram had called their children in the farewell he gasped out to his wife.

Like her famous son, given to memoir writing, she records that she sold off fifty acres, retaining thirty and their cabin—"first home we ever owned." She could split her own fence rails, make all the clothes needed, fashioning the woolen garments from fleece of sheep she raised. She thought nothing of walking three miles every Sunday to the Disciple meetinghouse where she joined heartily in the hymns. She sang at home, too, by the hour—sacred songs, ballads of the day, and tuneful narratives about incidents in the War of 1812.

Annals of northeastern Ohio are rich in Garfield lore, all of it extolling "the General," the region's own. He is the Lincoln of the Reserve. And, indeed, the life patterns of the two presidents are not unsimilar: log cabin origins, poverty, passion for education, platform genius that won a following and led to the White House and martyrdom.

Focal point of the Garfield saga is Hiram College, in Hiram, thirty-five miles from Cleveland. Founders, short on cash and cautious, established it as Western Reserve Eclectic Institute, not quite a college. During its first year Jim Garfield walked over from the next county to enroll. Such a fine physique as his in a college boy today would be labeled athletic and the coach would tag him immediately for the football team.

Everything was raw and unfinished. The campus was a cornfield. Amidst the sheaves in orderly ranks, rose the single building, today's much remodeled Hinsdale Hall, so called for a later president of Hiram College. He would write his recollections of this famous student.

Leaders of the new educational venture were Disciples. Though unlearned themselves, they wanted their children to know Latin, Greek, and Hebrew so they could read the Bible in the original to make their own interpretation.

Hiram village was selected as the site because it was "high on a hill and healthy," away from the miasma and ague of the lowlands, and, more important, away from the allure and worldliness of city living.

The village's first settlers, Royal Arch Masons from Connecticut, christened the place for a chief Masonry character, Hiram Abiff, skilled carpenter employed on Solomon's Temple. Masons and carpenters themselves, they hauled and sawed lumber, dug stone, and made bricks for the Eclectic's first building. One who supervised every stick and stone and lent a hand with the carpentry was the earnest Disciple deacon, Zebulon Rudolph. It was his daughter, Lucretia, whom Jim Garfield had met at Geauga Academy.

In that unhurried age antedating timesaving short cuts, Zeb had time to greet each sunrise, sitting at the big east window in the farmhouse he had built near the campus. He read aloud from his Hebrew Bible. He was self-taught in the ancient language, a favorite passage being: "If I take the wings of the morning and fly. . . ."

According to Hiram archives, the big lad from Orange took on the task of janitor at the solitary campus building. He swept its halls, prepared kindling, and pulled a rope reaching as far down as the cellar to toll the hours from five o'clock rising time to curfew at nine. No menial, he handled his tasks with dignity, wore calico shirts and homespun breeches with an air.

Adding to his income as carpenter assistant to his future father-in-law, he was strong enough to lay, without help, the tongue-and-groove oak flooring in what now is the college president's house. Such laborious work ordinarily required two men.

His candle often flickered until midnight as he gorged himself on New Testament Greek, Virgil's *Georgics,* the *Agricola* of Tacitus, geometry—a fresh field to him—and the "new" science of geology.

Awards came. The faculty, few in number and hard-worked, in no time asked the janitor-student to teach—salary eighty dollars a month. And he fell in love with "Crete" Rudolph. She was reserved, "never one to push herself forward," and Garfield was not an impetuous lover. It would be some years before he would consider he could support a wife.

Straining for wider cultural challenges, he went to Williams College, where he was graduated at twenty-five. A six-foot-two, yellow-bearded giant, he was as handsome as a god. The two years in far-off Massachusetts, however, did not cut his Ohio links.

Hiram called him back to teach, soon to be the Eclectic's principal and to marry Crete. He had not sought the school offer. It became almost a superstition with him never to press for preferment—not even for nomination for U.S. President.

Manlike, Garfield the bridegroom left selection of a home to his wife. She picked a pleasant house that long since has had other owners but continues to be pointed out as "the Garfield House," one of the sights of Hiram. It looked out over the campus, radically face-lifted by the new principal. One of his first acts was to level the cornfield, plant it with trees, and encircle the whole with a yellow fence against the community's wandering cows.

Students came to discuss personal problems with the vigorous young principal—politics, too, for he was participating in local affairs. Table talk was laced with quotations from Greek and Latin classics. William Dean Howells, also Ohio born, described one of his visits. They sat on the front porch "when whippoorwills whirred and whistled in the dusk." Garfield's stentorian shouts brought students vaulting over the fence. Their principal summoned them to hear Howells. Then employed in editorial work on a Columbus newspaper, Howells was talking informally about Longfellow, Lowell, and Whittier, with whom he already was familiar and whom he shortly would know better.

An energetic pedagogue and money raiser for his struggling school, Garfield was on the go, with many interests: he studied law and was admitted to the Cleveland bar; he appeared in surrounding small towns for evening debating programs, and he preached sermons Sunday mornings at Disciple churches in the area. Now a well-known figure, he was elected to the Ohio legislature. His mother saw him off to the state capital with tears, as if sensing the tragedy for him in the political road ahead.

At the outset of the Civil War he went about the Western Reserve recruiting a regiment of infantry. Everyone knew him. Men flocked to his call for patriotism. Church steps where he stood, bandstands on village greens, courthouse lawns—wherever he appeared—today are honored landmarks because "Garfield was there."

He was made the regiment's colonel. No finer-looking man ever wore a Union uniform. At thirty-one he was given the rank of brigadier general, after Shiloh, and the next year, following Chickamauga, there was added another star to his epaulettes as he became major general.

In the meantime voters sent him to Washington as a member of the Congress. Here, for seventeen years, he represented the Reserve he knew so well. The Garfields owned a home in Washington, but the family roots were deep in Ohio, and he bought a 152-acre homesite in Mentor, Lake County.

No fancy country estate in his eyes, he planned what the family called Lawnfield as a practical farm with extensive crops and cattle. He enjoyed taking part in daily chores, reviving memories of his boyhood.

Mrs. Garfield and the children were enthusiastic about the property. The old farmhouse was remodeled with a broad entranceway veranda. Before many years it would serve as forum for his presidential electioneering.

In 1880, as United States Senator-elect, Garfield was a delegate to the National Republican convention in Chicago. He placed the name of his fellow Ohioan John Sherman in nomination for the presidency. A deadlock developed involving Sherman, James G. Blaine, and Grant, who was trying for a third term. Garfield's proverbial luck came to the fore—he witnessed his own name as nominee being presented to the convention. Chosen on the thirty-sixth ballot, he, of all who had preceded him, was the only one present at his own nomination.

Lawnfield, more field than lawn, was the mecca of thousands who came to hear his utterances as he stood on his front porch. They trampled down the grass, marching in from near-by communities to the din of raucous bands, lighting the night sky with smoking torches. Admirers streamed in from distant parts. They disembarked from trains at a temporary depot installed by the Lake Shore & Michigan Southern Railroad on the grounds to mill about with the crowds listening attentively to the man on the porch.

Peculiarly an Ohio political flowering, this front porch technique became the forerunner for other presidential candidates from the state: William McKinley, who spoke from his home in Canton, and Warren G. Harding, in Marion.

Garfield, inaugurated in March and dead in September, was President of the United States a bit under seven months. In July, 1881, en route to the twenty-fifth reunion of his class at Williams College, he was fired on as he entered a Washington railroad station. The assassin, Charles J. Guiteau, was disgruntled at not being appointed a U.S. consul at Marseilles.

Even Lincoln's death had not stirred the nation to deeper sorrow. Bedside bulletins showed Garfield a valiant fighter during the long weeks when hope was held for recovery. The chronicle of the self-made statesman, widely revealed at the recent election, struck the people's imagination.

Homey, moving stories from the sickroom increased his popularity. He longed to visit Hiram and Orange Township once more. "How good it would be to have some of Aunt Alpha's Indian corn bread," he commented wistfully to an attendant. He talked about picking wintergreen on Ohio hillsides and he wondered if there had been any rain at the Mentor farm. And what were the prospects for a good harvest!

It was fitting that he was brought back to Ohio. When his towered mausoleum . . . financed by popular subscription . . . was dedicated on Decoration, or Memorial, Day in 1890, on the highest point in Cleveland's Lakeview Cemetery, the speaker was the President of the United States, Benjamin Harrison. Presiding at the ceremony was former President Rutherford B. Hayes. Among other notables was a President-to-be, William McKinley. All were Ohioans.

Mrs. Garfield occupied Lawnfield until her death thirty-seven years later. In the interim she saw to it that the mass of papers relating to her husband and the family was collected and systematically arranged.

Five Garfield children grew up here. Two others had died in infancy. Lawnfield was home, too, to "Grandma Garfield," the President's mother, who survived him seven years. If she was not always gently mellow or easy to live with, she was until her end the stalwart, independent frontier widow who never doubted her James was born to greatness.

All the rooms, with intimate personal mementos in every corner, remain as the Garfields left them. Lawnfield, viewed annually by thousands, has taken its place among American historic sites open to the public. It gives a glimpse into the private life of a President and also is an authentic example of domestic furnishings and architecture of late nineteenth-century America.

Beside this commodious home of James Garfield's affluent days stands a replica of the log house in which he was born—two symbols of the course mapped by his years.

Delia Bacon

STRATFORD-ON-AVON citizens grew accustomed to the tall American woman who hovered about Holy Trinity, the church that shelters Shakespeare's tomb. She was a distinguished person, despite shabby, careless dress, and still handsome, though gaunt and ill-looking. One night she arrived late. She had a key for the door and carried a lantern that twinkled in the darkness like a glowworm. Groping her way up the aisle to Shakespeare's burial place, she seated herself beside it. The marble slab was level with the floor.

Now and then she raised her lantern so its feeble shaft illumined the poet's bust on the wall, placed as if to guard his own immortal dust. The rest of the church was inky darkness. It was very quiet—save for an occasional stealthy footstep at the rear. She was not afraid—that was the clerk, she knew, come at the bidding of the vicar who reluctantly had lent her the key. The clerk would see she kept her promise: not to try to lift the slab from Shakespeare's grave, not tonight at any rate, though this had been a major purpose in coming to England. Later . . . soon, despite the doggerel over the tomb:

Good frend for Jesvs sake forbeare,
To digg the dvst encloased heare;
Blest be ye man y spares thes stones,
And cvrst be he yt moves my bones.

She must learn if the messages, as she believed, really were buried in the crypt—secrets long hidden, that would confirm her contention regarding the true authorship of the plays heretofore credited to William Shakespeare.

As dawn crept into the sky, she broke her vigil and went quietly to her rooms near Shakespeare's New Place, home of his affluent days.

The woman was Delia Bacon, born in 1811, forty-six years before, in Tallmadge, Ohio, a town her missionary father, the Reverend David Bacon, founded four years previous to her birth.

She had been in England for several years and had accomplished a part of her mission—publication recently of a 600-page book, *The Philosophy of Shakespeare's Plays Unfolded.*

Repetitious and involved, the weighty tome was a presentation of what she considered God had picked her to disclose—that Francis Bacon (no relation) and a brilliant coterie of Elizabethans, including Sir Walter Raleigh and Edmund Spenser, were the real authors of the plays ascribed to Shakespeare. For political reasons they had refrained from attaching their own names to these works.

Her "proof" was in the text of the plays themselves, along with some reliance on ciphers and cryptograms. It was scorned by the world, except for a few eccentrics.

Even the preface by Nathaniel Hawthorne could not save it, nor the kindly interventions of Ralph Waldo Emerson and Thomas Carlyle. All of them rejected Delia's hypothesis. Yet, they admired her and helped her launch her book.

The most remarkable aspect of her story is the way prominent individuals, and humble folk, too, on both sides of the Atlantic were attracted to Delia Bacon and often, at great personal sacrifice, befriended her.

Any list of such allies should be headed by Hawthorne, American consul at Liverpool, widely acclaimed for his *Scarlet Letter.* He was so moved by her desperate desire to get her magnum opus into print, and her financial plight, that he advanced her $1,100 he really could not afford, for the American publication. His contact with her was the impersonal one of consular duty. He kept his generosity a secret from Delia herself, from her family, and the public. He had no prospect of repayment.

Mrs. Hawthorne's sister, Elizabeth Peabody, the Boston intellectual, introduced Delia to Emerson. He, in turn, commended her to his dear friends Thomas and Jane Carlyle, when Delia embarked for England.

Such luminaries as William Cullen Bryant, Washington Irving, and the eminent historian George Bancroft sponsored her lecture series. James Buchanan called on her in London. Astronomer Maria Mitchell was solicitous of her when Delia was ill at Stratford.

President and Mrs. Polk entertained her along with Mrs. Madison at the White House. Delia knew the ubiquitous Beechers from girlhood: Catherine, her first teacher; Harriet, the author-to-be; and their clergymen brothers, the lordly Henry Ward and Edward.

All that constituted a rich background. She had accomplished the great objective, the obsession of her later life, publication of her "discovery" about Shakespeare. But now she was spent—at the end of her endurance. For her book she had sacrificed everything—family ties, social connections, her slender means . . . and her health.

She had been insisting, but in vain, that she must open Shakespeare's grave. Finally the vicar surprised her, agreeing to supervise such an investigation.

But Delia declined! Her book was in print. She was beyond necessity of such further evidence.

Or, did she fear that findings might upset her conclusions? So near to her own grave, she was too ill, no doubt, to care longer about Shakespeare's!

Before Delia Bacon's time, an occasional daring doubter had questioned the authenticity of the Bard, but she was the first person to issue a comprehensive refutation of him as the dramatist.

After her, "Baconians" and others, spurred by her pronouncements, have come forward repeatedly. Her idea that mysteries are buried with Shakespeare recurs perennially.

Delia Bacon's *Philosophy Unfolded,* dismissed less lightly of late, is currently conceded to have contributed scholarly insight into both Shakespeare and Francis Bacon. Her volume, however, remains a literary oddity. And because of it, Delia Bacon, linked with Shakespeare's name as his foremost detractor, has a place in the ranks of the remembered.

What a long road she had traveled from the lonely cabin in Ohio's New Connecticut! Under divine guidance and wholly on credit, David Bacon, her father, had contracted for twenty square miles of uninhabited land from a Connecticut real-estate company. A leading stockholder was the wealthy Revolutionary War veteran of Litchfield, Benjamin Tallmadge. Bacon chose his name for the settlement which was to be a Christian Utopia.

David Bacon was a missionary who expected to discharge his indebtedness by sale of the acreage, but only to righteous Congregationalists. One of the first town planners in Ohio, Bacon platted his domain with eight roads leading like spokes of a wheel to a center. At this hub would be a church, Congregational, of course. For its maintenance he affixed to each deed schedules of perpetual taxation: two dollars for every hundred acres; twenty dollars for a pair of oxen; fifteen dollars for a cow. With a New Englander's twin passions for education and evangelism, Bacon envisioned a college. Aspirations for a western college were being realized, too, but not in Tallmadge. However, Tallmadge Academy, organized after Bacon's death, became a feeder for the new "Yale of the West," Western Reserve College, its first building then going up in Hudson.

Today, Tallmadge, encircled by greater Akron, is a busy place, retaining the stamp of its founder's layout. Under Bacon, however, Tallmadge did not prosper. Even the devout objected to forced support of the church. His exclusive Calvinism barred desirable colonists. For example, a much-needed blacksmith was rejected because he was not a confessed Christian and was given to swearing. Ultimately accepted by the church, however, he soon departed—suffocated by piety, he said.

An adverse factor developed. Westward immigration lessened due to "tight money" in New England because of a foreign shipping embargo enacted by the Jefferson administration.

When Delia was born, the sound of the ax and the smoke of land-clearing operations filled the air. A handful of Connecticut stalwarts were staking out new homesteads. But their numbers increased too slowly.

Delia's father organized the church in the Bacon cabin with nine charter members. It was in time for his little daughter's baptism. How could any of them suspect that this unusually beautiful baby, the Bacon's fifth, would become Tallmadge's most famous citizen!

Mrs. Bacon, still girlish of figure, sensed that her husband's lofty scheme was doomed. It had happened before in the unchartered spaces at the Straits of Mackinac. Bacon and she, a bride of seventeen, had gone out from Hartford, Connecticut, to convert the Ojibway Indians, traveling by oxcart and sleigh, by sailing vessel and on foot.

Those had been futile years of untiring service to God and bitter privation for themselves. The tribes, warmed by the rum of white traders and inclined to the gentler preachments of the Jesuits, were repelled by Bacon's harsh hell-fire and damnation doctrines. Bacon was censured by his board of trustees and recalled to missionary headquarters. He had failed to win the heathens.

En route to Connecticut he passed through the future Tallmadge and left his family in near-by Hudson in the cabin of the village founder, David Hudson, whom he had known "back home." Shaking with ague, Bacon started out from here in a November sleet storm, walking the entire distance to Hartford to account for his stewardship of souls and for the $1.10 a day he had been allowed for salary and expenses.

He reached his destination in January. By March he was again in Hudson, exonerated but with a consuming new project. He was chosen by God, he believed, to establish the community of Tallmadge.

In 1807 Bacon had taken title to this sweep of dense woodland, and moved his family into a lonely new log house he and a helper had built.

After four years of heroic, dedicated effort, disaster loomed again. Mrs. Bacon speculated on this one night as she moved about her tiny home. Winter's early dusk was closing in. But the wide earth countered with a rosy glow. Her husband was away, "missionizing" somewhere, following rough roads on horseback, carrying the Word to isolated newcomers. He would not return tonight. She was never at ease during such absences, though she should be accustomed to them. Snow was on the way. Wind and wolves chorused outside.

Baby Delia was snugly blanketed in the battered cradle, but not asleep. Her eyes (what beautiful eyes they were!) followed her mother as she pulled the leather latchstring inside the door, pushed a cumbersome, homemade chest against it and, in final preparation for the night, drew a calico curtain over the grease-paper window.

Leonard, nine, eldest of the children, and all his life to be their *alter* father, was helping his mother, glad of the battening down. He knew black bears lumbered to the very threshold when hungry. Indians straggled in over old trails that cut close to the clearing, routes that ran from the Cuyahoga as far south as the Muskingum River. More than once the Bacons had looked up to see a brave leering at them through that window, asking in broken English to be admitted, or for whisky . . . Delia whimpered. Leonard put a practiced toe to rocking her . . . He would always try to respond to her calls.

Stockholders of the land company were demanding their money. David Bacon had none. The settlers he had enticed here were worried about their titles. They accused him of misrepresentation. So, a few months after Delia's first birthday, when General William Hull's surrender at Detroit was terrifying northern Ohio, the Bacons packed their poor little lot of household goods on a creaking wagon and turned once more to Hartford. The few men in the township were organizing a volunteer rifle company to combat possible attack from

British and Indians. They had no time—nor inclination—to say farewell to David Bacon.

It was his final retreat. Five years later—whether more from a broken heart or a wasted body, it was hard to say—at forty-six, he died, blessing God for His mercies to the end.

Like him, his daughter Delia would also give her life a half century later, and at about the same age, for a cause heaven-sent for her fulfillment.

Bacon's legacy to his young widow—she was in her mid-thirties—was poverty and seven boys and girls. She soon found she could not support them all.

Mrs. Bacon had named Delia for her girlhood friend, now Delia Williams, a well-to-do and childless matron of Hartford. Mrs. Williams took her namesake into her home. The foster parent was cold and austere, and Delia, then about eight, missed her lively brothers and sisters.

Bustling, mellow Hartford, with its classical buildings and monuments to the past, awakened the keen mind of the little girl from the Ohio frontier. The city whetted her eagerness for an education—to learn more of what those landmarks signified. When she was fourteen and on a visit to her mother in New York State, word came that Mrs. Williams would pay her expenses for a year at Catherine Beecher's Female Academy, opened the previous year in Hartford. Leonard, now a Congregational minister in New Haven, provided seventy dollars from his first salary for Delia's return to Connecticut.

That year (1825) Tallmadge dedicated its new Congregational Church, located on the green as David Bacon had planned. Its tower, soaring a hundred feet into the treetops, and its massive pillars make it today a gem of pioneer Ohio architecture. It is heir to Bacon's dreams, a fitting monument to him. The cost, $3,500, subscribed in labor, lumber, and grain, would have staggered the missionary.

Delia, unconcerned with such happenings at her birthplace, plunged hungrily into Miss Beecher's rich curriculum. This egotistical member of the Beecher clan was to shape her new pupil's life in many respects, A fellow scholar was Catherine's sister, Harriet, born the same year as Delia.

Catherine Beecher, twenty-five, an able teacher, stressed original thinking, the unity of all knowledge, as well as self-expression. She offered a prize for the best composition.

Delia, convinced that authorship was her forte, confidently submitted a piece which Miss Beecher criticized devastatingly. The award went to Harriet.

In Delia was born a determination to show the world she could write. Harriet and she never were very friendly. When both were grown women, and in London, where Harriet was being lionized for her *Uncle Tom's Cabin,* Delia did not look her up.

At the year's end, her only bit of formal schooling ended, Delia wrote Leonard that she was ready to support herself. The schoolroom offered the usual means to a livelihood for women. At fifteen she assumed the first of many posts that she would pursue for years, the while battling illness and inadequate income.

An ambitious effort to establish a boarding school, which Delia operated with her sisters, ended in failure after a two-year struggle. Delia was left frail from a near-fatal bout with malaria, and in debt . . . which Leonard paid off.

Never relinquishing the promise of her pen, Delia at twenty brought out her first book, *Tales from the Puritans,* three stories about early New England. It received some favorable commendation, though it seems stilted today. Leonard thought she might better have written Old Testament sketches for Sunday schools. Like other contemporary women authors, Delia kept her book anonymous. It gained her no fame, nor fortune either.

For her next output, *Love's Martyr,* she won a prize that was a real fortune to her—$100 in cash. She had first-page attention from the donor, *The Philadelphia Courier.* Among the contestants she had downed was one Edgar Allan Poe!

Now she tried a drama, *The Bride of Fort Edward,* based on a true occurrence. To smooth her own religious scruples regarding the theater and thwart Leonard's, she labeled it a dialogue. Never staged, several hundred copies were sold, but there was a deficit she had to share with the printer.

As Delia continued her teaching, she devised what she termed "classes" for teen-age girls, the technique that of the modern seminar. Her lessons ranged over a wide scope with considerable emphasis on Shakespeare, for she already was deep in the study of his plays. Brilliant and stimulating, she was thought fascinating by her girls, even though she held to strict discipline.

Inaugurating a kind of finishing school, she guided her pupils in grooming and deportment. To round out their social graces, she invited students from Yale, who came most willingly and were received in like manner.

At thirty-four she herself fell in love. Her affection centered on one Alexander MacWhorter, a Yale divinity student, ten years her junior. She scarcely could have selected one less worthy of her, or more of a cad.

The story is an incredible one of a man trifling with an accomplished woman, capable and poised in apparently all realms but that of the heart. He met her at their boardinghouse and constantly sought her company.

When Delia went to Brattleboro, Vermont, for the popular water cure after a siege of sickness, MacWhorter soon appeared there too. Delia was surprised to find two other guests, Catherine Beecher and her sister, Harriet, now wife of Calvin Stowe. He was caring for their children back home in Cincinnati and teaching under his father-in-law, Lyman Beecher, at Lane Seminary.

Catherine and Harriet observed with unabashed interest, and not entire approval, the romantic goings on. Catherine presumed to make outspoken inquiries as to the young man's intentions.

MacWhorter proposed marriage to Delia while at Brattleboro, later publicly denying it. At length Delia came to her senses and broke with the man. She asked that her letters be returned, only to learn they were being passed from hand to hand among her erstwhile suitor's friends.

Matters worsened. Leonard demanded that MacWhorter be brought before Congregational Church authorities. Charges listed calumny and falsehood, along with conduct unbecoming a candidate for the Christian ministry. Delia and her brother felt the trial would vindicate her, feeling sure God was on their side.

The ordeal dragged through two laborious weeks of confused testimony. Tempers and emotions quickened. Delia suffered intensely. All New Haven was interested.

The verdict was equivocal, the judges not in unanimous agreement. MacWhorter was censured, but not on every count. Delia, bruised and battered, went into seclusion at Leonard's parsonage.

She was about recovered when another blow fell. Catherine Beecher, indignant at the outcome of the trial, was meddling, taking the situation into her own hands. She was writing a book, *Truth, Stranger than Fiction*, to clear Delia's name! Despite Delia's pleadings that she drop the work, Miss Beecher continued.

Avowing its lofty purpose, Catherine circulated her book freely, careful to indicate its price, which was $.62½ a copy. She had procured a transcript of the hearings from Leonard without his knowledge of her intention. Her book is the record of what must be considered one of the oddest trials ever to take place in an ecclesiastical court.

Somehow, Delia righted herself to launch her most successful venture, her lectures "for ladies"—and some gentlemen. Her triumphs were achieved over the stiff competition of an era given to lectures on every conceivable subject.

Here was a woman born for the platform, graceful, attractively gowned, with charming manners, dark, flashing eyes, and a quick smile. She captivated her audiences at once. She spoke easily, without notes.

Glibly, she discussed the Acropolis at Athens, ancient Assyrian culture, the cryptic mysteries of the Rosetta Stone. Her programs featured readings from Shakespeare, one of her top accomplishments. The heady fare was popular.

A group of leading men in Brooklyn petitioned her to repeat for an evening program a morning lecture, "The Origin of the Oriental Element in Our Civilization." Best-seller William Makepeace Thackeray, on a speaking circuit in this country, received no more space in newspaper accounts than Delia Bacon.

Restless, on the *qui vive* for new adventure, she moved about in the East, even risking her powers in Boston and New York City. Attendance was good, sixty signing up in one place, a hundred in another. Fees, at first as little as five dollars for extended courses, rose to one hundred dollars as her name became known.

Subscribers and backers represented the first families: women relatives of the Cabots and Lowells, wives of Harvard and Yale professors, conservatives as well as the "new feminists." Often a guest in their drawing rooms, Delia met the V.I.P.s of the day. Samuel F. B. Morse, who could talk with equal eloquence about his portraiture or his experiments with the telegraph, introduced Delia to Charles King, president of Columbia College, not yet Columbia University.

Benjamin Silliman, at that time rated America's foremost scientist, who had enjoyed Delia's fiction, shared with her his enthusiasm for Francis Bacon, and first aroused the interest that was to dominate the rest of her days.

It was not until she was well into her anti-Shakespeare views that she met Emerson face to face. They had corresponded. (What letter writers these people were! And all by hand.) Delia had sent

Emerson a detailed outline of "the enigma unfolded." He had replied, inviting her to call on him and his wife. It was out of the question for him to call on her as: "I very rarely get so far [as Cambridge] from home where I am detained by a truly ridiculous complication of cobwebs."

Emerson and his invalid wife welcomed Delia warmly in their Concord home, though afterward he wrote that: "Mrs. Emerson is mortified at her heedlessness in putting you to sleep in a chamber certain to be disturbed by too-early-rising washers."

But the visit pleased both Delia and Emerson. The two sat in his study, now such a tourist mecca, Delia pouring out her iconoclastic arguments, and her decision that only in England could she finish her enterprise.

Emerson thought her "proposition immensely improbable" and later was critical of her book's style and argument. But he listened, entranced at her sparkling conversation.

She reminded him of the late Margaret Fuller—high praise, indeed! He sent off letters in her behalf to acquaintances in this country and abroad, persuading others to do likewise. Out of it all came introductions to publishers, literary figures, officials of the British Museum, and, most significant of all, to Carlyle.

One stumbling block remained—finances. Her speaking engagements brought her independence, but on too modest a scale to permit a trip abroad. Someone always emerged to bridge over her crises. At this point it was Charles Butler, who had heard of her from a relative, one of her sponsors, a friend of Emerson.

Butler, a wealthy New Yorker, dedicated to education and the church, had been a founder of Hobart College and Union Theological Seminary. Also, he was something of a student of Francis Bacon. In an interview, Delia so impressed him with her personality and her knowledge of Bacon that he advanced her $500 for what she wanted to do in England.

Keeping the identity of her backer from Leonard, who disapproved both of her proposed book and journey, Delia sailed in 1852. She was excited and happy, completely confident of her aims.

For nearly five years she kept doggedly to her objective. Her hopes and her health dwindled with her resources. Butler, meeting reverses and impatient as Delia prolonged her stay, refused further aid. She managed to spin out a pound "to serve for two," as she wrote Emerson. She practiced near-starvation economies in inexpensive lodgings in London and Stratford, where she came to feel much at home.

With her lengthy findings completed, there began the continually disappointing search for a publisher. Carlyle in England and Emerson in America wrote endlessly to recommend her to bookmen, Hawthorne later taking her under his benevolent aegis.

To them all she sent "packets of manuscripts" which they apparently read conscientiously, deciphering her difficult penmanship as best they could.

Emerson complained of her deletions and interlinear editing. Few authors have had such high-placed friendships. They decried her ideas, but they remained steadfast to her.

The Carlyles received her cordially. Carlyle wrote Emerson: "There is not one least possibility of truth in the notion she has taken up, but we find her, with her modest, shy dignity and her solid character a real acquisition."

Carlyle kept in close touch with Delia, sending her practical suggestions about publishers, lodgings, research in the British Museum, and hospitable invitations: "Come and see us . . . Almost every evening we are both of us at home (tea at 7) and at 3 I am visible."

Aware of her painful financial straits, he pressed her to "come off at once to the vacant room Jane and I keep in readiness for you in our home" in London's Chelsea. Infrequently she did break what had grown into a recluse's routine and could write: "Carlyle has been to see me, though I am miles away from his house. I was out when he came, but he left word . . . so there was no alternative but for me to go.

"It was very, very pleasant. I went at 5, stayed for tea and dinner, until 11, and Carlyle spent all the time with us, though he was very busy."

But at her Bacon authorship notions the blustery Carlyle "shrieked so you could hear him a mile at my audacity." And when she called Shakespeare a "booby," "I thought he would have the roof off the house."

For the most part she shrank from seeing anyone. Replying to Hawthorne, who had asked to call on her, she wrote: "If you will let me know when you are coming, I will put on one of the dresses I used to wear . . . for three years I have lived alone with God and the dead . . . but I will try to look as much like a survivor as possible."

Hawthorne has recorded his impression of that first meeting: "I had expected to see a very homely, uncouth, elderly personage and was quite agreeably disappointed . . . she was rather uncommonly tall and had a striking and expressive face . . . dark eyes that shone with an inward light . . . I could suppose her to have been handsome and exceedingly attractive once."

After listening more than an hour to her theme, he departed convinced "it would be a difficult and doubtful matter to advocate publication of Miss Bacon's book." Nevertheless, before long Hawthorne had set himself to accomplish exactly that. And he succeeded.

The year the book appeared—1857—Tallmadge held its semicentennial. Principal orator at the celebration was the Reverend Leonard Bacon, D.D., the "nineteenth century's greatest polemical writer," known for his hymns and essays, among them a series on slavery later quoted by Lincoln.

The dignified divine from the fabled East reminisced about his father's "covenant with God" on this spot, their lonely cabin home, and the Indians who so frightened his "sainted mother." His remarks, duly recorded in pamphlet form, are a vivid chronicle of frontier Ohio.

Delia's plight by now was serious. Reviews of her book were disheartening. Critics either ridiculed or ignored it. Her "discovery" stirred no clamor from the world. Weak physically from her intense preoccupation, with no longer a goal to challenge her, she collapsed. Her fine mind tipped off balance.

Faithful to his self-assumed responsibility as long as he was in England, Hawthorne saw to it that her landlord was paid and a doctor was provided, and he wrote to Leonard.

Delia was asking for her brother. Someone should come to take her home, Hawthorne said. But neither Leonard, important person though he was, nor any of the family had the means for the journey.

Leonard's son, George, was Delia's rescuer this time. Returning from a world cruise, on which he had been a paid official on the ship, he stopped off in England to look up his favorite aunt, not knowing of her difficulties. To his consternation he traced her to a private sanitarium near Stratford where her doctor had placed her.

Selling a collection of curios gathered on his travels, he accumulated money for the passage and brought her to America—to a sanitarium in Hartford, where Leonard could see her often.

After more than a year they buried her, age forty-eight, beside her relatives in New Haven.

Delia, like her father, finished with life's heartaches, had come to rest forever in her ancestral Connecticut, a far distance from her birthplace in the Ohio wilderness.

John Brown's Wives

MUCH PRINTER'S INK *has been spilled on the epic of John Brown, Ohio-reared, militant abolitionist. Revered as holy martyr, called crazy firebrand, few figures in American annals are more controversial.*

The two who knew him best (his wives, Dianthe Lusk and Mary Day) have received scant attention from posterity. History has been busy with John.

Dianthe, mate of his youth, married him at nineteen and mothered seven of his children. Mary, seventeen when she became his wife, gave birth to thirteen, endured the Harpers Ferry cataclysm that brought death to two sons, her husband's conviction as a traitor, and his hanging.

The first wife spent twelve years with John Brown, the second, twenty-six—strenuous years, every one. With babes in arms and babes in wombs, with offspring of varying ages, the women were moved from place to place, from home to home. Brown was a true son of his era, when families were large and the frontier lured.

John Brown's role, however, was more than that of a pioneer. For weeks, for months, he was away from home, following the voice of God, as he believed, commanding him to break the shackles of the slave.

His wives, first Dianthe and then Mary, the more heavily burdened, were left to care for his children, sick, well, and dying, to fight poverty and put up with loneliness. Their husband exacted from each woman the same sacrificial dedication to Negro freedom as his own. And they conformed. He appears neglectful, even cruel at times. But both wives gave him unwavering loyalty.

John Brown has inspired tributes and indictments beyond the lot of most men. Yet every indictment weakens before the record of his wives' steadfastness. No tribute is as eloquent as their devotion.

Dianthe was born in Bloomfield, New York, January 12, 1801, married John Brown in Hudson, Ohio, June 21, 1820, and died in Crawford County, Pennsylvania, August 10, 1832. Her successor, Mary, was born in Granville, New York, April 15, 1816, married John Brown in Crawford County, Pennsylvania, July 11, 1833, and died in San Francisco, February 29, 1884.

John Brown had not noticed Dianthe until his father, Owen, began dropping broad hints about the girl. She and her mother, the Widow Lusk, came regularly to help John's stepmother, Sally Root Brown, with the cooking, the washing, and the weaving.

Owen Brown operated a tannery on high-lying land at the outskirts of the young settlement of Hudson in Ohio's New Connecticut. His house overflowed with children—John's brothers and a sister, children of Owen's first wife, Ruth, and now of the second wife, Sally, with a new baby seemingly always on the way.

Crowded out by the steadily increasing brood, John and a foster brother, Levi Blakeslee, built themselves a log house near the tanyard, where they were learning the trade. John left briefly to attend an academy in Plainfield, Massachusetts, preparatory to entering Amherst College to train for the ministry. An eye infection cut short his schooling and he returned to continue curing hides for his father.

John knew how to cook. His choicest dish was corn-meal mush, done to a crusty gold, baked at his log fire and spooned up with rich cream from his own cows.

Bachelor John was a tidy housekeeper. But he had little time to give to such tasks, for he and Levi put in long hours in the fields and tannery. They persuaded Mrs. Lusk and her daughter to take care of their quarters, along with the work at Owen's house. The two often stayed to prepare supper for the youths.

After one particularly grueling day at the tan vats John came in while Dianthe was lifting browned loaves of bread from the tin reflector at the fireplace. The little cabin was filled with that most delightful of all odors—the fragrance of baking bread.

The sleeves of Dianthe's linsey-woolsey dress were rolled back revealing plump, well-turned arms. Firelight tinted her cheeks, usually so pale, to a delicate, becoming flush. John saw the young woman for the first time.

From now on he watched her as she went quietly about her duties, observed with approval that she scrubbed the wide plank floor to a gleaming whiteness, then sanded it with care. The bread served on his table was mighty good, and it was Dianthe's, her mother said.

John concluded that after all there was something in what his father had been saying about this Dianthe Lusk. When the supper things were cleared away one evening, Mrs. Lusk began to press John's Sunday shirt. It was white and had a plait. She pushed the clumsy sadirons to the heat of the hearth . . .

John asked Dianthe to walk out with him. They strolled as far as a great flat rock. Yellow light from the cabin's candle and a red glow from the fireplace filtered out to them. Spring had come to the knoll in the clearing—and romance to the hearts of Dianthe and John.

On the twenty-first of June, 1820, they were married. The Reverend William Hanford, first "settled" pastor of Hudson's Congregational Church, officiated. John had just turned twenty (May 9). His bride was a year younger. She had a wedding dress, made of home-woven stuff bleached to a near white.

John had been "examined and admitted" to the church in 1816, shortly after the arrival of Hanford, who was not long out of Yale College and Andover Newton Theological School. Dianthe was accepted into the fold in 1819. Church membership, like domestic skill, was a marriage prerequisite in young Brown's mind.

Religion was as serious a concern to Dianthe as to her husband. She had a place in the woods where from childhood she had gone alone to pray. When she sang it was always sacred tunes or hymns. She soon learned her husband's favorites: "Blow Ye the Trumpet, Blow," "Ah, Lovely Appearance of Death," "Why Should We Fear To Die," and "Sweet Is Thy Word, My God, My King."

Dianthe came of aristocratic stock. Her mother, a widow when Lusk married her, was born Mary Adams and traced her lineage to the second President, John Adams, and the Revolutionary War patriot Samuel Adams. Amos Lusk, Dianthe's father, also well born, was a natural leader, a founder member of the Hudson church and captain of the militia unit he drilled on the village green in the War of 1812. He led his company to meet other Ohio frontiersmen at a Lake Erie rendezvous and died of yellow fever near Sandusky in 1813.

Dianthe, destined for a brief but telling role in history, was twelve at the time of her father's death. Already she possessed certain advantages; she was reared in a home of above-average pioneer standards and in a community that fostered knowledge and a vigorously progressive spirit. It is probable that she attended the same school where John was a pupil, a log building early erected on the green. It served also for Sunday worship and prayer meetings until a church went up the year the two were married.

Captain Lusk left nine children, some very small, as well as a stepdaughter. Mrs. Lusk found ancestry little aid in providing necessities. She went to work in the homes of neighbors.

Amos Lusk had migrated to the Ohio country from New York State in 1801. Dianthe, who was six weeks old, came near to never reaching her new home because of a mishap en route. After a night's stopover at a tavern, Mrs. Lusk was preparing breakfast, while her husband, eager to get his slow-moving ox team on the road as soon as possible, was packing up.

Unaware that Baby Dianthe had been left blanketed and asleep on the bed, he hurriedly tossed a feather tick and bedclothes on top of her, then bundled and tied the whole of it, and rolled it down the stairs. Mrs. Lusk, missing the baby, rescued her as she was turning blue from near suffocation.

No likeness of Dianthe is known to exist. Nevertheless, we are sure she was "plain." In an autobiographical letter written in 1857, two years before his death, John Brown accords her this grudging flattery: "She was remarkably plain but a neat industrious & economical girl; of excellent character; earnest piety; & good practical common sense." (Punctuation John's).

Her brother Milton, who calls her his "guiding star" and "guardian angel," also describes her as "a plain person." She was "not as tall as my father but about her mother's height." However, she had an "amiable disposition" for this is what "attracted John." She "was pleasant and cheerful" and "she never said anything but what she meant." Evidently, like John, she lacked a sense of humor, for Milton describes her as "never funny." Though he professed to adore this plain sister, he had no use for her husband.

At sixteen, apprenticed to David Hudson, founder of the village that carried his name, Milton was free only on Sunday. One day after church he walked the considerable distance to John's cabin to call on his mother and sister. John, who observed the day with Calvinistic rigor, considered visiting on the "Lord's Day" a desecration and ordered the lad away. Milton had no other time to see his relatives and never forgave his future brother-in-law. When Dianthe and John were married, he refused to attend the wedding.

Dianthe, on the other hand, seems to have accepted everything about her austere mate, from his family dictatorship to his abolition fervor. An early and strong, but by no means unanimous, antislavery sentiment already existed in this part of Ohio. Owen Brown, active in the freedom movement from the first, set the example for John. From John's boyhood on, the Brown farm was a frequently used stop on the underground railroad.

Many a night Dianthe rose from her bed to prepare food for fugitives knocking furtively at the door. They were fed, given fresh clothes, and sheltered in the house, unless there was fear of pursuers. At such times John or Dianthe would pilot them across the pasture to a hide-out in the woods. In the pitchy darkness the timid young woman was as nervous as the Negroes, but she carried out her husband's injunctions regarding them.

Shortcomings were not countenanced by John. He beat his four-year-old son, John, Jr., his first-born, for relating a childish tale of fancy. Albeit the parent's cheeks were wet with tears, he put all his sinewy strength into the blows, for God guided the rod in the name of the child's salvation.

Afterward Dianthe may have comforted the exhausted boy in secret, but before her lord she yielded unquestioning acquiescence.

Later in life John Brown expressed regret for what undeniably was severe punishment inflicted on his offspring. Nonetheless, all of them appeared to hold their father in the same deep affection that Dianthe's daughter Ruth, when grown, expressed:

> He sometimes seemed very stern and strict . . . yet his tenderness made me forget he was stern. A few years before his death he urged me to reason calmly with my children . . . and never punish them, whatever they had done, if they told the truth about it. Said he: "If I had my life to live over I would do very differently with my children."

Whether or not he mellowed in later life, in this period when Dianthe knew him, Hudson tradition paints him as uncompromising and opinionated, a patriarchal despot, not only regarding his family, but in all his dealings. The journeymen whom he employed, to hold their jobs had to attend church every Sunday and join in the Browns' family worship at every dawn. An excellent craftsman himself, he tolerated only top-quality products, his exacting discipline making him a feared employer.

Substantial prosperity began for the Browns. Four years after their marriage, with two sons and another child expected, the cabin was outgrown. John could afford a new house, a frame one that stands to this day. Though much remodeled through the years, its core is John's. Frame houses, not too common, were a symbol of success in the era of primitive log construction.

Hudson was becoming one of the important centers in the Western Reserve. With the Canal Age launched by the Erie Canal's opening in 1825, Ohio was embarking on its own waterway network that would infuse new vigor in the economy of the entire state. Scheduled for completion in 1826, the first segment was to connect Cleveland with the young town of Akron, thirteen miles from Hudson. With land and a generous sum of money donated by Deacon Hudson, the much-talked-about Western Reserve College, "Yale of the West," was coming into being in the village.

The settlement David Hudson platted, a bit of transplanted Connecticut, reflected its sturdy New England heritage of industry and culture, school and church. It would seem a good place for a young man to plant the roots of his future.

However, John, never one to hold with roots or security, was overcome by the pioneer urge to venture into fresh fields. This restlessness, which beset him the remainder of his days, made life with him an arduous and at times a well-nigh-unbearable experience for his wives and children.

As a youth he had studied Flint's textbook on surveying. The skill was in demand in those days when unchartered regions were opening up everywhere. Explorations with rod and chain took him into far places. On one such journey he was introduced to wilderness lands in Western Pennsylvania. The virgin territory appealed to him. Oak forests provided bark for a tannery. The land lay along a direct route to Pittsburgh, a ready market for cattle. He took title to extensive acreage here.

Returning to Hudson in April, a few days before his twenty-sixth birthday, he was in time for an impressive ceremony. His father, Owen, with other members of the building committee of the new college, presided at the cornerstone laying of the first structure, Middle College. Whether or not John witnessed the event is not recorded.

He was preparing to leave this promising community and the considerable stake he had established in it—his farm, his tan vats, his growing reputation as a cattle- and sheepman and his new house.

If Dianthe was consulted about the uprooting, which is doubtful, she would not have uttered a murmur of dissent.

The Hudson home John had built so short a time before was on a lane connecting two main roads. Around it he maintained a thrifty kitchen garden. Near-by he had planted a select variety of apple trees in a fine orchard, now a burst of bloom. At the rear, the woods, so often a slave hide-out, topped a scenic knoll. From it flowed a clear little stream supplying water for the tan vats. His fields' rich earth fanned out over many acres, ready for the spring plow.

A relative had given Dianthe a slip from a bluebell clump, carried west from some far-off New England flower bed. It was blooming now, its tall stalks bending to the wind beside the wide stone doorstep of the little house. Around the well, functioning today on that hilltop, Dianthe had arranged a row of cockleshells, treasures of her girlhood.

They were leaving it all. Five Browns were moving on. On the high wagon seat Dianthe cradled in her lap the littlest son, two-year-old Owen, named for his grandfather. She bent to cuddle closer her other two, John, Jr., who was five, and Jason, four. Beside them, her husband, a silent, forbidding man, slapped reins on horses fretting to be off. They were fine horses, for John Brown knew animals and always had the best.

Brakes groaned, the heavily loaded wagon creaked forward. Dianthe was heading into the unknown. Her eyes caressed the little house behind her on the hill as long as she could see it—the bluebells and the orchard's froth of pink. She was quitting the best home she would know in the few grim years left to her . . . Her wedding dress, carefully folded, was tucked beneath the family's small store of clothes in a wooden box under the seat.

The new home was in an untamed part of Crawford County, Pennsylvania, in the vicinity of present-day Meadville. The woodlands, one of the attractions for John, closed menacingly about them. They lived as best they could until John finished a stout cabin. He felled twenty-five acres of timber, sunk vats, and built a tannery shed—all before the first frost. Whatever John Brown's faults, indolence was not among them.

Brown always "liked to be head of the heap," as Milton Lusk said of him, and in this scene he soon was just that. With his surveying knowledge he set about at once laying out roads. He had a school going shortly, and he organized church services in his barn. In intervals between infrequent visits of saddlebag missionaries, he himself preached. The church he started survives, now known as Guy's Mills Congregational.

The Bible John used was a stout volume often in his hands. He read aloud from it morning and evening to Dianthe and the children submissively assembled before him. He could quote entire chapters from memory. The book was bound in fine sheepskin of his own tanning.

President John Quincy Adams, unaware he was rewarding the husband of a distant kinswoman, appointed John the first postmaster of the district. The franking privilege was for Randolph, but the settlement stood on the map as Richmond. A sign over some crude shelves in the Brown home designated one corner as the post office. Dianthe often handled the letters. It was an extra burden, but welcome, for people came now and then for their mail and there was someone to talk to.

John was away a great deal, carrying the mail, going on long treks to Pittsburgh for supplies, and trading in hides and beef. Dianthe was homesick for far-off relatives and friends she would never see again. After lively Hudson, where she grew up and knew everyone, the Pennsylvania outpost was lonely, indeed, and sometimes terrifying, especially when wild animals crept stealthily into the Brown dooryard.

Some local contacts did develop for her, however, through the little school run co-operatively with their neighbors, the Delamaters, to whom she was related. Sessions alternated between the Brown and Delamater cabins, pupils lodging for a term at each home. When school kept at the Browns', Dianthe prepared breakfast as usual in winter darkness, for John tolerated no overstaying in bed.

Following the meal, John prayed long and fervently, then passed Bibles to each child, requiring them to read a goodly number of verses.

They had been in their forest home only a few months when their three boys acquired a brother, Frederick. He was named for John's brother, whose farm adjoined Owen's Hudson holdings. When four years old, the boy died, the first of many family deaths John was to know. He was buried in a field near the tan vats.

Shortly after this death another son was born and received the dead child's name, a custom in those days of high infant mortality.

Between the births of the two Fredericks, the Browns had a daughter, Ruth.

The sixth year in the bleak house, when Dianthe was thirty-one, her seventh child was born—dead. Dianthe died three days later. She was shrouded in her wedding dress, which someone found packed in dry lavender blossoms in the cabin loft.

Her husband's chroniclers pass briefly over Dianthe, except to state invariably that she was insane at death. However, a letter written by John to his father that came to light some years ago and is not included in any standard biography should refute the allegation for all time.

Under date of August 11, 1832, writing from Randolph, Pennsylvania, John announces in characteristic prose:

> We are again smarting under the rod of our Heavenly Father. Last night about 11 o'clock my affectionate, dutiful and faithful Dianthe (to use her own last words) "bade farewell to earth." My own health is so poor that I have barely strength to give you a short history of what passed since I wrote you last. Her health I think I mentioned in my last letter was very poor, partly owing to her pregnancy, but more perhaps to a difficulty about her heart. She, however, kept about a little when she was brought to bed of a son (not a living one). We called a good physician who was obliged to take the child with instruments. The presentation was wrong & could not be corrected. Much time elapsed before the Dr. procured his instruments & he advised her situation was most critical, but this information did not depress her spirits. She made answer that "I thought I might go to rest on God's Sabbath." At her request her children were brought to her and she with heavenly composure gave faithful advice to each.
>
> Our hopes were quite revived for the first 24 hours. About that time her difficulty of heart palpitation became so great that we thought her dying for some hours. She, however, revived, but not to gain much strength after.
>
> Her reason was unimpaired & her mind composed with the Peace of God. Tomorrow she is to be laid beside her dear little son.
>
> From your sorrowing son, John Brown.

In other words, then, it was Dianthe's body and not her mind that gave way. A just appraisal at last attaches to Dianthe, so long misrepresented.

She and her stillborn child were buried beside the little mound rounded over the grave of "her dear little son," the first Frederick. The marker carries the legend:

In memory of Dianthe
wife of John Brown.
She died August 10th
1832. Aged 31 years.
Farewell Earth.

Widower Brown found he could not meet the varied demands of making a livelihood and at the same time manage his household with five children, the eldest John, Jr., eleven, and the youngest, Frederick, just learning to walk.

For a time they boarded at the home of a young man in John's employ, who had been recently married. Understandably, the arrangement proved unsatisfactory.

John re-established his home and engaged a neighbor girl as housekeeper. She soon found her job a heavy one and brought along a younger sister to do the spinning. Her name was Mary Anne Day.

The girl's father, Charles Day, once a prosperous blacksmith in the township, had lost his property through injudicious signing of notes. As a consequence, his daughters had had few advantages and only the limited schooling available in the Pennsylvania wilds.

Mary seemed older than her seventeen years. Tall, big-boned, she was not pretty, but had the good looks of youth and vigorous health. Her chestnut hair was heavy and, with a bit of encouragement, might have waved. She talked little and carried herself with a certain confident dignity.

Mary kept the spinning wheel twirling by the hour and the little house echoed with her treadle's busy, cheerful tune. Under her expert hands the fleece John clipped from his sheep quickly was converted into excellent yarn.

The widower eyed her with approval. Here was a young woman in looks not at all resembling the wife he mourned, but one who showed the same diligence and capability. He noted particularly that the children liked her and that she was very attentive to baby Frederick. She could not quite take Dianthe's place . . . but Mary Day had her own good points . . . He presented his proposal of marriage by letter. John was a great letter writer!

Sensing its message, Mary carried the envelope around in an apron pocket for a couple of days. She fingered it fearfully, lacking courage to open it.

John grew impatient. Following her to the well one evening as she went to bucket up water, he demanded her answer. Mary still hesitated.

The stĕp would mean raising another woman's children and union with an awesome being nearly twice her age.

Photographs show John Brown at this time clean-shaven, not yet a sign of the familiar beard. Gimlet eyes described as "ice blue," thin lips pressed together in an unsmiling, implacable line. There was little about such a bridegroom to inspire sentimental longings in the breast of a seventeen-year-old girl.

But Mary sensed that her marriage would lighten her parents' heavy load, and there were few opportunities of any kind to look forward to in the sparsely peopled region . . .

Frail Dianthe had been resting almost a year amidst the rank grasses of the meadow near-by. Weeds choking the path to John Brown's cabin door were dry and dust-powdered in the blistering sun of a mid-July afternoon . . . Mary came into the log house without her sister, now to assume all the household responsibilities and all the mothering of five little Browns, instead of merely the spinning.

John Brown's new mate was unlike slight, meek Dianthe. Mary Day was above the average woman's height. Hers was a spare and rugged frame. Product of poverty-struck pioneering, harsher than that in Dianthe's girlhood background, Mary showed a resourcefulness and inborn self-assurance beyond her age. These qualities, that never were Dianthe's, would strengthen in Mary and serve as bulwark for buffetings to come.

Since, except in myths, humankind is vouchsafed no preview of the future, Mary was spared foreboding of the tumult and tragedy ahead for her as partner of John Brown. Dianthe had succumbed as his wife during the early, easiest years. Mary, made in a stauncher mold, survived him a quarter of a century.

Mary Day Brown became the mother of thirteen children. Nine died during her lifetime, four within the same month. Her first child, Sarah, was born in the spring (1834) following her marriage, the next year her first son, Watson. He was to die twenty-four years later at Harpers Ferry, wounded while his father clutched his last night of freedom in the abortive arsenal raid.

Before Watson was a year old, John Brown's roaming nature once more got the best of him. After the Pennsylvania tract had held him ten years, he pulled up stakes. He moved Mary, her two wee ones, and Dianthe's five, to Franklin Mills, today's Kent. It is in Ohio a few miles from Hudson, always "homeland" to John.

Here at Franklin Mills he expected to establish a tannery, but this fell through. Subsequent speculative operations in a real-estate allotment and mill sites also collapsed, largely because of diversions of water power in the Pennsylvania-Ohio Canal through here. The general panic of 1837, which tumbled many fortunes, was a final blow for him.

From this date on Brown's financial situation worsened. While not assailed as intentionally dishonest, his reputation suffered. The Franklin Mills fiascoes and future impractical ventures led him to bankruptcy, and plunged him into endless litigation with creditors nagging him to the end of his days.

After the Franklin Mills episode, for a brief interlude, he installed his family in Hudson, unfailing refuge. With his fortunes at a low ebb and his plans unsettled, John and his family flitted between Hudson and Franklin Mills.

Shunted from home to home, worried by scanty means and her husband's legal troubles, Mary continued to have babies every year or two. The sensitive Oliver was born in 1839, during one of the short stays at Franklin Mills. He, like Watson, lost his life at Harpers Ferry, dying on the brick floor of the engine room.

It was about the time of Oliver's birth that the event occurred which shaped the fate of the Browns—and of their country, as well.

John persuaded Mary and Dianthe's oldest sons to join him in a holy pact "to do all in their power to abolish slavery."

Liberation of the Negro loomed more and more prominently in his innermost thoughts until the cause obsessed him, as, in his own words, "the greatest or principal object of my life." Early he concluded that the black man's chains could be broken only by armed aggression, with bloodshed unavoidable. In such a mood he committed Mary and his sons to his enterprise.

This was revealed years later by John, Jr., who, in a reminiscent vein, gave the world the story. He was not certain of the exact date, but he remembered the place of the oath-taking as Franklin Mills in the "old Haymaker house," their home more than once. It is more likely the Browns were living near that village, on the Chamberlain farm, from which they were later evicted in a series of court actions. At the moment of the historic pledge John put lawsuits out of his mind.

> Father, mother, Jason, Owen and I were . . . seated around . . . the open fire-place of the kitchen [John, Jr., begins] and there he first informed us of his determination to make war on slavery . . . war by force and arms. He said that . . . he believed it was his duty to devote his life, if need be, to this object . . . After . . . setting forth in most impressive language the hopeless condition of the slave, he asked who of us were willing to make common cause with him in doing all in our power to "break the jaws of the wicked and pluck the spoil out of his teeth," naming each of us in succession, Are you Mary, John Jason and Owen? Receiving an affirmative answer from each, he kneeled in prayer [the first time John, Jr., had seen his father kneel while praying] . . . he asked us to raise our right hands, and then he administered to us an oath . . . [that] in substance . . . bound us to secrecy and devotion to . . . fighting slavery by force and arms . . .

John Sykes Fayette, "a colored theological student" who was graduated from Western Reserve College in Hudson in 1836, apparently then living with the Browns, was present, but he appears not to have participated.

If the compact was made in 1839, John, Jr., was eighteen, Jason, sixteen, and Owen, fifteen. Dianthe's fourth son, Frederick, was nine, too young presumably to be included. Yet, the oath left a mark on him, for in his young adulthood he followed his father to Kansas, where he was shot to death during free-soil exploits.

John, Jr., states that the evening gathering was the first time the family realized the full import of John Brown's Negro freedom aims. However, others had heard him so declare himself two years before.

The 1837 killing, by slave sympathizers, of the Reverend Elijah P. Lovejoy, abolition editor of an Illinois religious publication, roused the North. A memorial prayer meeting was held in Hudson's Congregational Church. Owen Brown, for once unimpeded by stuttering, rose to proclaim undying hostility to human bondage. His son John in his pew echoed the same pledge "with God's help."

Mary may have been present, but evidently John, Jr., was not.

The fireside covenant that John initiated and imposed upon his family motivated his actions for the next twenty years, the remainder of his life. Its influence also underlay Mary's attitudes and actions during this entire period. In 1860, shortly after her husband's execution, she told his friend, F. B. Sanborn, that she "had known his design and had been pledged to aid it for more than twenty years." Two years before, John Brown had confided similarly in Sanborn, who promised to divulge nothing.

The pact binding the older boys gripped the younger children as they grew up and was extended to include their husbands and wives. This explains the willingness of John Brown's sons and sons-in-law to go along with him, some unto death.

The Brown clan conspiracy to end slavery, unsuspected by outsiders, cannot be overemphasized as the background force in the family for two fateful decades.

When the contract was entered into, the boys were in their teens and impressionable. Mary was twenty-three, not much older or more experienced. It is difficult to conceive of any of them hesitating at this time to comply with John Brown's dictates.

The mature Mary, on the other hand, appears to have developed misgivings and reservations both about her husband's free-soil exploits and the finale at Harpers Ferry. At the same time she accepted his departures on these expeditions as inevitable flowering of his plan, sending him off on one occasion with bandages of her own making and with medicines for possible wounded.

She indicated no interest herself in going to Kansas, though some of the Brown women did go. Nor did she heed her husband's urgings that she join him in the Maryland farmhouse during his summer prelude to the raid.

Likewise, John, Jr., and Jason, despite the oath, failed to take part in the Harpers Ferry attack. Mary and the boys in these later years always gave John their respect and they could not be said to have defied him. Rather, they denied him the blind obedience of the past when his commands were heeded as the prerogative of a husband and parent. Watson expressed it when he blurted out to his father:

> "Trouble is, you want your boys to be as brave as tigers and still afraid of you."

As long as he could, John held tight reins over his household—his animals, too. During their Akron sojourn he was greatly vexed by a horse he could not break. As they started for church one morning, he ordered Mary to mount a pillion behind him on the animal. Knowing how intractable and dangerous the horse was, strong-minded Mary refused. But eventually she had to give in. She was thrown twice. Setting her mouth as firmly as her husband's she resolutely dusted herself off each time and silently remounted. The two rode on together and were only a few minutes late for the opening hymn.

The Browns' migrations took them to Richfield in 1842. It was about twelve miles from Hudson, near enough for John to keep in touch with an integration agitation that racked the village. That year, when members of Hudson's Congregational Church objected to Negroes seated beside them, Owen Brown, a deacon, led in forming the "Free," or "Seceder," Church. It also was known as the Oberlin Church, for its endorsement by Oberlin College abolitionists.

A small building was erected at a corner of the green, now a much-altered structure housing an ornamental ironworks. Fiery anti-slavery rallies addressed by the Browns, Frederick Douglass, and others were held here until differences were healed a few years later, the "Free" Church was dissolved, and the parent organization rejoined.

Mary, who was twenty-six and expecting her seventh child, Austin, was too busy to enter the strife. John was bankrupt, stripped by law of most of his livestock. He could retain only two mares, two cows, and two hogs, ten sheep, and nineteen chickens.

The court allowed him to keep eleven Bibles, two religious treatises, three pocket knives, and some miscellaneous items. With these, and a few other chattels, Mary and John were starting anew.

The first home in Richfield was a log structure. Mary had barely time to arrange their few possessions before Austin was born. In the two years in Richfield she moved twice again.

Captain Nathaniel Oviatt, one of the leading citizens, employed John as a shepherd. From its founding, the village was a sheep center and derived its name indirectly from these animals. A variety of grass particularly good for sheep grew so "richly" in the fields that Richfield seemed a natural appellation.

The Browns had been here a year when catastrophe struck. John was in New England, ostensibly concerned with sheep and wool, but also developing contacts with important abolitionists. More and more the Negro cause was absorbing him.

Meanwhile, early in September, Mary was confronted with a houseful of very sick children. Six-year-old Charles died. Neighbors procured a coffin, dug a grave in the cemetery, and stayed with her as the small body was lowered into the ground.

Three other children grew steadily worse. Someone sent for Mrs.

Mason Oviatt, her husband being related to the man for whom John worked. Pioneer women "did" for each other in times of trouble. Mrs. Oviatt was known affectionately as "Aunt Fannie" for her ready ministrations.

She lived some miles away and negotiated the rough mud roads by horseback. When she reached the Brown home, Peter, three, was dead, followed by Sarah, nine, the next day. Sarah was Mary's first-born and already a joy as a "mother's helper." Before September was finished, baby Austin died, a week after his first birthday.

Again Mary's neighbors took charge, helped her lay three little bodies in one coffin, bigger than the first, and placed it in a fresh grave beside the one of a fortnight earlier.

A single headstone marks the children's resting place in the lovely hillside cemetery, now called Fairview. Beneath their names is this dimming inscription:

> Through all the weary world of death
> In peaceful slumber may you rest.
> And when eternal day shall dawn
> And shades of death have passed and gone
> Oh, may you then with glad surprise
> In God's own image wake and rise.

The disease that smote the children is described usually as dysentery, which is what John called it when reporting the tragedy to John, Jr., in a letter.

Aunt Fannie disagreed. She always insisted the children died of "black diphtheria," according to her granddaughter, the late Miss Jennie Oviatt, a lifelong resident of Richfield. Considering that John was not at home, and Aunt Fannie was present throughout the ordeal, her testimony would seem to be more reliable.

Worn out by nursing and grief, Mary almost died. She was pregnant again. Her next baby, Anne, was born three months later, two days before Christmas. The birth did not interfere with any holiday celebration, for John's Puritan conscience disapproved of such festivity.

The following year, 1844, Mary and the children were uprooted once more. John concluded the most auspicious business venture of his career—partnership with Colonel Simon Perkins, Jr., a wealthy man of Akron. His father, General Simon Perkins, one of the founders of Akron, owned extensive Ohio lands. John was to take charge of Perkins' 1,500 sheep pastured on hills that now overlook rubber factories. Also, he was to act as commission merchant for the wool produced.

Best of all, from Mary's point of view, they were given a good home, now the property of the Summit County Historical Society. Well might John exult: "this is the most comfortable and most favorable arrangement of my worldly concerns that I have ever had."

Sorrow invaded the idyllic situation. Mary's ninth child, Amelia, born the first year at Perkins Hill, fell into a tub of wash water and was scalded fatally. John was away this time, too.

Two weeks after the funeral Mary had his letter:

> This is a bitter cup, but blessed be God . . . Divine Providence seems to lay a heavy hand and burden on you, my dear Mary; but I trust you will be able to bear it in some measure as you ought. I exceedingly regret that I am unable to return . . . to share your trials with you.

He hoped no undue censure would devolve on Ruth, Dianthe's daughter, who was caring for the baby when the accident befell her. She was helping Mary—help most needed—for Mary had had a new baby the previous month. The new baby was christened Sarah for Mary's first-born, one of the four left behind in Richfield.

After tending flocks for two years on Akron hills, John opened a wool headquarters office for Perkins & Brown in Springfield. He was away from home so much that he decided to transfer his family to the eastern city. Mary went through the well-known routine of boxing and bundling her humble store of goods for the faraway abode.

The dwelling John selected was "a small wooden building on a back street" in an undesirable part of town, as noted by Frederick Douglass. The eloquent former slave had been in touch with John since first meeting him with his father, Owen, in Hudson.

The Springfield house contrasted sharply with the impressive warehouse. The Browns' furniture "would have satisfied a Spartan . . . There was an air of plainness about it which almost suggested destitution" to Douglass.

The Negro did not know that money had been allocated for furnishings. For once, at long last, Brown could afford such expenditures. The flock of Saxony sheep he had fostered in Akron was reputed the finest in the country and worth $20,000. The warehouse was receiving large shipments from woolgrowers . . .

Calling Mary and the children to him in the bare sitting room,

John put his proposition to them: should they spend this money for their own comfort, or send it "to the poor blacks." With the Franklin Mills pledge in their memories, of course the blacks won.

Meals that Mary set out, Douglass found, were such "as a man might relish after following the plow all day, or performing a forced march of a dozen miles over rough roads in frosty weather." Everything suggested "stern truth, solid purpose and rigid economy . . . he [John Brown] was indeed master of it [the home] and was likely to become mine if I stayed long enough with him . . . His wife believed in him and his children observed him with reverence . . ."

The prosperous interlude was brief. Growers remonstrated at their wool piling up in the warehouse unsold. John was a better shepherd than merchant. Untrained in trade and price fluctuations, he involved the company in a series of disastrous deals. Perkins seems to have viewed with singular equanimity Brown's financial escapades. He concluded, as many before him had, that Brown had no head for money matters.

Doubtless sensing breakup of the partnership as inevitable, Brown looked about for another beginning. In his associations with eastern antislavery groups, he had become acquainted with Gerrit Smith, northern New Yorker, philanthropist, and landowner, who had strong convictions as to his obligations to God and the Negro.

Smith inherited a great primeval tract of thousands of acres in the Adirondack country. He offered plots to "worthy colored people" and escaped slaves, hoping they would clear the land, lay out farms, and generally find this an opening for profitable existence.

Brown called on Smith at his home in Peterboro, New York, and proposed to live among the colonizing Negroes, to oversee and guide their homesteading and their welfare in general. Smith was overjoyed at the prospect of co-operation from John, practical farmer and well-tried pioneer, and, to boot, a man as devout a Christian and as ardent an abolitionist as himself. He sold John and his sons, Jason and Oliver, two farms of over two hundred acres. The price was one dollar an acre.

The property was near North Elba, Essex County, three miles south of the present village of Lake Placid. It was land untouched by civilization, remote and inaccessible, with practically no passable roads leading to it. But John Brown would make North Elba known to the whole world!

Deciding to look over the new holdings, John took Mary and the current infant, six-months-old Ellen, as far as Whitehall, New York, where he left them at the home of Mary's brother. The outing was a rare treat for Mary. But it had its sad consequences.

Ellen contracted a cold and by the time they were back in Springfield she had developed what the jargon of the day labeled "quick consumption." John was at home this time untangling wool warehouse accounts. He walked the floor with his sick little girl, called her "kitten" endearingly, and sang hymns to her. She came to know his step. One day she reached her thin little arms to him as he entered the room. He picked her up, pillow and all, and she died as he held her.

His daughter Ruth described how her father broke down and sobbed. There is no record of what Mary did. Chances are she was more stoical. After all, she had more experience burying babies than he.

They were planning to depart for the new home in the north. Mary could not bring herself to leave Ellen's body, so it was interred temporarily in a vault and later removed to North Elba. It was the first burial in this now historic site.

A cold spring rain was falling when John Brown first took his wife and children to the property he had selected amidst untenanted mountains. The air was damp with a penetrating chill. Mists hung in every valley. Rain dripped from the massed dark pines.

John had piled his family and their few belongings into a sturdy wagon behind a yoke of plodding oxen. These were replaced on the way by a span of spirited horses. He hired as driver a colored man who was en route to take up Gerrit Smith land also. He was a cautious teamster, but the bumping over treacherous mountain roads alarmed the children.

Characteristically, Mary made little comment. John sensed her mood. She was wishing them all back in the Springfield home, plain and austere though it was.

To divert his companions John spoke of the perfume in the air from spruce, hemlock, and balsam. He stopped the wagon at foaming mountain streams to cup water for them to drink. He enthused over the scenery. Finally, to these paeans Ruth summoned a response.

"The view IS grand!" she conceded.

The available shelter was a tiny house, its main room "answering for kitchen, dining room and parlor." There was a pantry and two bedrooms, one equipped with four beds so that wayfarers might be accommodated. The unprepossessing cabin challenged even John's ingenuity to find space for everyone.

"The house is small," he admitted. "Main thing is for us all to keep good natured."

Next morning the sun was shining and spirits rose. Before noon a weary young fugitive slave, who had tramped cautiously all the way from Florida, came to the door. His name was Cyrus. He was welcomed as one of the family. That made ten in the little house.

Although matters were not going well for Perkins & Brown, the partnership held for several years. John Brown frequently had talked about going to England to market their wool in that country. In August, 1849, he proceeded on this ill-advised junket. British buyers rejected the American product. What he did dispose of was sold at ruinously low prices.

He crossed to the continent to study fortifications in Paris, Brussels, and the Waterloo battlefield. Though he referred to these excursions later in connection with his Harpers Ferry strategy, he could have absorbed little in his brief stops.

In October he was back in New York bringing most of his consignment with him, unsold. Resultant losses ran to an estimated $40,000.

While he was abroad, Mary, with children of varying ages to care for, was in charge of the farm's meager harvest and the blooded cattle John had imported. In addition, she faced constant problems concerning the Negroes for whom homesteading never was a success.

The burden overwhelmed her and her health gave way. She wrote John, Jr., that she was down to 142 pounds. In an age that knew nothing of the svelte figure, this was cause for concern. She betook herself to Northampton, Massachusetts, to a water cure establishment, a popular and much-patronized therapy. The proprietor was a Negro, David Ruggles, who had been a leader among members of his race in New York City. He befriended many escaping slaves, among them Frederick Douglass. It was through Douglass Mary learned of the place.

After Brown's return, unfinished business of Perkins & Brown confronted him on every hand. Perkins liked John. He admired his way with sheep, his ability to spot a poor one in a flock, to nurse to vigor a half-dead valuable lamb.

Despite the tumbling finances of their partnership, the long-suffering Perkins was reluctant to dissolve it. Its affairs now called

John back to Akron. His family had to make ready for the road again.

Mary was not sorry to go.

Ruth stayed in the Adirondacks, for she had married a local farmer, Henry Thompson. An early riser, he got his wife up before daybreak to prepare breakfast—a man to win approval of his father-in-law!

Writing to his son, John, Jr., from Akron in 1852, the father remarks about Ohio peach and apple crops and the weather . . . and adds casually:

> Your mother was confined by the birth of the largest and strongest boy she ever had, two weeks ago, and has got along well considering our difficulties. The little one took measles and was very sick and now has whooping cough so bad we expect to lose him.

The boy died before he could be named. Everyone in the family was ill, Mary taken with "bleeding of the lungs," in bed "now and then, but manages to be about a good deal and get much done." As he wrote, John himself "had fever and ague" which afflicted him often and contributed to his premature aging.

Two years later Mary's last child arrived—her thirteenth, John's twentieth. They named her Ellen in memory of the Ellen they had lost.

New babies were old stories to John Brown. In a long letter to his older children he discusses Kansas and free-soilers, refers to correspondence with certain prominent people, and with a colored family he is interested in. He finishes:

> We have a new daughter five days old, Mother and child doing well to appearances.

North Elba, never out of John's mind, now beckoned once more. In 1855 the wandering Browns set out for what would be their permanent base. From this date until Mary's widowhood, and afterward for four years, the outpost in the Adirondacks was home for all of them.

Their house, of flimsy construction, had four rooms with a dormitory loft. It was erected by Thompson and was unplastered and unfinished on their arrival. Life unfolded for Mary on as primitive a scale as if this were a century earlier.

The Browns had endured frontiering in Ohio and Pennsylvania, but no such poor land or harsh climate had confronted them.

The plow fought tree stumps. Winter lingered for six months. Certain grain products, like corn, never ripened. Mountain grandeur was all about, and hillsides were so eroded that crops scarcely could be coaxed out of the thin soil.

Transportation bogged down completely in bad weather. Inhabitants depended on their ingenuity to supply necessities. Mary got out her spinning wheel and loom, set up a cavernous iron kettle in the dooryard for hog butchering and rendering, tapped the maple trees for syrup, milked the cows, and gave thanks when she could hang a side of beef. Her husband's herds thrived on the steep slopes that supported little else.

John Brown shook off the encumbrances of the commercial world for which he was so ill-fitted and plunged zestfully into the rough life. He was at heart a pioneer.

The chronic hunger for roaming that never stayed long dormant began to goad him. One matter particularly upset his contentment. Five of his sons—Dianthe's John, Jr., Jason, Owen, Frederick, and Mary's Salmon—were in Kansas, the territory recently opened to colonizers. John wanted to see these far-off lands.

Letters from his boys in Kansas whetted John's longings, and one from John, Jr., brought him to a decision. The son reported the territory stirred to fever pitch over the Kansas-Nebraska Bill passed the previous spring (1854.) It permitted settlers to determine the slavery issue in the territories and voted them into the Union either as free or slave states.

John, Jr., wrote that they needed Minié rifles and revolvers to defend themselves and the cause of the Negro against proslavery "scoundrels who would fasten slavery on this glorious land by any means, fair or foul . . ."

That was rhetoric the father could not resist: fresh, empty land to explore; reunion with his boys from whom he never liked to be separated; above all, his cause and God's, summoning him in the name of the downtrodden slave . . .

Mary laid a simple meal on the table. The family and three Negro hands took their places, John seating himself last. He was absent-minded. The letter from Kansas that had come the day before, he laid beside his plate, stroking it with his work-roughened hands. Suddenly he focused his penetrating eyes on those about him. He announced he was going to Kansas. Straight off!

He departed in August (1855) when summer green softened the rocky slopes and the landscape lost some of its bleakness in the sunshine. For nearly four years he would give himself to this self-assumed mission of keeping Kansas and adjoining western territories free from slavery. He would spend his energies either maneuvering in the West, or traveling about in the East and Middle West, back and forth from New England to Chicago, raising funds and winning supporters for Freedom. He would be home very little—on one trip he was away almost a year and a half. But Mary would seldom be out of his thoughts. He wrote to her regularly, more often than she to him. Letters were not one of Mary's accomplishments. Besides, most of the time she had no idea where to address her husband. John Brown was associated with many women in the promotion of his cause. But there was never so much as a hint that his interest or loyalty ever wandered to anyone but Mary, the wife he left in their lonely northern homsestead.

These Kansas years were a prelude and preparation for the climax of John Brown's life, the thrust on Harpers Ferry, for which he paid with that life. Details and locale were not formulated immediately, though in his own mind Brown was committed from the first to armed intervention. This conviction he was careful never to divulge. When he asked for donations, he omitted mention of bayonets or bullets.

Henry Thompson had gone with John to Kansas. His brother, William Thompson, soon followed. Oliver went. Mary, though inured to giving up, found it hard to say good-by to him, her youngest living son.

It was October before John reached his sons' makeshift shanties at Osawatomie. He was exhausted in strength and funds. The young Browns were worse off, shivering in cutting winds, too ill to gather their poor crops. John wrote to Mary of their troubles, aggravated by lawlessness everywhere rife. Lest she bemoan her situation, he wanted her to know "those here are not altogether in Paradise."

In their faraway citadel, Mary and Watson faced the winter. It swept in early and stayed late bringing sub-zero temperatures, piling snow in drifts that clogged roads and lanes. The ill-built house was poor protection, a fact John seemed to have sensed. He wrote Mary "regretting the cold house" and sympathizing "with your widowed state." But, he reminds her, "the lot of the slave is worse."

Money is scarce, he tells her. What he has must go mostly to the Negro. Mary will make the best of what he can spare her. He is sending her a barrel of good flour. He cautions her to dig the potatoes "sparingly" and not "waste the hay."

John was "Captain Brown" now, or "Osawatomie Brown." From his letters and scanty newspaper accounts, Mary pieced together a bewildering concept of her men in Kansas "defending Lawrence," abetting fugitive blacks in Missouri, ever on the alert against mysterious "Border Ruffians."

Shattering news that she could not comprehend came to Mary. Garbled versions trickled through to North Elba of the Pottawatomie slaughter (May, 1856). In dark of night, five men, proslavery settlers, were routed from their beds and into their dooryards by John Brown and his sons. The settlers, clad in their night clothes, with no opportunity to defend themselves, were dispatched with saber and gunshot. Though John subsequently attempted to dodge responsibility and vindicate the massacre, he had ordered and planned the deed, whether or not he actually participated in the killings. The affair has left an indelible stain on his name that his most ardent advocates cannot eradicate.

To Mary, Pottawatomie was only a faraway place, vaguely associated with some terrible occurrence involving her husband and sons, until Salmon returned shortly to North Elba, and reported firsthand what had happened . . . John, Jr., washing the blood from his sword in Pottawatomie Creek, was sickened to temporary insanity . . . Young Oliver and Frederick turned away in revulsion, their hands clean—as Salmon's were not—of the carnage. . . .

The gruesome doings in Kansas were on their minds, but neither Salmon nor Mary discussed the subject at any length. Salmon shied away from memory of its horror. Mary was not given to talk.

Salmon and Watson were digging potatoes one October day when they learned of fresh violence in Kansas. Frederick, their brother, had been attacked—killed—at Osawatomie as he walked out unarmed to feed his horses. It was proslavery revenge for the Pottawatomie outrage in which he, ironically, had not taken part. His brothers dropped their shovels, left their big rush basket half filled with tubers, and made ready to go at once to Kansas.

Now there was no man at North Elba. Mary was in charge, left to care for the farm and the young women and children living with her and depending upon her. Two Thompson women, the stalwart Ruth, wife of Henry, and her sister-in-law, wife of William, with their husbands in Kansas, brought their babies. Watson's girl wife was here and Mary's baby, Ellen, and her two other little girls. The small cabin was near to bursting.

Winter was coming on apace, a hard winter. Warm clothing and food had to be found for them all, and fodder for the animals. Mary did not falter.

From travelers stumbling on the Brown home when wandering in the pathless region, a picture of Mary emerges. Her house was immaculate, despite overcrowding. No conveniences. Simple food in frugal quantity. A spotless white cloth on the table. Ruth Thompson, her deputy manager, devoted to her, as were all Dianthe's children. In the background, Mary, reserved, taciturn, overseeing everything. In neat, shabby dress, she was gaunt as an oak ravaged by many gales—and as unbowed.

John was on the move in "the Kansas Territories," or crisscrossing the country, exhorting before antislavery conventions in New York State, conferring with New England abolitionists, in Chicago one week, Cleveland the next, then on to Rochester, Philadelphia . . . there were frequent stopovers in Hudson, usually at the beautiful home of his brother Jeremiah, his unfailing ally. In Canada he held his Chatham Convention and put on paper its fantastic "Provisional Constitution," basis of a "free" United States. In these peregrinations he covered thousands of miles, a feat in that epoch of uneasy travel difficult to appreciate in the jet age.

He talked about his heaven-ordained assignment to rescue the slave before audiences who felt the same way about their own activities. If Pottawatomie crimes were mentioned, which was seldom, for they were not widely known, they could be shrugged off, glorified as bloodletting atonement for the sin of slavery, or as justifiable defense of free-soilers.

Brown was a striking figure. He was stooped from hard work and his rigorous life. His beard, the lines of weather and weariness in his face, all made him appear an old man. And he was only fifty-nine when he was hanged, in 1859. Under bushy brows his eyes glinted with a fanatic's fire. His worn, countryish clothes, abstemious habits, and his firm convictions won admiration and set him apart.

Welcomed in New England parlors, he counted as friends men and women like Theodore Parker, Wendell Phillips, Ralph Waldo Emerson, Lucretia Mott, Lydia Maria Childs, Horace Greeley, Henry D. Thoreau, F. B. Sanborn, Bronson Alcott, and his two most generous endorsers, Gerrit Smith and George L. Stearns.

Meanwhile, Mary carried on at her humble station, unacquainted and unconcerned with such notables . . . Her husband sent her $150 one time, telling her to buy a team of oxen with it, and to spend the balance on any debts she might have. Actually, this was a generous sum. John Brown was plagued eternally with lack of funds. Large sums were pledged to him, but invariably fell short of fulfillment. What he did acquire disappeared quickly as his aggressive program gained momentum.

Early in the fateful year of 1859, he left Kansas for the last time. During his sojourn there, while rustling cattle, leading escaping slaves to safety, and dodging posses out to arrest him, he had enlisted recruits for the "blow." Back in the East he conferred with committees and conspirators, drilled his "soldiers" in his own manual of arms.

He did not reach North Elba until April, and then for only a brief stay. He soon took to the road again.

Time was running out. Brown was looking nostalgically toward his mountain home. In June he wrote to Mary from Boston that he was "very confident of success" and that he soon would be home.

The intrigue afoot he shared at least in part with Mary, according to later statements of their daughter Annie. She overheard her parents in a whispered discussion mention armed assault, naming Harpers Ferry as the place. Her father swore her mother to secrecy, and Annie herself conscientiously kept her counsel.

However much he divulged to his wife, Brown's design was now complete. He planned an attack against the United States Arsenal at Harpers Ferry, Virginia (now West Virginia), located on a strip of land between the Potomac and Shenandoah Rivers.

He envisioned it would be a signal for Negroes everywhere to rush to his banner. He confidently expected colored men from the North and Canada to augment his forces that then would sweep into the South. Slaves, overthrowing masters and fleeing from plantations, would swell his ranks. Such an army would march on victoriously to cut a swath of freedom across every slave state and end human bondage forevermore.

After a few days John left home—for the last time. There is no record of the farewells between husband and wife, though one can be certain both had emotions well under control.

Brown's band of young men, foot-loose and ready for adventure, had no true understanding of where this odyssey would end. One of the men at Harpers Ferry on that fatal night declared, too late, he would have withdrawn had he realized the siege was against federal property and therefore traitorous. The Brown sons, Oliver, Owen, and Watson, were there because of the family covenant long ago in Ohio, which had influenced even the youngest of them.

A few weeks after leaving Mary, John Brown and his men were reconnoitering in Maryland on his country's Independence Day. They rented a farmhouse belonging to Widow Kennedy five miles from the "Ferry," representing themselves as coal miners. Guarding their identity and intentions, Brown and his sons masqueraded under the name of Smith.

Once in the farmhouse, John wanted his wife with him. He realized the importance of having women in the household to avert suspicion and curiosity of neighbors. Not willing to trust the mails, he sent Oliver to North Elba with a plea that Mary make him "a visit of a few weeks . . . I don't see how I can get along without you." If she could not come, he "would be glad to have Martha [Oliver's wife] and Annie come . . . You will have no more exposure than at North Elba."

He directed her to bring only her "plain clothes and a few sheets and pillow cases . . . Have your bag, or bags, marked 'I. S.' plain. I want you to come right off. It will likely to prove the most valuable service you can render the world. Do Not consult your neighbors at all about it . . ." The signature was: "Your affectionate husband, I. Smith."

Mary refused to go! Perhaps her husband's statement that she would "have no more exposure than at North Elba" carried too faint reassurance. She saw the girls off with Oliver, giving them a letter for her husband in which she wished him "success in your great and good cause."

The girls served faithfuly and well during the hot Maryland summer. Martha, who was seventeen, was cook. Annie, sixteen, acted as sentinel. She was keen-eyed and vigilant against prying outsiders or a casual passer-by.

Except for essential errands, the men hid in cramped, stifling quarters inside the small house during daylight, and relaxed only after dark.

Finally, the moment was at hand. Annie and Martha were sent home.

Brown staged his attack on Sunday (no Sabbath scruples now) October 16, 1859 . . . Mary and the young women, tense and worried at North Elba, were stunned at the bulletin that reached them a few days later:

> Osawatomie Brown, commanding 21 men stormed the Harpers Ferry armory and held it for two days until a detachment of United

States Marines under Col. Robert E. Lee overcame Brown and his "liberators." . . .

The gunfire at the Ferry had summoned no free Negroes to John's defense. One, Frederick Douglass, John had counted on, went to Canada. No slave deserted his owner. No groundwork of advance contact or publicity had been laid, and few Negroes, free or slave, knew anything about the assault. Five of John's men were colored, two from Oberlin, Ohio. One of them, John A. Copeland, Jr., later executed, was described by one onlooker as the bravest and manliest of the outfit.

What all this meant for Mary and the women around her at North Elba gradually formed in their consciousness: Mary's husband, badly hurt, fatally, it was announced at first; her two sons, Watson and Oliver, wounded—she did not know immediately that Oliver was already dead, Watson dying; others in the "army" dead or wounded; townspeople and Marines on the casualty list . . .

During the fighting, Oliver, desperately wounded, had begged his father for a shot to end his agony. John, trapped, but not yet vanquished, shouted back: "If you must die, die like a man!"

Oliver crawled for comfort to Watson, also in intense pain. A coward's bullet had caught Watson as he emerged from the arsenal carrying a white flag of truce. He died twenty-four hours later, propped on overalls improvised as a pillow by a Baltimore newspaper reporter on assignment there. Twenty years later the reporter, C. W. Tayleure, wrote John, Jr., of the episode, remarking on Watson's calm courage. "I did my duty as I saw it," he had said. John, Jr., forwarded the letter to Mary. It was a solace to her. Watson's body had not yet been found.

With the whole country, Mary followed her husband's short trial, the proceedings spread on the newspapers of the nation. John Brown, who recovered quickly from his wounds, won the respect even of his captors by his poise and obvious sincerity.

He forbade his lawyers to introduce a petition for his release on the grounds of insanity. The document was drawn up by friends in Hudson who had known him since boyhood and stated that frequently he had shown a streak of madness. Among the nineteen signatures was that of Dianthe's brother, Milton Lusk.

In a long letter to Mary, John recounted events of Harpers Ferry, the death of their sons, Oliver and Watson, his own saber cuts. "I have been tried and found guilty of treason and of murder in the first degree." Nonetheless, he felt "quite cheerful in the assurance that God reigns." He added in a postscript: "Yesterday Nov 2d I was sentenced to be hanged on Decem 2d next. Do not grieve on my account. I am still cheerful. God bless you all."

Brown spent the month of his imprisonment writing letters. They went to all parts of the country—to his family, to relatives, and in reply to messages from admirers everywhere. This correspondence, carried on in the steady hand of an undaunted crusader, did more than all his forays to win approbation for him and his cause.

For the moment Pottawatomie and other questionable acts were forgotten. From the Olympian heights of Concord, Emerson expressed the attitude of the antislavery North when he called Brown:

> That new saint . . . who will make the gallows glorious like the cross.

His execution was to clothe John Brown in the white robes of martyrdom and assure him the spotlight of history forever.

The prisoner had not seen his wife since his last visit to North Elba the previous June. He stifled his desire to have her come to him because it "would tend to distract her mind tenfold; and would only add to my affliction." Besides, it "will use up the scanty means she has to supply Bread & clothing, fuel &c. for herself and children through the winter."

However, she set out early in November. She had got as far as Philadelphia before John Brown heard of it. He sent word to her "for God's sake" not to proceed. Friends of her husband rallied to her and have recorded their impressions of her at this time:

> She is tall, large and muscular . . . her frame seemingly capable of great strength and long endurance . . . She was sober, rather than sad, her manner singularly quiet and retiring . . . Notwithstanding the cares . . . and her many privations . . . she appears as fresh and hale as if in the prime and vigour of life.

While waiting to go to her husband she was a guest of the Quaker abolitionists James and Lucretia Mott, and wrote to her children that "I expect to stay untill [sic] your dear father is disposed of. O what a terrible thought. But may the God of all peace be with us as he is with him. he writes very comforting letters."

Facing execution, John concentrated on penning instructions to Mary for their children's schooling. He reminds her that he "always expressed a decided preference for a very plain but perfectly practical education for both sons and daughters." They are to be trained "to be useful though poor . . . the music of the broom, washtub, needle, spindle, loom, axe, scythe, hoe, flail, should be first learned and that of the piano, etc., afterwards . . ."

In the meantime his precious interlude between life and death was two weeks spent before John informed Mary that she might come, but not until the end of the month:

> If you feel sure you can endure the trials and the shock . . . I should be most glad to see you once more . . .

Mary did not reach Harpers Ferry until November 30. The same day Colonel Lee returned to town at the head of an artillery unit to guard bridges and roads until after the execution. Rumors of schemes to free Brown and of threats to the peace had disturbed Virginia's jittery governor, Henry A. Wise.

Mr. and Mrs. J. M. McKim and another Philadelphia abolitionist accompanied Mary. Governor Wise had specified that John's wife alone could visit him in Charles Town, where he was held and where the execution was to take place.

It was now December 1, the last full day of life for John. At three in the afternoon a carriage escorted by eight Virginia cavalrymen arrived to take Mary to the prison. The sergeant in charge rode inside with her.

During the eight-mile drive Mary sat very still, staring blindly at the cavalcade surrounding them. Clatter of horses' hoofs was the only sound. She and the sergeant had nothing to say to each other.

Mary entered John's cubicle. There was a swift embrace. Mary gave way for the first quick moment. Her husband held himself with a composure verging on the casual. He pushed up two chairs. The two seated themselves to talk, in a matter-of-fact fashion, of family affairs—her future, that of the remaining children, John's will, and of Mary's single asset, the North Elba property. . . .

The precious hours melted away. John's jailer, Captain John B. Avis, who had shown him unusual consideration and kindness, now invited Mr. and Mrs. Brown to have supper with him and his family in his quarters adjoining the prison. Whether or not the Browns were able to eat anything at this, John's last supper, is not divulged to posterity.

Darkness fell. Avis led the two back to Brown's cell. John had one final favor to ask of his jailer—that Mary be allowed to spend this last night with him in his cell. The governor had decreed that John Brown's wife must be back in Harpers Ferry that night. No women were to view the hanging next morning—if Mary stayed, she might have this gruesome privilege.

Captain Avis reluctantly refused his prisoner's request.

John burst into angry grief, the solitary instance of his losing his self-control. He quickly recovered his composure, however. Stout-hearted guards were almost undone by the couple's iron fortitude at their parting.

Mary walked out without glancing back and John turned to his writing. He finished a long letter to:

> My Dearly Beloved Wife, Sons; & Daughters, Everyone . . . I am waiting the hour of my public murder with great composure of mind & cheerfulness: feeling in no other possible way could I be used to so much advance the cause of God; & of humanity . . .

After a bit he fingered his papers into a neat pile and soon was asleep.

At dawn, with men all about beginning to stir, he was at his Bible. Before he mounted the scaffold he had time for two more communications. With his scratchy pen he wrote Mary a short note, enclosing what he had forgotten to give her on the previous day. It was a memorandum of the inscriptions he wished on the monument at North Elba where he had asked to be buried.

The second letter, the last one he wrote, was addressed to Hudson. The town where he had lived longer than in any one area was in his memory at the end. He was replying to good wishes from Lora Case, a Hudson farmer, eleven years his junior.

In young manhood John had been Case's Sunday School teacher. John was sending him one final injunction:

> May you ever prove yourself equal to the high estimate I have placed on you. Pure & undefiled religion before God & the Father is as I understand it: an active (not a dormant) principle. . . .

The shadow of the noose arched closer, but his bearing was unflinching. As he left his cell he turned to officials about him and handed one of them what his biographer, Oswald Garrison Villard, calls "his final, wonderfully prophetic and imperishable message":

> I, John Brown, am now quite certain that the crimes of this guilty land will never be purged away; but with Blood. I had as I now think: vainly flattered myself that without very much bloodshed: it might be done.

John Brown, martyr, had now become John Brown, oracle. Sixteen months later, his last words echoing across the land, the curtain went up on the War between the States. . . .

From his jail veranda he surveyed the crowds of soldiers in the streets. Never before known to jest, he permitted himself a bit of macabre humor: "I had no idea Governor Wise considered my execution so important!"

True to the condemned's vision, many of the troops would shed their blood over this beautiful countryside before many years passed . . . The future general, Thomas J. (Stonewall) Jackson, one of the most religious among them, gazing up to the man on the scaffold, dignified and inspiring despite his ill-fitting, sloppy clothes, prayed Heaven to spare him . . . And Stonewall would himself die in this state before four years were gone. One, standing with rifle on shoulder, member of a Richmond company, was J. Wilkes Booth, oblivious at that moment of Abraham Lincoln, then talking against a "country part slave," jockeying for next year's presidential nomination. That very week Lincoln was in John Brown's old stamping grounds—Kansas.

They all were more tense than the condemned man himself. On the way to the rope he seated himself, relaxed and at ease, on his coffin in the wagon drawn by two white horses.

Down from the conveyance he climbed with alacrity, and up to the gibbet. He shook hands pleasantly with those about him and said good-by . . . He whispered two final words to Avis—"Be quick!" . . . The military below him wheeled forward and back, and forward in formation . . . And John stood patiently under the black hood, waiting . . . It was December 2, 1859.

Mary was at a Harpers Ferry hotel. In her long vigil from wife to widow she shed no tears. Those around her could not restrain theirs.

Her hands, with their rough uneven nails, were clasped in her lap. She wore her best clothes: a cheap black dress, modeless and poorly fashioned, faded into a shiny green. A shapeless black bonnet sat on her un-grayed hair, combed as she always combed it, parted in the middle, drawn tightly back to a full knot at her neck. Work in the fields had tanned her face, sorrow lined, and softened it. Mary was only forty-three. She barely moved or spoke . . .

Earlier in the day Colonel Lee had called on her. As kindly as he could, he explained that she would be required to identify her husband's remains so there could be no charge of any irregularity.

Toward evening soldiers brought the heavy coffin to her. Respectfully, they lifted the lid. Mary, composed and silent, stepped forward. For a long moment she gazed at the limp form, so strangely inert and shrunken in the rumpled garments. She turned away, and nodded. It was the body of John Brown . . . she would never lose memory of his face as the agony of the rope had left it . . .

At least she was to have this much from the Harpers Ferry debacle. She had not yet been able to locate the bodies of Oliver and Watson.

Mary took the corpse of her husband to North Elba. Wendell Phillips and McKim were with her. It was a journey of five arduous days. The country was in an uproar over the death. Mourning mass meetings and rallies were held in many cities in the North—in New York, Rochester, Syracuse, Ravenna, and Cleveland. A packed Anti-Slavery Association gathering in Boston was one of the largest known in that city. Brown was vilified as much as venerated, a controversial figure—as he has remained.

A reception committee met the train in Philadelphia on the afternoon following the execution. Reactions were explosive, the crowds far from friendly. Mary and those with her who had expected to stay over Sunday were asked by the mayor to leave—for their own safety.

Lest harm befall the body, a ruse was resorted to, whereby an empty hearse was driven up while the coffin was carried secretly in another car to the wharf and shipped by boat to New York City. Here a Brooklyn undertaker took charge of the body. Mary was impatient to be rid of the coffin and all the trappings from hated Virginia. She wanted her husband to have better clothes, too. Mary paid $45 for the mortuary services according to this itemized statement:

Removal of body to the undertakers	$ 3
Keeping corpse on ice	8
Washing and laying out corpse	3
5 ft 10 Walnut coffin	16
Case for coffin	4
Lawn Shroud Cravat Collar	3
Removal to R.R. cars	3
Attendance with help	5
TOTAL . . .	$45

As the party proceeded, the going grew worse. It was no simple undertaking to transport a body in those days through the far north's December cold. They spent a night in Troy. Church bells tolled and people came out to honor them here, also in Rutland, Vermont, and Virgennes. They now were in country that had known John Brown. At Lake Champlain by good luck a special crossing was maneuvered, but at great hazard. Arriving exhausted at Elizabethtown, friends gave them lodging. The coffin was placed in the Courthouse. Volunteers stood guard over it through the night.

Mary still had reason to be apprehensive. She and her companions learned that the son of a local sheriff had galloped out ahead of them, like Paul Revere, warning the populace of their approach. It was disheartening that here, so close to home, there were rumblings against "Old Osawatomie."

A wagon and team were hired. The trio with their burden rode off at dawn for the last twenty-five miles to North Elba, hardest part of the trip. Roads, never good even in summer, were choked with snow and ice. At Keene a freezing rain made progress near to impossible. The North Elba cabin was not reached until dark that night, Wednesday, December 7.

Dependable Ruth, her husband, Henry Thompson, and Salmon welcomed the weary travelers. Mary's girls were there—Annie, Sarah, and little Ellen, solemn and wide-eyed, shocked at their father's homecoming like this.

Next day Wendell Phillips read the funeral tribute in the crowded little house. He was one of the great orators of the day and the occasion was worthy of his talents.

Six neighborhood youths bore the remains to a grave, which was dug a few rods from the cabin beside a huge boulder. A tombstone already was in place. Two years before, John had brought it from Connecticut where it marked the resting place of his grandfather, Captain John Brown, a Revolutionary War soldier. Frederick's name, recording his death in Kansas, was inscribed on it. John had instructed Mary to have his, Watson's, and Oliver's added.

Members of a colonizing Negro family sang a selection that John liked from Watts's Hymnal. Services were in the hands of the Reverend Joshua Young, of Burlington, Vermont, for which his congregation dismissed him.

Three other women widowed at Harpers Ferry stood beside Mary: Watson's and Oliver's wives and Mrs. William Thompson. Isabella, Watson's widow, also mourned her brothers, William and Dauphine Thompson, both shot down at the armory. The third Thompson brother, Henry, Ruth's husband, had gone with John to Kansas but not to the Ferry.

Tragedy granted Mary only a brief armistice. On a blustery night in early February Oliver's delicate wife, Martha, gave birth to a girl, who soon died. Oliver's death had crushed his wife and with the new sorrow she wasted away.

The small room where Martha lay was unplastered, partitioned off from the main house. Snow sometimes sifted in over the coverlet . . . Mary was a skillful nurse and cared for the girl like a daughter. Martha died a month after her baby. It was a double blow to Mary.

John Brown's faithful friend, Sanborn, made it possible for Annie and Sarah to attend school in Concord. Mary decided to visit the city. Watson's widow and her little son, Freddie, accompanied her. There were many followers and associates of John Brown in the vicinity to offer hospitality to his relatives.

The women emerged from their North Elba seclusion unprepared for the double-barreled attention beamed on John Brown. In this center of the antislavery movement denunciations of him were disconcerting and barbed, in sharp contrast to the mild pro and con reactions of the far North. Typical of one point of view met with was the gathering held some time before in Faneuil Hall that branded Harpers Ferry as an outrage. . . .

John Brown's name in praise and in censure was tossed from tongue to tongue, and Mary found herself caught in the web of his renown. Honors or invectives—she liked one as little as the other.

A reception was planned for Mary at the Bronson Alcott home in Concord. Alcott, loyal supporter of John, taught in Sanborn's School. Mary saw to it that Mrs. Watson Brown and son were also present.

Alcott's daughter, Louisa, had not yet published her juvenile classic, *Little Women,* but she was writing regularly. She often jotted down daily happenings in a journal. One entry reveals how fame affected Mary:

> It had got about that Mrs. Captain Brown was to adorn the scene and so, many people came who were not invited and had no business there . . . The two pale women sat silent and serene through the clatter. The bright-eyed, handsome boy received the homage of the multitude like a little king . . . Mrs. Brown Sr. is a tall stout woman . . . with a strong face and natural dignity and showed she was something better than a "lady" though she did drink tea out of her saucer. . . .

The Browns returned to North Elba, but tranquillity was not to be Mary's fate. Freddie died before he was four and Salmon lost two children. Salmon, the only son left to Mary, lived near-by. Like his father he raised blooded sheep. His wife, the former Abbie Hinckley, called their place "a lonesome hole" but could count blessings, like a fine yoke of oxen, a cow, and poultry. They were content "not realizing we were cut off from the usual comforts."

Her uncle disrupted all that. He came from California and could talk of nothing but the glories of that state. While Abbie cooked dinner in the fireplace of the cabin's one big room, the visitor put toe to the cradle and rocked her baby to sleep. To the steady rhythm he recited his glowing tales.

Salmon and Abbie listened—and succumbed. Mary caught the fever. She was growing tired of the struggle to drag a livelihood out of her rocky fields. Her girls were excited. After many family conferences they determined to risk their lot in climate milder than this one that, Abbie reminded them, was "six months winter and the other six months very cold weather."

Mary wanted to sell her property but could not find a ready buyer. It was summer, the summer of 1863. Salmon and Abbie were impatient to be on the way. Annie, twenty, and Sarah, seventeen, were in a school not far from North Elba, St. Edward's Institute, where Sarah was showing promise as the accomplished artist she later became. Mary decided to take Ellen and go west with the Hinckleys, leaving the older girls to follow.

They left in September, 1863. Lyman Epps, one of the Negro neighbors who had sung at John Brown's funeral, drove them in his wagon to the "steam cars" at Keene.

The country was torn by the bitter passions of the Civil War that John Brown's raid had helped whelp but which he had hoped it would prevent. During the very month his family was headed to new homes, nearly 4,000 Americans killed each other at Chickamauga, while 30,000 others were wounded or missing after the onslaught. Four years before, on the threshold of death, John Brown had seen beyond his gallows to this bloodletting. . . .

By now he had become a kind of symbol of it all, revered by Union sympathizers, reviled by Confederates and also by certain groups in the North, like the Copperheads. The flaming prejudices for and against him soared beyond anything Mary had encountered previously. She was to find this growing more furious the farther she traveled.

Men in blue were tramping to their death, or were whiling away campfire evenings to the song:

John Brown's body lies a-mouldering in the grave . . .
His soul goes marching on! . . .
Glory, halle, hallelujah. . . .

It mattered not—nobody knew or cared—that John Brown of the catchy march was not her John Brown but a sergeant-at-arms of that name in the Massachusetts Volunteer militia stationed early in the war at Fort Warren in Boston Harbor. He was the butt of much teasing because of his name. When someone in the company came up with the line that the real John Brown lies a-mouldering in the grave, it was seized on instantly by an organist among them, James E. Greenleaf. He tinkered with an old Methodist hymn and the stirring tune evolved from the original of William Steffe, of South Carolina.

The following year Julia Ward Howe, wishing to write more appropriate words for the popular melody, composed "The Battle Hymn of the Republic."

There are those who believe "John Brown's Body" did as much as Harpers Ferry and his hanging to advance the abolitionist to the forefront of history and to make him immortal.

Mary and the westbound travelers broke their trip with a few days' rest at Put-in-Bay, Ohio. John, Jr., and his wife had a good-sized farm there, as did Owen, a bachelor. They were enjoying modest prosperity raising grapes for the community wine industry.

Owen was the only one of the five to escape from the Ferry who did not enter the Union army. John, Jr., who was not in the raid, had enlisted for a short term. Now both were leading peaceful lives in this lovely Lake Erie island where Commodore Oliver Hazard Perry had routed the British navy fifty years before, that very month.

The North Elba contingent pressed on to Decorah, Iowa. Here they planned to spend the winter and to go on to California in the spring. The locale proved so attractive they considered staying permanently and contracted to buy land. Salmon had managed to transport some of his fine sheep. Mary wrote they were much admired, for "there is no such sheep in this country." He raised quail and other game for city markets. Ready money was hard to come by and his mother noted gratefully that Salmon "earned twelve dollars last week chopping cord wood, he gets six shillings a cord."

Dated January 31, 1864, this letter was written from Decorah to Owen, thanking him for his kindness to Sarah, who had stayed with him en route to Iowa.

The expedition to the West was opening Mary's eyes. She concludes:

> I very much regret that I ever spent a cent on that farm in North Elba but I did not know what I know now. I am in hopes of selling it sometime so as to get back part that I spent there.

The Browns liked Iowa, but the winter turned unprecedentedly cold. California looked better than ever. As soon as spring broke they started, their transportation three wagons drawn by ox teams. Salmon and his family were in the first. Mary helped drive the second, with Ellen, Sarah, and Annie, who by now had joined them. The third, hauling six valuable Merino sheep and a couple of cows, was in charge of two California-bound young men who earned their passage this way.

When the Browns reached Council Bluffs, Iowa, they found to their consternation that five hundred wagons milled about ahead of them in a seemingly endless line. They were waiting their turn at the ferry that would take them across the Missouri River to Omaha.

This meant a halt of several days, a drain on their diminishing assets. Mary was particularly straitened. She had relied on money from her North Elba property, but it was still unsold.

From time to time numerous and differing accounts have appeared in California publications about this overland safari of the Browns. All accounts agree, however, that the enterprise involved great hardship and just avoided being fatal for all of them.

The trail wound over such rough terrain that the wagons' roll often churned daily milk supplies to butter. The Browns were on the lookout for Indians on the warpath against the white invasion. Stories were bandied about of as many as two hundred emigrants scalped within recent months while en route over the plains.

Someone stood guard at every night encampment and vigilance was maintained by day. Nonetheless, marauding tribesmen ambushed them. But a caravan of eighty wagons came up and frightened off the attackers. The Browns now were invited to join the newcomers' wagon train, a better protection against the Indians.

The strangers were Southerners and were aghast when they learned the people they had saved were kin of "John Brown of Pottawatomie." At once they hatched a plot to murder them all—to mete out to all of them the same "justice" he had dispensed in Kansas.

Two men crept to Salmon's wagon after nightfall and warned them of the threat. He aroused his relatives. They snaked out their wagons and dashed off.

But the rebels were not to be cheated. They bolted after them. The Browns lashed their oxen to the breaking point—and held their lead. For a terrifying week they managed to elude their pursuers. But the latter were gaining on them steadily.

Three wagons of dust-covered, unnerved Browns thundered into the Union garrison at Soda Springs, Idaho, the oxen lathered and nearly done for. They were only three hours ahead of their foes.

Soldiers intercepted the Southerners and forced them to take an oath of allegiance to the United States. After the Browns had rested here in the compound for several days, they were given military escort for two hundred miles as they moved on.

"We reached Red Bluff, California, a hungry, almost barefoot, ragged lot of emigrants," Mrs. Salmon Brown wrote.

It was prelude to the first happy days in Mary's experience. Citizens of Red Bluff came to the aid of all of them, provided them with emergency food and clothes.

True, Mary's funds were practically vanished, but she had managed with so little so long she was an expert in the art. Soon a campaign was launched in California newspapers to provide her with a home. Contributions came from every corner of the state. A little cottage was built on Main Street and presented to her along with a sum of cash.

The house, with a single gable in front and a steep-pitched shingled roof, became a landmark in the town. Salmon bought a 128-acre ranch and pastured a flock of the best sheep he could buy. He bought them all on time and in two years he was out of debt.

Mary supported herself and her girls as a practical nurse. She was much in demand. In the spring of 1866 a burden was lifted from her with the sale of her North Elba farm. The purchaser was Alexis Hinckley, brother of Salmon's wife. The price was $700.

She reserved the plot where her husband was buried, about half an acre. With sagacious regard for the future she provided also for a "perpetual right to pass to and from" over the other part of the farm to the grave.

The property remained in private hands until taken over by the Division of Archives and History of the University of the State of New York, which now manages it. Thousands find their way here annually, for it has become an international tourist mecca.

Mary and the girls lived in the little house California gave them until 1870. The climate proved too hot for these women inured to the cold of northern New York State.

They sold the house reluctantly and moved to a cooler location in Rhonerville, California.

Mary had a garden that yielded food generously—nothing like the scant harvests of North Elba. She bought a cow and a thoroughbred horse. The tall woman sitting straight in her saddle was a familiar sight in the community. But she and her children held themselves aloof, for mention of John still precipitated arguments. He was either deity or devil. There were no halfway opinions about him.

Sarah, who never married, worked in the San Francisco mint for years and was Mary's dear companion. Sarah also was a painter of note. She persuaded Mary to move once more, this time to a mountain location. Ellen and her schoolteacher husband, James Fablinger, and their children lived here with them. Annie married and lived near-by.

They were not free of notoriety clinging to them as relatives of John Brown. Many Saratoga residents were natives of the South, among them Confederate veterans. The Civil War was as vivid as yesterday.

When word spread that the widow and children of John Brown were to be in their midst, the former Southerners sounded a hue and cry against them. There was the touch of mob violence in it.

The moment was one of cutting mortification and dark thoughts for Mary. Not one to retreat, she took possession of the new home as intended. Citizens beheld a poised, withdrawn woman marshaling a dignified, good-looking family and concentrating on her own affairs.

Tensions relaxed. Some who had been the most antagonistic became her fondest friends.

The Fablinger children, however, were disturbed and bewildered by references to their mysterious grandfather.

Counter it as she might, Mary was a conspicuous figure in the community. A San Francisco newspaper lost no time sending a reporter to see her. Queried about the fanaticism of her husband, Mary bristled: "He was anything but fanatic," she replied. "He was a clear-headed, sober-minded man in business and no less sober-minded if more pertinacious in his views on slavery. He abhorred the institution as a menace to the Union and for its wrongs against humanity."

She received the interviewer in her small parlor where she had hung an oval picture of John Brown, the pose where he stands full-bearded, with hands behind him under tails of a frock coat. It was a copy of the likeness he had given Thoreau. On either side she had a photograph of handsome Watson and of Oliver, with his smooth boy-face.

Mary hankered to see old haunts in the East, the grave at North Elba, relatives and connections in Ohio, members of her Day clan in Pennsylvania . . . She always had firm friends. Some of them, for her own sake and in memory of her husband, in 1882 presented her with funds for the journey.

She would have preferred to have made the trip without fanfare. But such a role was not possible for John Brown's widow. During a brief stop in Chicago, the *Tribune* ran an item about her presence in that city. Reading it, a Martinsville, Indiana, physician, Dr. Jarvis Johnson, was prompted to get in touch with Mary. He disclosed the amazing fact that he had Watson Brown's skeleton and would be willing to surrender it to her. He explained he had obtained it from a surgeon in Winchester, Virginia. The latter was given it by an officer of the Virginia troops immediately after Watson's death. In both cases the body was used for anatomical study and dissection, preserved carefully and marked with Watson's name.

John, Jr., went to Martinsville to investigate. He had studied phrenology and his measurements of the cranium satisfied him that this was his brother. He shipped the remains to his home in Put-in-Bay.

Mary came at once. Jason inspected the skeleton and verified John's conclusions. Owen hurried over from his vineyards and agreed this was Watson.

Mary was the center of an affectionate and attentive family of Browns gathered on the island at the time. They all were Dianthe's children. But they regarded her as their mother and she reciprocated, holding them as dear as her own. She leaned heavily on them in this extraordinary situation.

Mary wrote to Salmon about it:

> Sept 17th. The box that contains the remains of Watson was opened today. everything goes to prove it is pooer Watson. . . . Oh I am so thankful that God has spared my life to see this time.

She would take the remains to North Elba "to bury it beside of his Father . . . John is agoing with me."

Disclosure about Watson was flashed from coast to coast. The broadcasts resurrected Harpers Ferry and John Brown for the public. The furor headed up in Put-in-Bay. Residents clustered about the little building where John, Jr., had stored what was left of Watson. Mary summed it up in her letter:

> The country is all awake to the fact that one of John Browns Sons Should have been kept amongst them over twenty years . . . I wish I could get a newspaper to send you. It would tell you more than I could tell you.

She had not forgotten the other children she had lost. She told Salmon she would "go to the grave of six children in Richfield." She referred to the four buried in a single month of 1843 and two others in graves now unmarked, interred there following their deaths in Akron.

With forecasts of early winter, October had come to North Elba when Mary saw Watson placed beside his father, the man she had married almost fifty years before. Watson's widow, now Mrs. Salmon Brown, wife of Watson's first cousin, clung, arm-in-arm, to Mary.

All the Brown contingent accompanied her from Put-in-Bay. Their attention and support pleased Mary. But, mother-like, she wished "the rest of his brothers and sisters could be here . . ."

The tiny cemetery beside the great boulder contained the other Browns, Watson's little Freddie and Mary's first Ellen, John's "Kitten," the baby who died in Springfield.

Yet another grave would be dug here for a Brown—for Oliver. His body and those of several others killed at Harpers Ferry were wrapped in their shawls and buried in a common grave on the banks of the Shenandoah River. Forty years later, in 1899, the bodies were disinterred and Oliver at last was united with his own. But Mary was denied the consolation of this knowledge, for she was no longer living.

Experiences of the eastern tour had been gratifying, but a strain on her. Public receptions were held for her in many places—Boston, Springfield, Philadelphia . . . in Kansas, where, for the first time, she saw the battlegrounds that had figured so sensationally in her husband's life. Mary responded graciously . . . in her husband's name, discounting that she herself commanded respect and admiration as much as he.

She was happier in simpler hospitality, like that accorded her in Hudson. She stayed with the widow of John's brother Jeremiah, in the new house she had built near the center of the village. Hudson found Mary appreciative but diffident, better at listening to the conversation around her than contributing to it.

After return to California, she visited Salmon and his family on his sheep ranch in the north. Here she was taken ill with what developed into a "lingering and painful disease."

Dying was no easier than living had been.

She was lovingly watched over by Sarah and died in San Francisco. She lies in a beautiful cemetery in Saratoga, California, separated by a continent from John Brown.

The monument over her grave tells her story:

Mary
wife of John Brown
of
Harpers Ferry
Born April 15, 1816
Died February 29, 1884
"Enter thou into the joy of the Lord."

NOTES

Paul Laurence Dunbar

AMONG MANY PERSONS who helped me in preparing this chapter were two who knew the poet and his mother. One is Miss L. Pearl Mitchell of Cleveland, the other, Dunbar's niece, Mrs. Helen Murphy Gillim, of Dayton. Miss Mitchell, whose father, Samuel T. Mitchell, was president of Wilberforce College, Wilberforce, Ohio, as a girl went to Dayton to participate in a program honoring Paul Dunbar. He was already a very sick man, Miss Mitchell said. After giving his speech of appreciation, he hurried off the platform. Miss Mitchell, former probation officer and examiner, Juvenile Court, Cleveland, kindly read the manuscript and made numerous suggestions from her knowledge of the poet's life and work.

Mrs. Gillim contributed firsthand impressions of her Uncle Paul, whom she remembers with affection for his attention and gifts to her as a little girl. She was acquainted with Alice, who visited in Mrs. Gillim's parents' home. I have followed her interpretation of the rift between the poet and his wife as due basically to Alice's intolerance of the Dunbar mother complex, rather than to his drinking. This was not excessive, Mrs. Gillim contends, as many biographers depict. She added that both her grandmother, Matilda Dunbar, and Alice were strong-willed and possessive of Paul. Since Paul always wanted Ma to live with them, a clash was inevitable, though Alice and Paul were deeply in love, she believes. Mrs. Gladys Ware, curator of Dunbar House, and her husband, Marvin, were cordial and helpful in acquainting me with Dunbar background. Mrs. Diane R. Meyer, secretary to Charles C. Pratt, head of Division of Properties, Ohio Historical Society, supplied valuable material from the Society's files.

For an evaluation of Dunbar poetry, I am indebted to Loring Williams, of Cleveland, himself a poet who has published six collections of his own, and is editor of *The American Weave,* a member of the Board of Editors of the Book Club for Poetry, and past president of the Ohio Poetry Society. Granting that Dunbar's dialect verses have popular appeal, Mr. Williams feels "his prestige as a poet should rest on his formal pieces that depend neither on dialect or easy melody, but which have depth of thought and great poetic insight. His poem, 'Compensation,' for one, should be included in any comprehensive anthology of American poetry."

I wish to thank Dr. Charles H. Wesley, president of Central State College, Wilberforce, Ohio, for his suggestions. His booklet, "Negro Americans in Ohio" (1953) was a valuable source of general data.

Dr. James H. Rodabaugh, formerly of the Ohio Historical Society, now a member of the faculty at Kent State University, an authority on the Negro in Ohio, is author of several publications that have been used in this study, including his "The Negro in Ohio," (*The Journal of Negro History,* Volume XXXI, January, 1946) and "Paul Laurence Dunbar House," (*Ohio Historical Society's Museum Echoes,* XXIX, 1956).

Other publications consulted: "Paul Laurence Dunbar and William Dean Howells," by James B. Stronks (*Ohio Historical Quarterly,* LXVII, 1958); *Paul Laurence Dunbar and His Song,* by Virginia Cunningham (Dodd, Mead and Company, New York, 1948); *Paul Laurence Dunbar, Poet of his People,* by Benjamin Brawley (University of North Carolina Press, Chapel Hill, 1936); *Dunbar Critically Examined,* by Victor Lawson (The Associated Publishers, Washington, 1941); "Paul Laurence Dunbar," by C. A. McGinnis (*Negro History Bulletin,* May, 1942); *That Dunbar Boy,* by Jean Gould, Dodd, Mead and Company, New York, 1960; *The Life and Works of Paul Laurence Dunbar,* by Lida Keck Wiggins, Austin-Jenkins Company, Washington, D. C., 1907, and *Harper's Weekly,* June 27, 1896, containing the Dunbar criticism by Howells.

Poems quoted are from the numerous books and booklets published during Dunbar's lifetime, including *Oak and Ivy, Majors and Minors, Lyrics of Lowly Life, Lyrics of the Hearthside, Lyrics of Love and Laughter, Lyrics of Sunshine and Shadows. The Complete Poems of Paul Laurence Dunbar,* with an introduction by Howells to *Lyrics of Lowly Life,* was published in 1960 by Dodd, Mead and Company, New York.

Ulysses S. Grant

FOR MUCH OF the Georgetown story of Lyss Grant, I am indebted to J. W. Bier, owner of the Grant boyhood home, where he lives when not at his home in Miami, Florida. Mr. Bier, former writer on the local *News Democrat,* has spent years investigating Brown County and Grant lore. He has collected so many documents and photographs that he had to build a cabin to house them, in the

Brown County Fairgrounds at Georgetown, opening the display to the public during fair week.

I hereby express my thanks, also, to another Georgetown authority on Grant, John Markley, who contributed little-known details about Lyss.

My guide on Portage County history in many instances has been James B. Holm, of Kent, whose research developed the Prudence Hall-Jesse Grant courtship tale.

Personal Memoirs of U. S. Grant, two volumes (Charles L. Webster and Company, New York, 1885) contains details about his boyhood. Some of the facts about these years are unreliable, such as the statement that his father worked for "a Mr. Brown, father of John Brown," in Deerfield, the Browns' residence being Hudson.

Other publications consulted are *Captain Sam Grant,* by Lloyd Lewis (Little, Brown and Company, Boston, 1950); *Portage Heritage, History of an Ohio County,* James B. Holm, editor (Portage County Historical Society, Kent, Ohio, 1957); numerous articles touching on Grant's boyhood in publications of the Ohio Historical Society and issues of *Civil War Times,* Gettysburg, Pennsylvania.

Robert G. Ingersoll

ROBERT GREEN INGERSOLL's Ohio boyhood is described by Clara Caldwell Hubbard in an article in the *Cleveland Plain Dealer,* December 20, 1896, detailing his stopover in Ashtabula the previous April. While there on a lecture tour, he looked up former haunts and recalled earlier days with old friends. His reminiscences at that time confirm much of the lore that is abundant about him in this section of northeastern Ohio, where his father served as pastor of churches in Ashtabula, North Madison, and Rome. Robert Ingersoll refers to the Ashtabula visit in a letter a few days later, April 8, 1896. This is quoted in *Letters of Robert G. Ingersoll,* edited by his granddaughter, Eva Ingersoll Wakefield (Philosophical Library, New York, 1951).

Oberlin events of 1839, as well as John Ingersoll's varied connections with contemporaries prominent in Ohio and New York State, are largely from *A History of Oberlin College from Its Foundation Through the Civil War,* by Robert Samuel Fletcher (two volumes, Oberlin, 1943).

Also consulted were: *Cultural Story of an American City, Cleve-*

land, by Elbert Jay Benton (Western Reserve Historical Society, 1944); issues of the *Herald and Gazette,* 1839, at Western Reserve Historical Society Library; *Directory of Cleveland and Ohio, For the Years 1837–38; Cleveland, the Making of a City,* by William Ganson Rose (The World Publishing Company, Cleveland and New York, 1950).

In gathering data about the little-noted Ohio years of Robert Ingersoll I have had invaluable aid from many persons, including: Miss Ethel J. MacDowell, librarian, and Mrs. L. D. Artman, reference librarian, Ashtabula Public Library; Mrs. Arthur Kellogg, librarian, Madison Public Library; Walter H. Crosby and the late Mrs. Thaddeus Curtiss, both of Rome, Ohio.

Miss Harriet Carroll, Pittsburgh, during her former residence in Ashtabula, carried on extensive research about the Ingersolls and made her finds accessible to me.

Reverend Roger L. Robbennolt, minister of education at Oberlin's First Church, and Donald M. Love, secretary emeritus of Oberlin College, supplied details about John Ingersoll and his boys at Oberlin.

Lyon N. Richardson, director of Western Reserve University Libraries, put at my disposal *Beriah Green, the Reformer,* by Muriel L. Block, of Syracuse University, an unpublished thesis now at Freiberger Library of the University. It is the source of my data on the colorful Green.

I am indebted especially to Dr. C. H. Cramer, dean of Adelbert College, Western Reserve University, author of the definitive life of Robert G. Ingersoll, *Royal Bob* (The Bobbs-Merrill Company, Inc., New York and Indianapolis, 1951). Dr. Cramer reopened his notes and files on Ingersoll to answer my questions. He also shared with me correspondence since his book's publication that reveals for the first time the name of John Ingersoll's second wife, as well as the place and date of their marriage. The information was uncovered in records of the Probate Court of Lorain County, Ohio, by J. P. Reed, attorney, of Emmett, Idaho. Heretofore the only known reference to her was that in *The History of the First Presbyterian Church of Ashtabula,* published in 1939 by Reverend Robert H. Rolofson, D.D.: "Mr. Ingersoll married a local widow who had several children of her own."

Lastly, I am grateful to Dean Cramer for reading my manuscript and offering corrections and valuable suggestions.

Annie Oakley

ANNIE OAKLEY stepped from legend to life for me as I listened to her niece, the late Mrs. Annie Fern Swartwout, of Greenville, Ohio, talk about her beloved "Little Sure Shot." Mrs. Swartwout's treasured Annie Oakley souvenirs—guns and gay circus posters, marksmanship cups and costumes—are now in Greenville's Darke County Museum. I am indebted to the curator, Mrs. Gertrude Holzapfel, for Annie Oakley data. Local tales about the colorful Oakley-Butler team abound in this area and I have used many of them in this chapter.

Mrs. Swartwout published a book about her aunt: *Missie, Life and Times of Annie Oakley* (Brown Publishing Company, Blanchester, Ohio, 1947). The definitive biography is *Annie Oakley of the Wild West,* by Walter Havighurst (Macmillan Company, New York, 1954). This well-known author, in his usual delightful style, gives a vivid picture of the American Wild West show and circus of the Annie Oakley era. Another biography consulted is *Annie Oakley, Woman at Arms,* by Courtney Ryley Cooper (Duffield and Company, New York, 1927).

Woodrow Wilson

THE SETTING of this chapter is the former Thomas Woodrow house on South Paint Street, Chillicothe, Ohio, for many years the residence of Mr. and Mrs. Philip Butler, who have maintained it little altered from the way Woodrow's nephew, Thomas Woodrow Wilson, knew it. Mr. and Mrs. Butler generously turned over to me the stories and anecdotes they have collected about the house and the illustrious Woodrow and Wilson clans.

My authority for this story of Wilson's youthful romance is an article, "My Mother and Woodrow Wilson," by Harriet Woodrow's daughter, Helen Welles Thackwell, in the *Princeton University Library Chronicle* (Volume 12., No. 1, 1950–51). It is the basis for "Woodrow Wilson's First Romance," by George C. Osborn (*Ohio Historical Quarterly,* January, 1958).

Helpful in tracking down further details of this episode was the late David K. Webb, never-failing guide on the history and folklore of Chillicothe and Ross County. I express my thanks also to

Mrs. Ruth P. Story and Mrs. Violet D. Wissler, former and present curators, and Eugene D. Rigney, director, the Ross County Museum, Chillicothe, and to Mrs. Everett T. Perrin, librarian, Freiberger Library, Western Reserve University, Cleveland. Little attention is given this early love affair in formal biographies of Wilson, though brief reference is made to it in: *Woodrow Wilson, the Fifteenth Point,* by David Loth (J. B. Lippincott Company, Philadelphia-New York, 1941) and in *Woodrow Wilson, Life and Letters,* by Ray Stannard Baker (Doubleday, Page and Co., Garden City, New York, 1927).

Isaac M. Wise

I AM INDEBTED TO the late Rabbi Abba Hillel Silver of The Temple, Cleveland, a distinguished graduate of Hebrew Union College, for his kindness in reading this manuscript and for his corrections and suggestions. In Dr. Silver's student days, Rabbi Wise was already a legend, a campus personality held in reverent memory. His anti-Zionist views showed he was no prophet, according to Dr. Silver, who was past president of the Zionist Organization of America and chairman of the Jewish Agency of the World Zionist Movement in the United States. Dr. Silver, who built a home in Jerusalem, spent part of every year there.

I express my appreciation, too, to Dr. Jacob Rader Marcus, archivist, Hebrew Union College, who first interested me in Isaac Wise and supplied me with a wealth of material. I have made free use of two scholarly pamphlets by Dr. Marcus, "The Americanization of Isaac Wise" and "Isaac Mayer Wise and the College He Built." Both are Founders Day addresses given by Dr. Marcus at the college.

The chapter is based to a great extent on the writings of Rabbi Wise himself, including especially his *Reminiscences,* translated and edited by David Philipson (L. Wise and Co., Cincinnati, 1901) and *The World of My Books,* translated and edited by Albert H. Friedlander (offprint from *American Jewish Archives,* June, 1954).

Other sources include: *Isaac Mayer Wise, Founder of American Judaism,* a biography by Max B. May, A.M., Wise's grandson (G. P. Putnam's Sons, New York, 1916); *The Serene Cincinnatians,* by Alvin F. Harlow (E. P. Dutton and Company, Inc., New York, 1941); "Isaac Mayer Wise," a biographical sketch by Stanley F.

Chyet, of the faculty of Hebrew Union College, in *Ohio Authors and Their Books,* edited by William Coyle (The World Publishing Company, Cleveland and New York, 1962).

Thomas Alva Edison

THE BASIS for this chapter on Edison's Ohio boyhood is largely Edison lore collected over the years by the writer, in visits to Milan, Ohio.

Some of it is word-of-mouth stories handed down through the generations, or recorded in local newspapers.

I am particularly indebted to Wallace B. White, retired public school superintendent, whose long and careful research on Edison and Milan history have been the subject of some published articles; also, his pamphlet, "Milan Township and Village, One Hundred and Fifty Years, 1959."

The latter commemorates the sesquicentennial of the community. Much of Mr. White's material is in manuscript and in notes, all of which he generously shared with me. In addition, he read this manuscript, making numerous suggestions.

Also helpful and patient in answering my numerous questions have been Mrs. Ruth S. Esgar, librarian, Milan Public Library; Mrs. Marion Wheeler, of the Edison family, and Mrs. Edward Collister, of Milan, a descendant of early settlers.

Books consulted include: *Edison,* a biography by Matthew Josephson, (McGraw-Hill Company, New York, Toronto, London, 1959); *Cleveland, the Making of a City,* by William Ganson Rose (The World Publishing Company, Cleveland and New York, 1950).

Harman Blennerhasset

AS I FOLLOWED the Blennerhassett trail in Ohio and West Virginia, and as far away as Ireland and Guernsey Island, in preparation of *Plain Dealer Magazine* articles on the subject, many persons welcomed and aided me. Grateful acknowledgment is tendered: Mrs. Edith Reiter, former curator, and Mrs. Catherine Remley, her successor, of the Ohio Historical Society's Campus Martius Museum, Marietta, who gave me the advantage of their familiarity with this episode in Ohio Valley history and put me in touch with original manuscripts and relics of the island mansion in the museum collection; Miss Frances A. Inslee, of Parkersburg, West Virginia, for generously sharing with me her extensive information and accumulated memorabilia on the Blennerhassetts; Norris F. Schneider, of Zanesville, Ohio, recognized Blennerhassett authority, whose pamphlet, "Blennerhassett Island and the Burr Conspiracy," is an invaluable contribution to the island history.

I am especially indebted to Dr. and Mrs. Morris Thompson, of Cambridge, Ohio, who, while I was in Ireland, introduced me to their cousins, the Blennerhassetts of County Kerry. They, in turn, received me, a stranger, with the famed hospitality of their country, and they filled in for me Irish family background. It is a pleasure to thank Miss Hilda Blennerhassett, of Ballyseedy Castle, Mr. and Mrs. Frank Blennerhassett and Mr. and Mrs. Thomas Blennerhassett, all of Tralee.

In St. Peter Port, Guernsey Island, Harman's will was unearthed for me by tireless work and no mean sleuthing on the part of Her Majesty's Greffier James E. Le Page, and his deputy, George Cohu Naftel. I express thanks to them and their staff, as well as to Mr. and Mrs. W. W. M. Cooper, who searched property files to verify the fact that their home, No. 1 Mount Row, Guernsey, had been the Blennerhassett residence. Blennerhassett's will carried his sister's name as "Avice," a spelling I have followed.

Publications consulted include: *The Life of Harman Blennerhassett,* by William H. Safford (Ely, Allen & Locker, Chillicothe, Ohio, 1850), much of this narrative based on conversations with eyewitnesses of island events and on early Blennerhassett documents; Safford's more detailed volume, *The Blennerhassett Papers and a Memoir of Blennerhassett* (Moore, Wilsrach, Keys & Co., Cincinnati, 1861) with illuminating correspondence of the principals involved; *History of Ohio,* five volumes, by Emilius O. Randall and Daniel J. Ryan (Cent. History Company, New York, 1912), a comprehensive account in Volume III by Ryan; *Aaron Burr,* a biography by Nathan Schachner (Frederick A. Stokes Company, New York, 1937); *Joseph Barker, Recollections of the First Settlement of Ohio,* edited by George Jordan Blazier, librarian and archivist, Marietta College (published by Marietta College, 1958); *Historical Collections of Ohio,* by Henry Howe, two volumes (published by the State of Ohio, 1904)—Volume II contains Washington County reminiscences; Dr. S. P. Hildreth's chapter in *Historical Memoirs,* 1852, and his article in *The American Whig,* April, 1848; Fortesque

Cumming, *Sketches of a Tour,* Pittsburgh, 1810, an eyewitness account; numerous articles issued by the Ohio Historical Society.

The libraries of the Ohio Historical Society and Marietta College have important letters and other documents pertaining to the "conspiracy," which have been made available to me.

Events on the Ohio River island have been woven into fiction, including C. F. Pidgin's novel, *Blennerhassett* (C. M. Clark Co., Boston, 1901) and Walter Damrosch's opera, *The Man Without a Country.* Marion Boyd Havighurst, Oxford, Ohio, utilized her lifelong interest in the Blennerhassett saga for her entertaining juvenile, *Strange Island* (The World Publishing Company, Cleveland and New York, 1957).

Marshall Field

THE TRAGIC EVENTS connected with the wedding of Marshall Field and Nannie Scott, including the death and funeral of the bride's sister, were recorded in the *Ironton Register,* June 19, 1862. The *Ironton Tribune,* successor to the *Register,* printed an article by Min Grimes on the Field-Scott nuptials in its centennial edition October 9, 1949. Lawrence County Probate Court records disclose the marriage as finally taking place January 8, 1863, Reverend John Boul, the officiating clergyman.

I wish to express my appreciation to Mrs. Grimes, now managing editor of the *Tribune,* for her considerable research on the subject in my behalf. I also wish to thank the *Tribune's* former editor, Don Mayne, now editor of the Huntington (West Virginia) *Herald-Dispatch,* who opened his files for my use.

Don Rist, Ironton, was painstaking in supplying original and valuable data otherwise unavailable about the Hanging Rock Iron Region and its early furnaces, and I take this opportunity to express my gratitude for his assistance.

Other sources of information include: *The Hanging Rock Iron Section of Ohio,* Eugene B. Willard, General Supervising Editor, two volumes (Lewis Publishing Co., Chicago (?), 1916); "The Resounding Clash of Ironclads," by Glenn Tucker, in *Civil War Times,* Gettysburg, Pa., 1959; *The Marshall Fields, A Study in Wealth,* by John Tebbel (E. P. Dutton and Company, Inc., New York, 1947). The true story of the wedding has escaped the author.

Katharine Wright

REMINISCENCES OF Oberlin College faculty members and fellow students, contemporaries of Katharine Wright Haskell, as well as friends of her brothers, in the main, supplied the story of her romance.

The writer has been greatly aided by Miss Susan Zearing, of Oberlin, and Miss Pricilla Lord, Cambridge, Massauchusetts, both in college with Mrs. Haskell.

I wish to thank Miss Lelia Holloway, reference librarian, Oberlin College Library, for her assistance. She supplied me with a body of valuable material from college files and alumni records, such as trustee reports and resolutions, issues of *The Oberlin Alumni Magazine,* as well as *The Papers of Wilbur and Orville Wright,* sponsored by Oberlin College, 1953, Marvin W. McFarland, editor.

Other sources consulted include: *The Flight Into History, The Wright Brothers,* by Elsbeth E. Freudenthal (University of Oklahoma Press, Norman, Oklahoma, 1949), and *Miracle at Kitty Hawk,* edited by Fred C. Kelly, and *The Wright Brothers,* by Fred C. Kelly (Farrar, Straus and Young, New York, 1951).

Wayne B. Wheeler

MATERIAL FOR this chapter has been gathered largely from the extensive files and reference library of the World League Against Alcohol, successor to the Anti-Saloon League, in its headquarters at Westerville, Ohio. The Reverend E. H. Dailey, League secretary, was of great assistance. Much data was supplied by the massive publication, *Standard Encyclopedia of the Alcohol Problem,* edited by Ernest Hurst Cherrington and Albert Porter (six volumes, Westerville, Ohio, 1930). Helpful, also, was *Wayne Wheeler, Dry Boss,* by Justin Steuart (Fleming H. Revell Company, New York-Chicago, 1928).

Many facts and intimate details about Wayne Wheeler's life were supplied by his son, Robert Wayne Wheeler, Cleveland attorney, who kindly read the manuscript and added important details.

Mark Twain

My interest in Mark Twain-in-Cleveland was aroused first by Leo Weidenthal, scholarly editor of Cleveland's *Jewish Independent,* and a collector of memorabilia of historic Cleveland. He turned over his files of clippings, photographs, broadsides, and theatrical programs relating to Mark Twain, Editor, and Mrs. Fairbanks, the Severances, and the Cleveland scene of their day. I wish to express my special thanks to him for his never-failing willingness to permit me to tap his rich knowledge of Cleveland's cultural background of this and many similar projects I have undertaken.

Severance Millikin, grandson of Solon and Emily Severance, gave valuable co-operation and kindly let me have use of one of the scarce copies of his grandmother's *Journal Letters.* It was published by the Gates Press, Cleveland, 1938, under the direction of Mr. Millikin's mother, Mrs. B. L. Millikin.

The March-April, 1960, issue of *The Open Shelf,* published by the Cleveland Public Library and ably edited by Bernice Bollenbach, contained helpful material, including literary evaluation of Mark Twain by Marie C. Corrigan, head of the Literature Department of this library.

Other sources consulted, and which supply the reader with further details of the *Quaker City* tour, are: *The Innocents Abroad,* by Mark Twain (Samuel L. Clemens) in two volumes (Harper and Brothers, Publishers, New York and London, 1869); *Mark Twain to Mrs. Fairbanks* (letters), edited by Dixon Wecter (Huntington Library, San Marino, California, 1949).

Philip Sheridan

I am pleased to be able to express my thanks to Mr. and Mrs. Ross Underwood, owners of the house General Sheridan built for his parents, the main body of which they have retained unaltered. Mr. Underwood, prominent merchant on Somerset's Square, and his wife are enthusiastic collectors of Sheridan mementos and authorities on the family's Somerset years. Both have given me generous assistance on several occasions, looking up data for me I otherwise could not have obtained. Mr. and Mrs. Lawrence Guinsler, who live in Sheridan's boyhood home, have been most co-operative. Miss Stella Fink (sometimes spelled Finck) and descendants of the late Linus Dittoe, prominent Somerset families, gave me such information about their ancestors' part in establishing St. Joseph's Catholic Church. For further details about this first Ohio outpost of Catholicism I am indebted to the Very Reverend Robert Edward Brennan, O.P., S.T.M., author of a history of St. Joseph; Reverend Michael Barrett, O.P., and the late Reverend Gabriel Scanlon, O.P., all of St. Joseph's Priory.

Publications consulted include: *Personal Memoirs,* by General Philip H. Sheridan (two volumes, published in 1888); *The Life of Philip H. Sheridan,* by Frank A. Burr and Richard J. Hinton (J. A. and R. A. Reid, Brace and Company, New York, 1932); *The Right Rev. Edward Dominic Fenwick, O.P.,* by Reverend V. F. O'Daniel, O.P., S.T.M. (The Dominicans, Washington, D.C., 1920); *The Heartland,* by Walter Havighurst (Harper and Row, New York and Evanston, 1962).

Warren G. Harding

THIS SILHOUETTE OF Warren G. Harding in his Marion, Ohio, setting reflects impressions and information gathered during visits made over the years in that city where he was beloved during his lifetime and cherished in memory. This phenomenon of persisting community devotion, far from diminishing, I discovered, has been carried on by younger generations.

I wish to thank Harding relatives and friends who on numerous occasions have shared with me their recollections, interpretations, and personal estimates of this controversial Twenty-ninth President. Especially, I express appreciation to Miss Pansy K. Rauhauser, president, Marion County Federation of Women's Clubs, and former high school history teacher.

Mr. Ralph T. Lewis, whose first wife was Abigail, Harding's sister, and Dr. Carl W. Sawyer, son of Harding's personal physician, have been particularly helpful.

Mrs. Ada Dickerson Denman, double cousin of Harding through both her mother and father, remembered her Aunt Phoebe Dickerson, the President's mother, as a person loved and admired in her home and community. She became a devout Seventh Day Adventist, a denomination to which most of the Harding and Dickerson clan, Warren Harding excepted, have belonged ever since.

Mrs. Chester Roberts was a mine of information on the Harding epoch. Acquainted from girlhood with Warren Harding and his wife, who were friends of her parents, she is the sister of Harding's secretary, the late George B. Christian, Jr., and distantly related to Mrs. Harding. As a student at National Park Seminary (its campus now absorbed within the Walter Reed Hospital grounds) she roomed with Emily Daugherty. Emily was the daughter of Harding's attorney general, Harry M. Daugherty, whom Mrs. Roberts recalled as a kind and indulgent father. Mrs. Roberts was often one of the party when Daugherty gathered up Emily and schoolmates—with chaperon—for dinner at the Willard Hotel, pointing out celebrities in evidence there. Mrs. Roberts' girlhood memories also include glamorous moments at the White House as guest of Mrs. Harding, who was never too busy to give attention to home folks.

Quite different from the ceremonious person she often is pictured as, Mrs. Harding frequently came on horseback in Marion to call on Mrs. Roberts' mother. Some years before the Hardings were in the White House, Mrs. Roberts' parents had accompanied them to a Michigan sanitarium where Warren Harding was treated for a heart ailment. Consequently, it was puzzling to her family that speculation developed as to what had caused the President's death.

The late C. E. Schaffner, Harding's executor, when interviewed some years ago, like many when they refer to Harding, soon was wet-eyed as he told me that "the closest scrutiny by government officials of Mr. Harding's affairs here revealed not the slightest irregularity or involvement on his part in Washington deals."

Published references consulted on the Harding period include: *Our Times,* by Mark Sullivan, Volume VI (Charles Scribner's Sons, New York, 1935); *The Incredible Era,* by Samuel Hopkinson Adams (Houghton Mifflin Company, Boston, 1939); *The Epic of America,* by James Truslow Adams (Little, Brown and Company, Boston, 1931); *The Inside Story of the Harding Tragedy,* by Harry M. Daugherty in collaboration with Thomas Dixon (The Churchill Company, New York, 1932); *The President's Daughter,* by Nan Britton, publisher not identified; *The Answer,* by Joseph de Barthe, privately printed. The latter is a repudiation of the Britton book on the premise that fatherhood was an impossibility for Harding as a result of complications following a youthful attack of mumps.

A particular rich source of data was *The Cleveland Plain Dealer,* in issues from Harding's nomination for President in 1920 through subsequent years covering investigations in Washington and Washington Court House, Ohio, hometown of Daugherty.

James A. Garfield

REFERENCES TO James A. Garfield abound in publications about the Western Reserve. Representing the district in Congress for seventeen years, he traveled the length and breadth of it, preaching in its churchs, recruiting for the Union Army, addressing civic gatherings, and campaigning for office. He was a handsome, holy man whose popularity never waned. A varied body of publications, letters, and documents, including pamphlets and reprints on the Garfield home and family, are to be found at their Mentor homestead, Lawnfield, maintained as a museum by Lake County Historical Society. The curators, Mr. and Mrs. J. A. Cooper, authorities on the Garfield story, have given me a great deal of time and attention, for which I express my appreciation.

Edward W. Garfield, of Cleveland, and the late Abram Garfield, grandson and son respectively of President Garfield, have filled in family background for me, for which I am most grateful.

Miss Thelma Bumbaugh, librarian at Hiram College Library, has directed me to the productive field for Garfield research here, including "Pickups from the American Way," published by Hiram Historical Society. Two selections from Series II have been helpful: "Early Life and Civil War Reminiscences of Captain Joseph Rudolph," edited by Adelaide Rudolph, 1941, and "The Garfield-Hinsdale House of Memories," by Ellen C. Hinsdale, 1947. Other sources: *Life and Letters of James A. Garfield,* edited by Theodore Clarke Smith (two volumes, Yale University Press, New Haven, 1925); *Life of James A. Garfield, Our Martyred President,* by James D. McCabe (W. E. Dibble, Cincinnati, Ohio, 1881); *Years of My Youth,* by William Dean Howells (Harper and Brothers, New York and London, 1916).

Delia Bacon

DELIA BACON'S NEPHEW, Theodore Bacon, wrote her life story, *Delia Bacon, a Biographical Sketch* (Houghton Mifflin Company, Cambridge, 1888). However, in the spirit of Victorian "good taste," he omitted a good deal, particularly details about her unhappy romance. Catherine Beecher's *Truth Stranger than Fiction* (Phillips, Sampson and Co., Boston, 1850) fills in gaps of this episode. I am indebted to Mrs. Grant Robley, New Haven, Connecticut, who assisted me in research on the Beecher volume in Yale University Library. I am grateful to Ernest Wessen, of Mansfield, Ohio, for whetting my interest in Delia Bacon.

A recent biography of Delia Bacon is *Prodigal Puritan,* by Vivian C. Hopkins (Harvard University Press, Cambridge, Mass., 1959).

Impressions of her magnetic personality are gained obliquely from references to her in writings and letters of those who knew her, like Emerson, Carlyle, and Hawthorne, the latter describing her in "Recollections of a Gifted Woman," one of a collection of essays, *Our Old Home* (Ticknor and Fields, Boston, 1863).

The Ohio period of her visionary father and of the rest of the remarkable Bacon family appears in manuscripts originating in Tallmadge and Hudson, many in the archives of the Tallmadge Historical Society and the files of the author, among them: "The Flitting of the Fenns," by Mrs. Urania D. Ashley, as told by her mother, Mrs. Miranda Fenn Ashley; "Events Leading to Building of the Church," by Mrs. Henry Bierce, 1924; "Early Days in Tallmadge," by Mrs. Myra Seward Pitkin; "Historical Papers," 1802–1902, by Emily Metcalf, Hudson, 1902. The pamphlets "Tallmadge Semicentennial Anniversary," 1857, and "90th Anniversary, First Congregational Church, Tallmadge" were helpful, as well as *Western Reserve University, the Hudson Era,* by Frederick C. Waite (Western Reserve University Press, Cleveland, 1943).

The late Leonard Bacon, poet and member of the American Academy of Arts and Letters, writing about his great-great-aunt Delia Bacon, to the author, from his home, Peace Dale, Rhode Island, said of her affair with MacWhorter: "I knew nothing beyond the bare fact she believed she had been jilted. Theodore Bacon II implies MacWhorter spoke disparagingly of her, which may or may not be true. And I fancy the Family were very uncomfortable a century ago about the pretty hateful publicity." Delia, he believes was "clearly a wonderful creature, whatever may be thought of her theory of which I personally do not believe one word. Nevertheless, she remains in my sight a noble woman with a powerful intellect." This correspondence is dated 1952.

John Brown's Wives

JOHN BROWN GREW from boy to man in Hudson, Ohio, spending twenty-one years here, more in his wandering life than in any other one place. I have lived even longer in this village. Coming a hundred years after him, I was struck at once with his imprint everywhere about.

First to tap this rich lore was Reverend Clarence S. Gee, minister of the First Congregational Church. His discovery that Brown joined this church in 1816 started Dr. Gee on what has become a scholarly lifetime avocation. Today, the varied and extensive material assembled in his Lockport, New York, home is nationally recognized as source material, while he himself is a much consulted expert on the enigmatic abolitionist.

At the time of Dr. Gee's pastorate, there were persons in the village who remembered John Brown, some of them kinfolk. Word-of-mouth reports that the clergyman gathered asiduously add luster and authenticity to his collection.

I was caught up in his enthusiasm for our village's early resident, and to Dr. Gee I owe my long-sustained interest in John Brown. Unstintingly Clarence Gee made available to me his documents, shared his exciting "finds," and discussed debatable points in connection with numerous articles on John Brown published in my regular series, "Ohio Scenes and Citizens," in the *Plain Dealer Sunday Magazine*. Dr. Gee's generous assistance and advice were invaluable. He kindly read the present chapter, making suggestions and contributing important data, some published here for the first time.

I am further privileged to have had John Brown tutelage under Boyd B. Stutler, foremost authority on the husband of Dianthe and Mary. A visit with Dr. Stutler in his home in Charleston, West Virginia, is an excursion into John Brown's era, for here is a repository of Brown memorabilia amassed during fifty years, and unrivaled anywhere. These papers, recently microfilmed under Dr. Stutler's direction for the Ohio Historical Society, Columbus, constitute the heart of a collection said to be the largest relating to Brown in any institution. Kenneth W. Duckett, curator of manuscripts, is in charge.

When first launched on John Brown's trail, I was fortunate to know his niece, Lucy Brown Clark, daughter of his half brother

Jeremiah. Through her I learned about various Brown landmarks in and around Hudson, such as the lovely home of her girlhood, now the Stanley G. Marks residence. Mrs. Clark told of her Uncle John visiting her parents when en route to Kansas. This was probably in the summer of 1855. He took her on his knee and confided to her that boxes stored in her father's barn contained guns. She recalled Mary Brown stopping in 1882, staying with her mother, Mrs. Jeremiah Brown, then widowed, in the latter's new house in Hudson, now the H. E. Benhoff home.

Mrs. Clark recalled John's frame house as Dianthe knew it, today the much-changed residence of Mr. and Mrs. Herbert S. Karch. By a queer quirk of history, it was the home in the 1940s of Mrs. Earl Johnson, niece of Richard Realf, the English poet who was secretary of John Brown's Chatham Convention but not with him at Harpers Ferry. Mrs. Johnson had Realf mementos and recounted John Brown anecdotes she had heard from her mother, Realf's sister.

Mrs. Clark's son, Howard Clark, of Kent, and his daughter, Mrs. Burton Morgan, of Hudson, put into my hands family documents of many sorts. Details about Dianthe, so little chronicled, were gathered from the Clarks and from Congregational Church records. Milton Lusk papers searched by his Hudson grandsons, Joseph W. Pettingell and his brother, the late Raymond Pettingell, produced fresh information about John's first wife.

A copy of the little-known letter to Owen Brown, refuting Dianthe's alleged derangement at the time of her death, was sent to me by her granddaughter, Mrs. Ella J. Towne, West Hollywood, California, daughter of Ruth Brown Thompson. Dianthe's grave is within the Pennsylvania estate of the late Dr. Charles Wesley Olsen, of Chicago.

I was greatly aided in research about Mary Day Brown in the tragic Richfield years by Mrs. W. R. Simpson, of Kent, granddaughter of Edward—half brother of John—and herself a storehouse of Brown family facts; Mrs. Eunice Merton Bordner, of Peninsula; Mrs. Dorothy Sykes, librarian, Richfield Public Library; the late Miss Jennie Oviatt, of Richfield, whose grandmother helped Mary at this time; and the late Mrs. Charles Perkins, who, through letters and recollections concerning her father-in-law, Colonel Simon Perkins, had much to offer about the Browns' Richfield-Akron period.

Through the years I have collected diary notes, letters, and vivid reminiscences generously shared with me by Hudson neighbors whose antecedents were contemporaries of the Browns, including:

Julian W. Scott, grandson of Lora Case; Miss Anna V. Lee, direct descendant of David Hudson; F. Howard Mills, whose great-grandfather, Gideon Hayes Mills, and John's mother, Ruth, were brother and sister; the late Arthur N. Waite, twice mayor of Hudson, and his brother, the late Dr. Frederick C. Waite, Western Reserve University, whose father, Nelson, was indentured to Oliver O. Brown, John's brother. The late Janet and Charles Read, whose father, Mathew, circulated the petition for John, spoke of seeing Mary in Hudson in 1882 when she mentioned helping drive one of the wagons on the western exodus. The Read residence on Baldwin Street is now owned by Ralph W. Miner.

For John Brown contributions I wish also to thank: Dr. and Mrs. Harlan L. Trumbull, W. D. Shilts, Mrs. Virginia Grazier, librarian of the Hudson Library and Historical Society, Mrs. J. Fred Waring, librarian of Western Reserve Academy Library, all of Hudson; Mrs. Cyril Sumner, Damariscotta, Maine, and Mrs. Donald Stem, Chagrin Falls, Ohio.

Also consulted were: Lora Case, "Reminiscences," both as published in the *Hudson Independent*, 1897, and *Hudson of Long Ago, Reminiscences,* as edited by Frances B. B. Sumner, 1963; manuscript of address, 1902, at centennial, First Congregational Church, Hudson, by Miss Emily Metcalf, related to Sally Root Brown, John's stepmother; manuscript, "History of Hudson," by Mrs. H. N. Wood, about 1924.

Rare letters and excerpts from such letters by John and Mary Brown have been freely used from the Gee and Stutler collections, especially notable those by Mary from Put-in-Bay; from Lucretia Mott's home, original owned by Mary Fablinger, of Campbell, California, Mary's granddaughter; the letter from Decorah, discovered by Dr. Gee in the Lake Placid Club Library and believed unpublished up to now.

Addenda on Mary's California period are from "Threats, Then Friends, for John Brown's People," by Sam Hanson, the *Los Gatos Daily Times,* March 26, 1953; *Here Lived the Californians,* by Oscar Lewis (Rinehart & Company, Inc., New York, 1957); and an article in the *Lake Placid News,* September 29, 1916, by Mrs. Salmon Brown; and letters from Annie Brown.

References to Mary and the family covenant appear in "Pioneer Reminiscences of the Western Reserve" (*Northwestern Congregationalist* [Minneapolis], September 23, 1902), by Reverend Edward Brown, and in "The Soul of John Brown" (*The American Magazine,*

October, 1909), by Eleanor Atkinson. Mary's part in her husband's funeral is from several sources, including an account by Dr. Joshua Young in *The New England Magazine,* April, 1904; "The John Brown Farm," a pamphlet issued by the Division of Archives of the Education Department, University of the State of New York (undated); *History of the Adirondacks,* two volumes, 1921, by Alfred Donaldson, The Century Co., New York, n.d. and "The Stone on the Grave," pamphlet, reprinted from *New York History,* vol. 42, April, 1961, by Clarence S. Gee.

The history of the song "John Brown's Body" is based on an article under that title in *Civil War History,* September, 1958, by Boyd B. Stutler and in a communication in "Letters," published by Time, Inc., July 22, 1935, from Fletcher Hodges Jr., Indianapolis, Indiana.

Two interviews with Mary reveal her on the way to Harpers Ferry, one by Theodore Tilton, correspondent for the *New York Independent,* the other by J. Miller McKim in the *Anti-Slavery Standard,* both quoted in *Captain John Brown of Harpers Ferry,* by John Newton (The Wessels Company, New York, 1902).

Among many volumes on John Brown, three were especially relied on in preparing this chapter: *Life of Captain John Brown,* by James Redpath (Thayer and Eldrige, Boston, 1860); F. B. Sanborn's *Life and Letters of John Brown* (Roberts Brothers, Boston, 1891); and *John Brown,* by Oswald Garrison Villard, first issued, 1910 (Houghton Mifflin Company, Boston and New York), which remains the definitive biography. All contain some references to Mary, but comparatively little about Dianthe.

Index

ABOUT THE AUTHOR

GRACE GOULDER, whose famous column "Ohio Scenes and Citizens" (from which this book draws its source) has appeared in the Cleveland *Plain Dealer* for more than twenty years, was born in Cleveland into a family which had settled early in Ohio and was brought up on the history and lore of her native state. A graduate of Vassar College, Miss Goulder has been the recipient of the coveted Ohio Governor's Award and has been cited by many Ohio organizations and historical societies for her contributions to the culture and education of Ohio citizens. Miss Goulder frequently lectures to clubs and societies and is the author of *This Is Ohio*. She now resides with her husband, Robert Izant, in Hudson, Ohio.